To Juliette.

Thank you,
thank you,
thank you.

Pat

April '92

WE'VE ALL HEARD of the Third World's debt crisis, of hopelessly poor nations unable to pay their debts, and of the human suffering and environmental consequences of their desperate predicament. Amid emotional calls from some to forgive the debt outright come the sober solutions from bankers and bureaucrats, with their seemingly unending stream of Brady and Baker Plans, and bewildering variants of them.

Yet despite the raging world-wide controversy over the Third World's debt, no one has posed these most elementary questions: who lent what and to whom, where did the money go, what did it do there, and where is it now.

In this brilliant hybrid of detective work and policy analysis, Patricia Adams has unraveled a rats' nest of Third World lending to describe the debt crisis in its startling simplicity. Her conclusions are equally startling – not what many might have expected from a prominent environmentalist heading an outspoken advocacy organization.

Through a straightforward exposition of the facts, you will come to see the debt for what it is – the sum total of thousands of loans, some illegitimate, justifying repudiation, others legitimate, meriting repayment. Surprisingly, you will learn that the Third World's environment – so ravaged through decades of degradation – has often been spared by virtue of the debt. And that legal mechanisms – first used by the U.S. to repudiate Cuban debts after the Spanish-American War – are in place to resolve the debt crisis far more equitably than political solutions cooked up in Washington and the capitals of Third World countries. Odious debts are well established in international law; through this doctrine Chase Manhattan, the World Bank, and other lenders would collect on their debts – not from the people of the Third World but from the Marcoses and Mobutus who would be liable.

Patricia Adams is an economist and the author of *In the Name of Progress: The Underside of Foreign Aid*. She lives in Toronto and is the Executive Director of Probe International, a think-tank concerned with Third World aid and trade policies.

Other Books by Probe International

In The Name of Progress: The Underside of Foreign Aid (*by Patricia Adams and Lawrence Solomon*)

Damming The Three Gorges: What Dam–Builders Don't Want You To Know (*Edited by Gráinne Ryder*)

This edition made possible through grants from the Charles Stewart Mott Foundation and the Margaret Laurence Fund for Peace and the Environment.

First edition published simultaneously in the United Kingdom by
Earthscan Publications Ltd., 3 Endsleigh Street, London WC1H ODD; and in Canada by
Earthscan Canada, 225 Brunswick Avenue, Toronto, Ontario M5S 2M6.
Telephone (416) 978-7014, Fax (416) 978-3824

British Library Cataloguing in Publication Data
Adams, Patricia
Odious Debts: Loose Lending, Corruption and the Third World's Environmental Legacy
I. Title
336.309172

I.S.B.N   1-85383-122-0

Earthscan Publications Ltd. in the United Kingdom is an editorially independent subsidiary of
the International Institute for Environment and Development (IIED; charity number 800066).

Canadian Cataloguing in Publication Data

Adams, Patricia, 1953-
Odious Debts

Includes bibliographical references and index.
ISBN 0-919849-16-4 (bound). - ISBN 0-919849-14-8 (pbk.)

1. Economic development projects – Environmental aspects – Developing countries.
2. Economic development projects – Developing countries – Finance. 3. Developing countries –
Economic policy – Environmental aspects. 4. Debts, External – Developing countries.
5. Developing countries – Foreign economic relations. 6. International finance – Law and
legislation. I. Earthscan Canada. II. Title.

HC59. 72. E5A32 1991   332. 6'73'091724   C91-094729-5

Probe International is a research division of EPRF Energy Probe Research Foundation

Produced by Environment Matters, Toronto, Canada
Printed using recycled paper by Bookcrafters, U.S.A

ISBN Summary
0-919849-14-8 Softcover Canada
0-919849-16-4 Hardcover Canada
1-85383-122-0 UK Softcover

Patricia Adams

ODIOUS DEBTS

Loose Lending, Corruption,
And the Third World's
Environmental Legacy

Probe International

1991
EARTHSCAN
London . Toronto

Contents

Acknowledgements

Friends and colleagues have been exceptionally generous in helping me finish this book. Margaret Barber deserves special thanks for her painstaking research, and for her good cheer throughout. I am also especially grateful to Susan Fitzmaurice for her artistic judgment and for her commitment to the complicated task of producing this book. Both made an otherwise stressful job a joy.

To those who shaped this book with their thoughtful comments on the manuscript and their advice along the way, I am particularly indebted: Elizabeth Brubaker, Gawin Chutima, Marcus Colchester, Chad Dobson, Philip M. Fearnside, Dipak Gyawali, Mary Hallward, Peggy Hallward, Alex Kisin, Larry Lohmann, Juliette Majot, Richard Owens, Magda Renner, and Gráinne Ryder.

Several people did research on my behalf, relentlessly pursuing all manner of sources: Asheesh Advani, John Mihevc, Geoffrey Patridge, and Ann Stewart. Others provided research material in other ways. I owe thanks to Ana Banachowicz for researching and translating material on Sicartsa, to Jessica Campbell for explaining scientific matters and for 11th-hour translating, to Olga Martinez for translating legal documents, to Kole Shettima for explaining traditional Nigerian lending systems to me, to Sheila Malcolmson and Tom Adams for clarifying many questions about electric utilities and nuclear power, and to Adam White for reviewing economic arguments and for being on computer call. I am also grateful to Professor Jim Boyce, to Leonor Briones of the Freedom From Debt Coalition in the Philippines, to John Cavanagh and Robin Broad, and to Peter Bosshard from the Bern Group for keeping me up to date on the campaign to recover the Marcos money and the legal challenge with respect to the Bataan nuclear reactor. Brazilian colleagues at Friends of the Earth - Brazil, Instituto Apoio

Judicial Popular, Programa Regional De Trabajo Popular, and Instituto Brasileiro de Análises Sociais e Econômicas (IBASE) were also the source of much inspiration.

I am especially thankful to lawyers Richard Owens, Sandy Walker, and legal scholar Dotse Tsikata for patiently explaining legal first principles to me, and for challenging everything I wrote.

Kathy Kehoe's editing and proofreading of endnotes, and Rick Archbold's and Joel Brody's publishing advice, have been extremely helpful. I am also grateful to Miguel Cea for technical production and design of the book.

I consider myself lucky to have had editor Norman Houghton apply his skills to several drafts of *Odious Debts*, and for being the ultimate and ever-reliable source on editing matters. Thanks go too to Janet Case for her valuable comments and careful editing of the final draft.

The overwhelming evidence of the damage done by past loans to the Third World made this book a necessity. The irrepressible communication between Third World citizens' rights groups and their counterparts in the lending countries made it possible. To my Third World colleagues, who have been generous in spirit and patient in explaining their part of the world to me, I owe my thanks. Many of them have risked a great deal in their pursuit of peace, order, and good government;to them I also owe my profound respect.

And finally, I will always be thankful to my husband, Lawrence Solomon, without whose encouragement, companionship, and spirit this book would certainly not have been finished, and perhaps never started.

Responsibility for the analysis, opinions, and any mistakes that occur is mine alone.

Patricia Adams
July 15, 1991

To Robert Watson Adams

ODIOUS DEBTS

Loose Lending, Corruption,
And the Third World's
Environmental Legacy

INTRODUCTION

The Tragedies of the Commons

BEFORE THE WORLD BANK and other international institutions came to bring development to the remotest corners of the globe, the millions of villagers living along Northern Thailand's swiftly flowing rivers understood that they depended upon one another. Each community needed its river to irrigate its crops, water its animals, and provide for its members' personal needs. To ensure clean water for all, the communities negotiated rules governing who received how much water and when, and implemented those rules through adjustable weirs made of bamboo and teak poles: by adding or removing poles, by raising or lowering the weirs' height, by scouring the river and irrigation beds, they rationed water among its many claimants with uncanny precision.

Housekeeping and farming practices along the river were everybody's business because they affected rates of erosion, and thus contamination of the river and irrigation systems. Upland forests, vital to bringing the rains each season and controlling runoff, couldn't be cut without permission.

Upkeep of the 1000-year-old *muang faai* water management system, as it is still called, was proportional to landholding. Taxes to maintain the system were paid in the form of labor. Newcomers bought into the system through sweat equity – they needed to put in twice the labor to compensate for the past efforts of others. Absenteeism was penalized, volunteer work rewarded with extra water and sometimes with gifts of rice from neighbors.

The principle that everyone receive enough water to survive – an ancient version of the modern day "social safety net" – was paramount. In dry years, those with distant plots difficult to irrigate would receive water first; rice, a subsistence crop, had precedence over cash crops.

Out of this shared sense of dependence came a political structure that provided what would be called "due process" by modern-day legal theory: elected irrigation committees, guided by a duty to preserve the river for existing and future generations, had formal responsibility for monitoring water distribution and administering weir and channel maintenance. Theft of water and unauthorized cutting of forests were punishable by fines which, having a social stigma attached to them, were never treated as a mere cost of doing business. While these elected officials were responsible for administering justice, all community members, as proprietors of the *muang faai* system, were expected to enforce the rules. With everyone's side-channels in plain view of commuters between village and fields, weed buildup in the waterways or illicit tree cutting never went unnoticed.

Muang faai – which survives in much of Thailand – amounts

11

to a system of property rights in which private rights and responsibilities have been finely tuned over the centuries to maintain equity, protect the environment, and promote prosperity. Though hardly idyllic, frequently conflict-ridden, and constantly adapting through trial and error and discussion, the system worked well to protect those who lived along the river, and the river itself. From such an accountable environment came a degree of security that allowed all who were governed by it to produce amply and diversely for their families, enriching their communities in the process.

Then came progress. Thai government officials, armed with foreign money, concrete, and plans for a made-over agricultural system, started arriving in the 1950s, engineers in tow, to replace the old-fashioned bamboo weirs with the concrete barrages foreshadowing the Green Revolution. Those dependent upon the river could no longer regulate it along its path – a giant dam and reservoir upstream would now control the flow through a less intensive system of irrigation canals. How much water would flow down the river, and where it would go, would henceforth be determined by officials in the Royal Irrigation Department. The informal governments of riverine communities and their complex set of laws were thus emasculated.

The behavior of the river, and of the inhabitants, would change too. Traditional crops, found in ecological niches along the river valley and dependent upon timely irrigation, were no longer manageable by the riverine farmers. Too risky to invest in, they soon fell into disuse, ending the extraordinary diversity of old seed varieties that had been engineered by generations of farmers as insurance against blights. Modern varieties, well suited to the new centrally controlled water regime, were now sold by large seed companies or state agricultural boards. But these new seed varieties, which depended on the unknown and unknowable government authorities providing water at the right time, also required fertilizers, pesticides, and herbicides to protect them. To buy these, the government offered farmers credit, and the farmers soon fell into debt.

As the riverine communities of Thailand lost control over

12

their environment, they also lost control over their economy. Remote government officials at the Royal Irrigation Department were now in charge, dispensing contracts to dam rivers and log watersheds for their own rhyme and reason. Though the Royal Irrigation Department hoped to benefit the villagers, their concrete weirs were too blunt to allocate water reliably or equitably, and they themselves were too remote to police the river's uses. Since despoilers of the watersheds (often state officials and their friends who benefited personally) went unpunished, use of watersheds became a free-for-all.

The once lawful riverine communities, witnessing the government's arbitrary licensing of logging, soon took to logging the forests as well. As the complex, self-regulated property rights regime disintegrated, so too did the economy and the environment: with deforestation, silt clogged the rivers and irrigation canals, reducing them to sludge in the dry season and causing them to flood in the rainy seasons. With water so uncertain, many farmers gave up growing rice. What had once been a river ecology whose use was regulated in common purpose, became a lawless commons to exploit.

HUMAN BEINGS DO NOT WILLINGLY DEGRADE their environment. No farmer dreams of leaving his children a ramshackle farm, top soil swept away, eroded gullies pock-marking the terrain; no community willingly subjects itself to hazardous wastes. Passing on an environmentally sound world to the next generation is part of the moral code of all cultures.

People usually exercise similar caution in their personal finances. Most parents strive to leave their children wealth, not liabilities: to do so they try to maximize their assets and minimize their debts.

To ensure children don't inherit the excesses of their parents, most societies require debts to be extinguished upon settlement of the debtor's estate: societies that allow debts to be passed on to future generations are condemned by the United Nations for practising a form of debt bondage.

But all societies tolerate debt bondage when the creation of the debt is once removed: the state can and does borrow collectively on our behalf, and we then leave this collective debt to our children, often deluding ourselves that someone else's children will be responsible for repayment. Through this mechanism, and this mindset, is the financial commons created.

A commons need not lead to tragedy. The Thai river communities managed their common rivers and streams to their personal and communal benefit; the Thai government officials, managing the same resources, didn't. But tragedy will surely occur, whether in a financial commons or an environmental commons, when the beneficiary and the victim are obscured by space, time, and loose accounting. As long as they need not face each other on the street, along the river bank, or in the town hall; as long as they are remote and unidentifiable, the perpetrators of financial or environmental liabilities will escape an accounting, the victims will be denied a voice, and just about any practice will be justified in the name of the national interest or in the name of progress. As long as borrowing occurs on the environmental or financial accounts of everybody yet nobody, rights will be unhinged from responsibilities and the debts of the nation will grow.

PART I

The Environment's Demise

1

The Environmental Legacy of Yesterday's Loans

ONE MORNING IN FEBRUARY 1989, the citizens of the Amazonian village of Pedras awoke to find that the Uatuma River had died. From the foot of the mango tree that marked the river bank to the far side of the shore, the water was covered with a blanket of fish carcasses so thick that, according to village matriarch Fofrasia Castro da Silva, "You could have walked across the water and not even have gotten wet." Until that day, the river had been the source of the villagers' food and water, and of their livelihood.

"I sat right down and cried.... We had beautiful water, a beautiful river and life here was wonderful. But they killed our river and now life here is very hard. What they have done is a crime."

The "they" in Mrs. Castro da Silva's lament were the people at Eletronorte, the Brazilian state electric utility for the Amazon region. What they had done occurred almost a year and a half earlier – they had closed the floodgates of the Balbina dam.

The Balbina dam was conceived in the 1970s, at the height of the OPEC oil crisis and of the Third World's borrowing boom when big was still beautiful, when money was still easy, and when the generals still ruled Brazil. The country would need to increase its debt to finance Balbina, but such increases were considered necessary: Balbina would help Brazil shake its dependence on imported oil. At least that was the plan. But the dam was plagued with controversy: corruption was rampant, the economics were dubious, and the environmental damage staggering. Balbina's reservoir would flood 2,360 square kilometers of pristine tropical rainforest to build a modest 250 megawatt dam. In contrast, the Tucurui dam, also in the Amazon, would flood a comparable area to provide 8,000 megawatts. Before Balbina could be finished Eletronorte ran short of funds. Cash starved, Balbina's construction crept along at a snail's pace until 1986, when a $500 million World Bank loan allowed it to continue.

Criticism continued with it. The local press dubbed Balbina a "monument to institutional insanity." Environmentalists inside and outside the country criticized its grotesque inefficiency. Even the director of Brazil's Special Secretariat for the Environment described Balbina as a "disaster and everybody knows it ... one of the greatest errors committed in the Amazon."

Eletronorte responded to its detractors by launching a public relations blitz with Orwellian slogans such as, "Whoever is against Balbina is against you." In one radio advertisement broadcast every 15 minutes, the voice of Curupira – the spirit of the forest – assured listeners that he would not allow Balbina to exist were the dam not good for the fish and wildlife. A television

17

commercial showed a cave woman being clubbed over the head with a large bone, suggesting that Brazilians would revert to Neanderthal times without Balbina.

With opposition to the dam reaching a fever pitch, the Brazilian government decided to end the debate: without warning, Eletronorte closed the floodgates 30 days early.

The problems that many feared soon began to surface. The National Institute for Research in the Amazon discovered that the area to be submerged was grossly underestimated. To determine the topography of the ground that lay beneath the lush tropical forest canopy, engineers had mapped the top of the forest canopy using aerial photographs, and then subtracted what they thought was the average tree height. This method was unreliable in the extreme; some of the tallest trees obscured the network of ravines in which they stood. According to the engineers who worked on Balbina's topographic survey, its margin of error was so great that a 4,000-square-kilometer reservoir (almost four times the size originally estimated by Eletronorte) was "within the range of possibility."

Apart from the ravines, the surrounding terrain was flat, so flat (the reservoir's average depth was less than eight meters) that when Balbina's floodgates closed water spread as it would on any flat surface – everywhere. As the ravines filled up with water, they formed approximately 1,500 islands, 60 tributary streams, and a labyrinth of canals, disturbing an area twice that of the reservoir. The little hilltops that were all but submerged by the reservoir's rising water soon became the scene of appalling carnage.

The forest's animals had headed for higher ground as the water rose. Their refuge soon became overcrowded; unable to escape, they began to die. "It was a horrible thing to see," said one resident. "The islands are covered in corpses, corpses on top of corpses on top of corpses. There are dead turtles, monkeys, jaguars ... everything." This immediate aftermath of the floodgate's closing was only the beginning.

In its haste to fill the dam, Eletronorte had failed to clear the reservoir area of the trees and vegetation that were once home to

18

countless unknown species. The vegetation left to decompose soon depleted the river of oxygen, produced hydrogen sulphide gas, and turned the water acidic. The reservoir, with its millions of submerged and bleached-out tree trunks, became slick with scum, the smell unbearable. The once teeming river quickly became incapable of supporting its previous life forms.

According to Jamie de Neles Miranda, one of several thousand riverine people who depended on the river and the forest for their survival, many of the submerged trees were dangerous. The leaves of one tree, if brewed into a tea, would give a person a fever; the bark of another could be used to kill fish in ponds; a third was so toxic that food couldn't be cooked over its fire. "I know hardwoods and I know what's under that water behind the dam," he explained. "There are many, many kinds of poisonous plants under the reservoir and that's why the river is dead."

With the water supply poisoned and the fish and wild animals now gone, an epidemic of skin rashes, intestinal disorders, headaches, nausea, and vomiting broke out. To make matters worse, they were followed by malaria – a common occurrence around large stagnant bodies of water that provide a perfect breeding ground for malaria-carrying mosquitoes.

While the Balbina dam brought sickness and destitution to the riverine people, it brought death to the upstream Waimiri-Atroari Indians. With their numbers already halved by years of conflict with governments and corporations which had systematically appropriated their territory for highways and cassiterite mines, these unfortunate Indians in the 1970s found themselves in Balbina's way. The Brazilian agency for Amerindian affairs (FUNAI), to clear the area of Indians, began to relocate them. Their job became gruesomely easier by the day. From 1973 to 1979 the Waimiri-Atroari's population diminished from 3,500 to 1,100. By 1986, just a year before Balbina's floodgates closed, their population was reduced to 374 – mostly children. In fourteen years, more than three thousand Indians had disappeared.

Balbina was but one of many hydroelectric dams to wreak

havoc on the Brazilian Amazon. The Tucurui dam – the largest dam ever to be built in a tropical rainforest – required the relocation of 18,000 people, including an entire Indian tribe. Like Balbina, Tucurui's floodgates were prematurely closed to stem public opposition: a court order was threatening to prevent the reservoir from filling.

With the river's flow interrupted, the water was starved of oxygen, killing hundreds of thousands of fish and reducing the area to a stench-filled and macabre zone – so macabre that alarmed officials, prior to the ribbon-cutting ceremonies, ordered the fish removed by the truckload to avoid embarrassing the dignitaries performing the honors.

The environmental carnage didn't end with the dedication ceremony. Rotting trees, interrupted sediment flows, and leaks from 350 partially filled drums of dangerous defoliants bought in a failed attempt to rid the area of trees, and then forgotten, combined to poison the Tocantins River. Tens of thousands of people downstream had their lives all but destroyed. The dam also stopped the silt that had enriched the soil when the waters rose each year during the rainy season. Harvests of rubber and acai palm fruit from the Tocantins floodplains and islands fell dramatically as the riverside trees rotted away. The river, once a source of life, became devoid of fish and shrimp. "Before the dam, our life was good," one resident said. "It was bountiful. Everything – fish, shrimp, good water. Now all we have is the consequences of the dam and that's it: hunger and polluted water."

Ecosystems less publicized than the rainforest were also falling to the financiers who sought to redirect their fate. The once thriving agricultural community of Singrauli in India has been reduced, with foreign loans, to a destitute population eking out a living from soils contaminated by the twelve open-pit coal mines and the five coal-fired electricity generating plants they now have as neighbors. Water contaminated by coal-ash slurry and air laden with dust and sulphur dioxide have contributed to a public health disaster involving widespread tuberculosis, skin diseases, and digestive tract disorders: 70,000 now toil in the mines and the plants where their farms once stood. So blighted is Singrauli that the Indian press compares it to "the lower circles of Dante's Inferno."

Hydroelectric dams and thermal-powered electricity generating plants – long the darlings of international financiers – account for roughly 25 per cent of the Third World's debt. They are also responsible for much of the destroyed farmland and forests, for induced earthquakes, for the spread of diseases, for the alteration of hydrological regimes, for the erosion of coastlines, and ultimately for the reordering of river and land around which millions of people had organized themselves over the centuries.

Next to energy, agricultural projects – often irrigation schemes – contributed most to Third World debt.

In Ethiopia's Awash River valley, irrigation systems for sugar cane, cotton, and banana plantations destroyed the valley's rich floodplains – a mixture of savannas, swamps and riparian forests. To make way for the plantations, 20,000 people were expropriated from their lands, mostly without compensation. Forced to leave, the people and their livestock crowded onto lands held by other tribes near the newly irrigated plantations, forcing them, in turn, to spill onto the lands of their neighbors. Normal migration routes were blocked and tribal warfare intensified as the region's land base eroded. When the rains failed in the early 1970s and again in the early 1980s, the people, bereft of their former resources, became wards of famine-relief stations. To the Afar people of the Awash River valley, the misery wrought by this foreign-aid-financed agricultural scheme was so much worse than the droughts and other hardships of the past that they could only explain it as punishment from God.

Cattle ranching projects in Botswana promoted such intensive grazing that grasslands were destroyed and traditional pastoral people's economies decimated. Tobacco plantations in Africa, also recipients of foreign aid loans, wreaked havoc on tropical soils by draining them of nitrogen, phosphorous, potassium, and other vital nutrients, consuming one acre of forest to cure each acre of tobacco.

21

WHILE ILL-CONCEIVED agricultural projects would leave much of Africa in ecological ruin, industrial investments would earn for Brazil the title of the world's worst polluter. Brazil became home to many of the world's most polluted cities, including Cubatao, a place often cited as the worst on earth.

Located between Sao Paulo, the country's biggest city, and Santos, its biggest port, Cubatao seemed a perfect site for development when Brazil's military government began its drive to industrialize in the mid-1960s. Petrobrás, Brazil's national oil company and largest borrower, was the first large company to open there, followed by another 25 local and multinational companies, turning the outskirts of town into a sprawl of steel, cement, and fertilizer factories.

As the *Wall Street Journal* explained: "From the start, the generals who ruled then made it clear that they cared less about pollution than about modernizing at almost any cost. That was good for industry, but disastrous for Cubatao."

Scores of factories spew pollutants into the atmosphere. The air in some sections contains twice the level of contaminants considered safe by the World Health Organization. Cubatao has the highest level of acid rain ever recorded. Up to half its 100,000 inhabitants are thought to suffer from respiratory ailments, and expectant mothers worry that their babies will be born deformed. Its river is a mass of sludge.

Cubatao became Latin America's most important petrochemical complex and one of the most polluted cities on earth: every day 800 tons of toxic gasses spewed from the 24 petrochemical factories, poisoning the air, water, and land. For 25 years, a lethal red rain fell daily on Cubatao. Authorities gave up attempts to measure the air pollution: the instruments would not stand up to the corrosion. Some 74 different pollutants burnt the eyes and lungs of Cubatao's inhabitants, earning for it the nickname, the "valley of death." Vegetation and wildlife disappeared, 44 per cent of the workers in the heavy industrial plants suffered from lung disease, and children died by the thousands from tetanus, tuberculosis, lung ailments, diphtheria and typhoid. Many never lived long enough to die of such diseases. For every 1,000 births, 40 babies were stillborn and another 40 died in the first few months of their lives. Cubatao also held the unenviable world record for anencephaly – the total or partial absence of brain tissue in newborns – with one case for every 250 births.

Next to Brazil, Mexico may be the world's dirtiest country, thanks to its rush to develop its oil and petrochemical resources, creating in the process another hell on earth.

In the Coatzacoalcos River basin, the leading oil-producing region in the Gulf of Mexico, researchers from Mexico City's Center for Ecological Development declared an 8,000-square-kilometer area to be "ravaged," calling every aspect of the ecosystem – water, land, and air – "severely afflicted" by the exploitation of petroleum deposits and the growth of refineries and industrial complexes. Nothing escaped the oil industry's assault, neither "flora, fauna, nor humanity," said the Center. River and coastal pollution achieved unprecedented levels: carcinogens were found in nineteen species of fish, crustaceans, and molluscs; nickel deposits in the river sediment "were much greater than those normally encountered in areas of human activity"; and air pollution in the form of high levels of sulphates and formaldehyde were nearly as high as those in Mexico City, accounting for the very high incidence of respiratory and eye illnesses suffered by the people in the area.

Mexico City's air is reputed to be among the world's worst, causing respiratory ailments, stinging eyes, skin rashes, intestinal disorders, and up to 100,000 pollution-related deaths annually. In 1986 it was blamed for birds dropping out of the sky and writhing in death throes on people's front lawns.

Third World governments and their international financiers have viewed pollution as both necessary and a sign of wealth. "We welcome pollution," one Third World delegate declared at the first-ever Stockholm environment conference of 1972. "Brazil can become the importer of pollution," elaborated Brazil's Planning Minister.

Hell bent on industrialization, Third World governments,

and those in the north who wanted their business, would build hydro dams, steel mills, roads, irrigation canals, petrochemical plants, mines, and smelters as if there were no tomorrow.

But tomorrow came all too soon, choking more than the environment: the hydro dams, steel mills and other investments were choked too.

2

The Environment Strikes Back

ATTEMPTS TO CONQUER the mighty Amazon have never been cheap, and rarely have they been successful. Gold diggers, grand old families in search of plantation lands, and traders of quinine bark and other exotic substances have for centuries plied their way up the Amazon. But Amazonia had its own defenses. So inhospitable to outsiders was the rainforest, so dense its vegetation, so difficult its climate, so dangerous its diseases, so swift its regenerative powers that intruders were quickly swallowed up by its seething life.

The Madeira-Mamoré Railroad, begun in 1872, was the first great contest between modern man and the Amazon jungle. Its European and North American backers simply intended to transport Bolivian rubber 230 miles to the markets and shipping routes of the eastern Amazon – a distance less than one-tenth that of the U.S. transcontinental railroad, completed just three years earlier.

But building the railway was not simple. Malaria, yellow fever, amoebic dysentery, beriberi, and typhoid killed an estimated 10,000 people, more than any other construction project in modern times, including the Panama Canal. "Under each crosstie a human skull," goes the saying of locals, who designated Madeira-Mamoré the Railroad of the Dead.

In five years only five miles of track had been laid. The rainforest was so dense that surveyors could measure only a few feet at a time. Routes were often abandoned for new directions when the track struck an impassable hill that had been camouflaged by jungle. The rains swamped roadbeds and shifting rivers carried them away.

The European owners, in a survey of their investment debacle, branded the region "a welter of putrefaction, where men die like flies. Even with all the money in the world and half its population it is impossible to finish this railway." The Madeira-Mamoré Railway thus lurched from one private owner to another, ruining more than one great fortune along the way. Finally, in 1931, the government stepped in. So often the investor of last resort, it mustered the money to finish it and to keep the debt-ridden railway operating until 1972. Then, a full century after its beginning, the government closed it in favor of a road through the Amazon.

Throughout these misadventures, history had kept repeating itself, attracting new adventurers – Henry Ford among them – who ignored the lessons of their predecessors.

In 1927, seeking to circumvent the British and Dutch rubber monopolies, Ford bought two and a half million acres of Amazonian river-front property, called his development project Fordlandia, and set about transforming it into a rubber plantation. Seven thousand acres were cleared while Ford's head office in Dearborn, Michigan shipped in houses, a school, a hospital, a sawmill, and other facilities. The sawmill processed the virgin hardwoods, and young rubber trees were planted.

But no sooner had the canopies of the young trees begun to close in upon one another than *Microcyclus ulei*, or South American leaf blight, struck savagely. Fifty-three other grafts and clones were then brought in from Sumatra and Liberia, but all became susceptible to the disease. To compound Ford's troubles, two dozen insect predators also attacked. In 1942 swarms of caterpillars nearly destroyed the trees. By 1945, after spending nearly $10 million, Ford admitted defeat and sold out to the Brazilian government for $500,000. Two decades would elapse before another developer dared defy the Amazon.

Then in 1967, North American shipping magnate Daniel K. Ludwig came to develop the Amazon, and on a still grander scale. Expecting the world to soon run out of wood fiber, Ludwig decided to clear 250,000 acres of native rainforest for plantations of his "miracle tree," *Gmelina arborea*, a fast-growing Burmese species. On his three million acres of Amazonian rainforest, Ludwig also envisaged the world's largest rice plantation, mining and livestock operations, nicely planned communities for workers, a 2,500-mile network of roads, and fifty miles of railroad track. With help from the Japanese Import-Export Bank and the Brazilian government, he brought in, by barge, preassembled, a 17-story-high pulp mill from Japan.

Ludwig's heavy land-clearing machines scraped and compacted the delicate soil, which retaliated almost immediately. Transplanted *Gmelina* grew slower than in its native environment. But Ludwig persevered, replacing *Gmelina* plantations with equally disappointing eucalyptus and Caribbean pine. The pulp mill processed what pulp it could extract from the rainforest while his billion-dollar investment faltered. After fourteen years, Ludwig gave up, losing an estimated two-thirds of a billion dollars.

Ludwig, Ford, and the original developers of the Madeira-Mamoré found their pockets too shallow to persist in fighting the

Amazon. The Brazilian government has no such limits with its Greater Carajás Development Program.

The Greater Carajás story begins in 1967 when a Brazilian geologist, whose helicopter was forced down in the Carajás region, discovered an El Dorado of mineral riches: mountains laden with gold, copper, manganese, bauxite, nickel, tin, and other valuable minerals. Eighteen billion tons of iron ore deposits – the world's purest – made Carajás among the world's two or three largest finds. Attempts to exploit these reserves went nowhere until 1980, when the Brazilian government announced a $62 billion plan to create an agro-industrial complex of mines, smelters, dams, railroads, ports, ranches, and plantations. This Greater Carajás Program encompasses an area in the eastern Amazon the size of Great Britain and France combined.

The Carajás plan includes 25 privately owned pig iron smelters, their investors lured into the Amazon by generous tax deductions. To fuel the smelters, some 58,000 square kilometers of primary Amazonian rainforest will be converted into charcoal. For the operation to be financially viable, the rainforest's trees have to come free and the environmental costs of destroying the rainforest have to count as zero. The Brazilian government made both assumptions in justifying the project. When the nearby stands run out, the private smelters will likely be forced to shut down, leaving a ruined rainforest behind them.

THE RAINFOREST may not have the strength to recuperate from these repeated assaults. With the incursions now so frequent, with roads now piercing the protective bubble that had previously protected the Amazon from man, the one species who could destroy it, the Amazon may fall along with its despoilers.

Some 500,000 landless peasants and 50,000 cattle ranchers, none of them individually as threatening as Ford, Ludwig, or the Brazilian government, have collectively become the major engine of destruction. Traveling along highway BR-364, the road which replaced the Madeira-Mamoré railway, lured by government ads promising free rich land and a better life, they would discover that the Amazon's verdancy sprang not from its soil but from the canopy of life above it.

Within a few years of their arrival, vast areas of destroyed Amazon rainforest could be spotted from space, clouds of smoke replacing what were once the rainclouds of the greatest river basin on earth. In this way, the world's most concentrated, diverse, and ordered habitat has become a commons that is fast devolving into a desert.

The peasants plant subsistence crops, exhausting the soil after a few years. When crops fail, they move further into the forest, burning and planting, failing, and then moving further in again. In their wake come ranchers who consolidate the cleared land to graze exotic species of cattle.

But Amazonian soils make poor pastures. The minerals held in the rainforest's lush vegetation, though released to the soils upon clearing, soon vanish. As the pastures' nutrient value declines, noxious weeds invade. Incapable of supporting grass-lands, the pastures are abandoned, usually within ten years of the initial clearing.

There was much to draw the cattle ranching industry into the rainforest: cattle are a symbol of prestige and the cattle rancher, flanked by gleaming white herds, is a potent image of the wealthy frontiersman. But status wasn't enough: the government needed to provide lucrative tax incentives, subsidies, and outright grants to encourage the massive livestock projects – average size: 60,000 acres – favored by its Superintendency for the Development of Amazonia.

According to the World Bank, livestock subsidies cost the Brazilian government over $1 billion between 1975 and 1986. The British magazine *The Economist* calls it "the biggest known subsidy in history for ecological destruction, unrelieved by economic gain."

Mammon, as much as nature, should persuade Brazil to conserve the Amazon. Much deforestation results from activities fostered by bad fiscal policies: from cattle ranching designed to mop up tax losses, from unprofit-able hydro-electric schemes built to provide under-priced electricity, from iron smelting built with lavish state aid, from small farmers displaced by the subsidised mechanisation of big farming in the south. President Sarney has begun to put a stop to cattle-ranching subsidies. A strong, sensible government would save itself money, and ultimately create more jobs, by ending all such fiscal folly. Many of the schemes that spring up where the trees come down are intrinsically uneconomic.

The World Bank, which had lent a half billion dollars to this giant road-building and agricultural colonization project – called "Polonoroeste" or "North West Development Pole" – eventually admitted its mistake. World Bank President Barber Conable, on the U.S. public affairs program *60 Minutes*, described the Polonoroeste project as "a sobering example of an environmentally sound effort which went wrong." He explained that "the bank misread the human, institutional and physical realities of the jungle and the frontier."

The Polonoroeste project, by providing access on a scale unknown before, threatens the destruction of an area of the Amazon the size of Great Britain. Indian lands are systematically seized, generally without compensation, and Indian economies destroyed. The livelihoods of non-Indian dwellers – mainly rubber tappers who for generations had collected rubber, Brazil nuts, and rainforest products – are also threatened.

Defying reason, the Inter-American Development Bank followed in the World Bank's footsteps and financed an extension of highway BR-364 still deeper into the Amazon, heightening tensions between the rubber tappers and Indians on the one hand and colonizers, especially the cattle ranchers, on the other. Their conflict over land led to hundreds of murders, including the assassination of Chico Mendes, the now legendary union leader of the rubber tappers.

With the razing of the rainforest came disease. The malaria-carrying mosquitoes, which had formerly restricted themselves to monkeys and other creatures in the jungle's upper canopy, discovered the ever expanding human population on the ground, making malaria endemic and leading the Brazilian government to declare the area a national public health emergency zone. To counter the malaria epidemic which threatened its development plans, the World Bank lent the state of Rondonia $99 million for a mosquito eradication program, with DDT its choice of pesticide.

IN INDONESIA, AS IN BRAZIL, the state spent billions of dollars – most of it raised through foreign loans or from oil revenues – to colonize the rainforest. The Indonesian program, called Transmigration, is a modern-day version of the old North American homesteading: residents of Indonesia's densely populated central islands were relocated in the sparsely populated, rainforested islands such as Kalimantan (formerly Borneo) and Irian Jaya (western New Guinea).

Those who originally challenged the transmigration program as a thinly veiled experiment in social engineering, and as an unprecedented gamble with the last great rainforests of Asia, have been borne out. Millions of dollars, many lives, and vast expanses of destroyed tropical rainforests later, transmigration is a dismal failure.

Thousands were moved to areas with water available only six months a year, with soil unsuited to farming. Many abandoned their plots only to join the ranks of shifting cultivators or illegal loggers: an estimated 300,000 of those who remain languish at impoverished farms. Exotic pests introduced by the transmigrants decimated crops. The rat population exploded on the rotting remains of burned and bulldozed rainforest. To counter these pests, peasants saturated their fields with chemicals, leading to humans poisoned by DDT and Klerat, a rodentcide. As in Brazil, malaria spread among the migrant population.

The native people, who once counted the rainforest as their home, have had their land and their means of subsistence mercilessly eroded, with clashes between them and settler communities on the increase.

The environmental horrors aside, there is not even a semblance of an economic argument to help justify this enormously destructive scheme: the World Bank, one of the main financiers

31

of the transmigration operation, merely explains that the project has "unquantifiable economic and social benefits," citing hoped-for benefits from increased food security and improved regional development – precisely the opposite of what transmigration has brought.

As in the rainforests of the Americas, investments in other environmentally risky endeavors the world over – especially large dams – were ending in financial disaster. What were touted as engineering miracles instead turned out to be technical nightmares and financial drains on the people they were meant to enrich.

Guatemala's Chixoy hydro dam was one such example. Completed in 1983, the dam was closed six months later when a 26-mile tunnel feeding water to the power station collapsed. This feeder tunnel, one of the longest ever built in Latin America, cut through unstable geological formations, including gypsum, a soluble rock, where the collapse eventually occurred. Repairing it – an operation that involved lining the tunnel with steel – took four years and helped triple the dam's cost to $1 billion.

Through this entire fiasco, the financiers of Chixoy were always at the ready to lend more money to help see the project through. The Inter-American Development Bank, with cofinancing from several commercial banks and the World Bank, financed the construction of the dam, then the repairs to the tunnel, and eventually when soil erosion threatened to cripple the dam they financed plans for corrective action including reforestation and soil reclamation. In the end, this hoped-for economic boon had become a boondoggle responsible for a third of Guatemala's $2.5 billion foreign debt.

In the Dominican Republic, the Tavera dam – its productive life already shortened – is threatened by swaths of hillside that sweep into the turbines with the rains. Dominicans have had to borrow more to dredge out the muck. Meanwhile, their Valdesia dam is impoverishing them as well, and for similar reasons. Because its deforested hills choke the reservoir with silt, it is becoming useless.

In China, siltation is so severe that the Sanmenxia dam had to be decommissioned just four years after completion, and the Laoying reservoir was retired even before dam construction was completed. In Colombia, the lower Anchicayá reservoir filled with silt within the first decade of operation, and the silt-laden Guatavita hydroelectric complex operates at one-sixth capacity.

When not crippled by high silt loads or by weed growth and acidic water, dams built in the last 40 years have often been crippled by lack of water. Ghana's Akosombo Dam – financed by the World Bank, various national aid agencies, and the export credit agencies of the U.S. and the U.K. – has for years provided between 40 and 80 per cent of its intended power because the Volta River has too little water to keep the dam's reservoir filled. In Peru, engineers designing the Carhuaquero dam discovered that the river had insufficient water before it was completed.

Brazil's Balbina dam similarly ran short of water. Its drainage basin – the surrounding area from which rainfall drains into the river – turned out to be only eight times larger than the reservoir itself, very small as hydroelectric dams go. As a result, water would flow into the reservoir too slowly to replenish the outgoing water generating the electricity: Balbina had only enough water to produce 112 megawatts – less than half the amount promised. Combined with cost overruns that doubled the original estimate, Balbina is doing more to bankrupt the economy than to enrich it.

Dams have also become nightmarish investments when they're designed for irrigation. Waterlogging from large irrigation systems has destroyed millions of acres of Third World farmland at a cost of billions of dollars. In the Indian state of Uttar Pradesh, a massive irrigation project designed to boost food production waterlogged 20 per cent more land than it irrigated, reducing overall food production. Throughout the Third World, irrigation takes as much land out of production each year, through waterlogging and salinization, as it brings into production.

Large-scale irrigation schemes were just one part of the Green Revolution – a package of agricultural techniques promoted to end hunger in hapless Third World countries forever. The rest of the package, which was promoted in the Asian countries in the 1960s, included fertilizers and pesticides, mechanization, and new seed varieties genetically engineered to provide higher yields. Like other revolutions blinkered by dogma, the Green Revolution has often failed spectacularly.

After 15 years of collecting data from Indonesia's rice fields, the International Rice Research Institute found that insecticides, though exorbitantly expensive, did not improve that country's rice yields. Several hundred species of insects normally live in a rice field, and for every insect that is a pest many more are natural predators which do not damage the rice but feed on the pests that do. By upsetting the delicate balance between pest and predator which had evolved over 3,000 years of rice farming in Asia, pesticides cause havoc.

Before the Green Revolution, the brown planthopper was a minor pest in the rice crops of Java and north Sumatra. By 1976, because it was resistant to the pesticides which were destroying its predators, the planthopper devastated over 500,000 hectares, destroying 350,000 tons of rice – enough to feed three million people for an entire year. Efforts to eradicate the planthopper with higher doses of pesticide proved a costly failure.

When another outbreak of brown planthopper plague appeared imminent in 1986, the Indonesian government reverted to pre-revolutionary techniques: it cut pesticide subsidies and banned many pesticides from rice fields. Within a year pesticide use fell by more than half, natural predators thrived, and the planthopper population in pesticide-free fields declined by 75 per cent. Crop yields soared, and the government saved a small fortune in subsidies.

Scores of debt-financed development projects have become outright money losers when their physical and environmental repercussions were ignored. But sometimes developers can insulate their projects from the environment's wrath, making the projects themselves appear viable. All too often, in those cases, society as a whole, and future generations, pay for the environmental sins of the destroyers.

34

3

The Environment Strikes Back: The Economy

AT THE CLOSE OF THE 1980s, with concern at its height for the Amazon's survival, researchers from the New York Botanical Garden, the Missouri Botanical Garden, and the School of Forestry at Yale University published a joint study on the value of the edible fruits and latex, known as "minor" forest products, harvested from a standing rainforest. The value of the produce, which the rainforest's inhabitants had for generations collected and sold in local markets, came to $6,330 per hectare, compared to only $2,960 from a hectare cleared for raising cattle, and

$3,184 from a hectare of fast-growing tree plantations.

Yet although the land was twice as productive in its pristine state, the importance of the traditional rainforest economy had been denigrated by government and business interests alike, with only "modern" businesses being accorded any respect. The study blamed biased public policy and selective economic accounting: "Tropical timber is sold in international markets and generates substantial amounts of foreign exchange; it is a highly visible export commodity controlled by the government and supported by large federal expenditures." On the other hand, the study explained, the more valuable "minor" forest products are "collected and sold in local markets by an incalculable number of subsistence farmers, forest collectors, middlemen, and shop-owners. These decentralized trade networks are extremely hard to monitor and easy to ignore in national accounting schemes." Most financial appraisals of the tropical rainforests simply didn't bother to count this difficult-to-identify rainforest GNP: the rare attempts made to quantify them had been half-hearted and grossly underestimated their true value, hence the myth that destructive logging and widespread forest clearance would yield more than an intact rainforest.

The same failure to count properly was being made the world over, in the rainforest and outside it. The Philippines, until the 1970s a super-achiever among Third World economies, had relied heavily on its minerals, timber, and other assets to increase its GNP. But the Philippines, like most countries, failed to account for changes in its natural resource stocks. When it sold its trees, for example, its GNP recorded the sale as an economic activity, as was the norm. But the Philippines' accounts didn't show the corresponding loss from its balance sheet of the assets (the trees) liquidated to generate that economic activity. Through this method of accounting, all appeared rosy for the Philippines until its forests were virtually wiped out – as happened in the late 1980s. Over a period of 30 years, the forest industry went from being the country's top foreign exchange earner to being the largest importer of raw materials and one of the largest drains on the country's foreign exchange reserves. Now destitute, the industry has become a national liability.

Such an accounting method has brought many to ruin. People who come into an inheritance and sell off the family treasures for imprudent investments or extravagances might appear to be successful to themselves and to outsiders. But if the sales don't generate new wealth, such people become destitute when there's nothing left to sell.

Most people (and all companies) judge their economic success by the wealth they are accumulating, not by the rate at which they are spending. Countries, however, do not record their physical wealth in their national statistics; they judge their success chiefly through statistics called gross national product (GNP) or gross domestic product (GDP). GNP counts all economic activities as positive – even if the activity diminishes a nation's store of natural resources – by measuring how much is sold, not how much wealth remains. To improve their country's GNP, government leaders thus attempt to increase economic activity, with little regard for the activity's profitability. They are often hailed as economic masters until there's nothing left to sell.

A study by the U.S.-based World Resources Institute estimated that growth in Indonesia's gross domestic product, when calculated properly to account for the loss or denigration of its natural resources, was only half the amount officially estimated. Taking into account only three assets – oil, forests, and soils – each of which was depleted to increase the country's output, Indonesia's GDP dropped from 7.1 per cent growth to 4 per cent. Had the World Resources Institute included other important assets such as coal, copper, tin, nickel, fisheries, and natural gas, the country's actual GDP would have been slashed further, possibly even showing a net loss of wealth.

The World Resources Institute's detailed examination of the degradation of Indonesia's soils illustrates how the country's expansion of modern agriculture proved to be a double-edged economic sword. On the central, densely populated islands of Java, Bali, and Madura, clearing steeply sloped highlands of their forest cover to make way for maize and cassava did increase agricultural output. As hillsides were cleared of trees, however, erosion increased dramatically, and each hectare now loses 60 tons of topsoil every year. The sedimentation clogs reservoirs, harbors, and irrigation systems, and harms fisheries and other users of the water downstream. Nutrients are also lost from the soil, which becomes thin and less fertile. Although improved seed varieties and fertilizers helped boost crop yields in the hilly areas, the annual loss of soil fertility, measured as the value of lost farm income, is as large as the annual production increase. In other words, each production increase becomes offset by an equal loss in soil productivity, a senseless bargain that puts Indonesia's economy on a treadmill.

"Natural resources are treated as gifts of nature rather than as productive assets whose value must be depreciated if they are used up," the World Resources Institute concluded, adding that "a country could exhaust its mineral resources, cut down its forests, erode its soils, pollute its aquifers, and hunt its wildlife and fisheries to extinction, but measured income would not be affected as these assets disappeared."

This negation of natural resources is deeply embedded in what has become the principal measure of a nation's economic progress – the system of national income accounts. Designed during World War II for the U.K. by John Maynard Keynes, the most influential economist of this century, national income accounting – the system that produces GNP and GDP – was soon adopted by other nations as an economic planning tool for wartime and peace. Keynes wanted governments to actively manage their economies to avoid another Great Depression. To serve this interventionist means to an end, he designed a system of national income accounts to allow governments to manipulate consumption, savings, investment, and government expenditures. To stimulate economic activity, governments would incur deficits by spending money on public works and other endeavors, thereby making the national accounts and the national economy look healthier. Limits to government pump-priming due to natural resource constraints were virtually dropped from the economic models of Keynes and his contemporaries: over the previous century productivity had advanced so greatly that resources had come to be treated as infinite. Economics in the Keynesian world of government intervention lost its theoretical underpinnings as the "science of scarcity" articulated by the classical economists Adam Smith, David Ricardo, and John Stuart Mill.

Keynes and the other Brave-New-World economists could hardly be faulted for being dazzled by the 19th century's extraordinary advances: steamships and railroads were dramatically lowering transport costs while food grains and raw materials came flooding in from North and South America, Australia, Russia, and the imperial colonies. "It was not that Nature herself had become more generous," explained Robert Heilbroner in his treatise on the history of economic thought. "On the contrary, as the famous Law of Diminishing Returns made clear, Nature yielded up her wealth more grudgingly as she was more intensively cultivated." No, Heilbroner went on, "the secret to economic growth lay in the fact that each generation attacked Nature not only with its own energies and resources, but with the heritage of equipment accumulated by its forebears." As that heritage grew – as each generation added its quota of new knowledge, factories, tools, and techniques to the wealth of the past – human productivity grew at an astonishing pace, and Nature's parsimony began to fade as a determinant of the wealth of nations.

FOR THE HALF CENTURY since the birth of the national income accounts, economic planners and governments the world over have assumed virtually limitless natural resources capable of virtually limitless exploitation, depreciating at such a vanishingly slow rate – if at all – as to not be worth counting. Unlike buildings, equipment, and other man-made assets, which accountants depreciate in value as they are used, the nation's natural resources are presumed able to generate a steady, unending stream of undiminished future income.

Those same resources, however, can trickle to naught or they can generate a torrent of debt, as the coincidence of debt-ridden and resource-rich economies shows: Mexico, Venezuela, and Nigeria are all oil exporters, and all became heavily indebted. With their economies in irresponsible hands, their national balance sheets deteriorated badly as they sold off their natural resource assets while borrowing wildly against the amount left unsold, using both sources of cash to finance consumption and all-but-worthless investments. In the end they, and the other Third World debtors who borrowed against their resource assets, have been squeezed between a dwindling asset base and soaring debt payments.

Low-income countries tend to be more dependent on their natural resources for employment, revenues, and foreign exchange. Ironically, the system of national accounting by which they measure their economic progress completely ignores their principal asset, sending out signals to exploit their resources when signals to preserve them are most needed.

The disregard for a country's natural assets stemmed from more than perverse national income accounting conventions: it also stemmed from a nearly total disregard for the value of other people's activities. The productive endeavors of millions of people have for the past half century been overlooked and left out of the cost-benefit calculations for the world's great development projects. When a farmer's fields are expropriated for irrigation canals, when nomadic peoples' grazing lands are plowed under for cotton plantations, when a community's forest lands are turned over to loggers, when prime agricultural farmland is submerged by a dam reservoir, assets are destroyed and go unrecorded in the selective and usually secret calculations of the development planners and Third World governments. These lost assets, and the lost productivity that springs from them, silently erode the economic wherewithal of a nation.

The staggeringly large costs of natural resource exploitation have escaped man's notice for the past century. But these costs will not escape the laws of nature, which in the end always demand an accounting.

4

The Asset Sale

LITTLE HAS CHANGED SINCE 1519, the year Hernando Cortés and his fleet reached Mexico's Yucatán peninsula in search of glory, conquest, and riches for God and Spain. Cortés was no ordinary conquistador: unlike his predecessors, who came only to loot, Cortés envisioned Mexico a Spanish province in Spain's service.

With cunning, and with the help of firearms, coats of mail, and mounted troops which the Indians considered supernatural, Cortés began a three-hundred-year subjugation. Under Spanish rule, looting ended and the state-sanctioned extraction of Mexico's assets began.

In the Europe of the fourteenth and fifteenth centuries, with the bourgeoisie rising, commerce expanding, and European kings needing to finance their wars, gold had become Europe's most prized commodity. Gold shipments from Mexico, at first limited to nuggets that Indians gathered from the ground and panned from rivers, steadily grew as rich underground veins were discovered. Silver and other precious metals soon followed, as did cochineal (dried insects yielding a scarlet dye), and indigo.

The Spanish monarchy bled the Mexican economy dry of any profits it might make: it wanted Mexico's resources and little else. Spain prohibited colonial industries that might compete with those of Spain, taxed producers of all precious metals, levied duties on other imports and exports, sequestered profits from government monopolies in salt, quicksilver and, in the eighteenth century, tobacco, and introduced a bewildering array of other taxes. In February of each year, these revenues sailed from Mexico in a treasure fleet to Spain.

The soil gave up its produce for Spain as well. All the land being the property of the crown, the Indian populations had little protection from encroachment by the *hacendados*, or large farmers. As the Indians' standard of living declined, that of the *hacendados* rose higher and higher.

Mexican industry zigged and zagged according to the imperial policies of the day. Sixteenth-century kings, promoting new export crops, planted wheat fields, vineyards, orchards of fruit trees, and groves of mulberry trees for silkworms, only to have seventeenth-century kings chop them down when Spanish manufacturers complained about this colonial competition.

Mining, which made large fortunes, was the only Mexican industry which Spain unswervingly encouraged: the mine's annual yield continued to increase, rising from about two million pesos in the middle of the sixteenth century to about thirteen million in the middle of the eighteenth.

Over the centuries, the population of Mexico and the other

colonies increasingly became European in character as Spanish immigrants came to the colonies to form the dominant class and the colony's viceroy ruled on behalf of the Spanish monarch. When the colonies of Spain and other European powers became independent in the 1800s and 1900s, the new, Mexican-born leaders no longer had to answer to an imperial power, but little else changed.

In most cases, the new governments inherited colonial systems that centuries earlier had dissolved the Indians' traditional property rights, deeming much of their resources to be state property. The new rulers, in Spanish America and elsewhere, pushed expropriation still further, adding oil, iron, lead and copper to the list of extractable assets. Under independent rule, the world's emerging nations began to export their assets with unprecedented vigor: rubber from Malaysia, timber from the Philippines, coffee from Tanzania, copper from Zaire, bauxite from Venezuela.

In the 1950s and 1960s, to further accelerate such exports, Third World governments decided to borrow money, mainly from the international aid agencies and other public bodies. And the public bodies encouraged them, believing that the Third World needed capital to earn foreign exchange for the technology and know-how to industrialize. How better to acquire it than by selling its abundant assets?

In the 1970s, when the price of oil, copper and other commodities soared, those assets became even more valuable, pushing the credit ratings of their Third World owners to unprecedented levels and resource exploitation to new heights. In the 1980s, when the world's economy reeled through recession, and the Third World's debt crisis hit home, among the few constants in that uncertain time was the Third World's asset sale, which continues, as it has from the start, unabated to this day.

Today's debt crisis has not authored the asset sale: with or without the debt crisis, the asset sale would continue. But one thing has changed. Where once the beneficiary was a conquistador, or a colonial power, or a local elite, today the Third World's foreign financiers are claiming a share of the bounty. To pay off existing debts – and also to reestablish credit for more borrowing – debtor nations are selling off their various resource assets.

Brazil is becoming the world's largest iron ore exporter, with roughly $2 billion a year from the Carajas mining operation alone. In petroleum-exporting Indonesia, when foreign exchange revenues fell with the price of oil the government increased its timber exports. A quarter of its non-petroleum exports, totaling some $3 billion per year, now comes from forestry products, increasingly from the last great tropical rainforest refuge found in the Indonesian archipelago on the island of Irian Jaya. By 1990, more than half of Indonesia's rainforests had been razed.

Forests in other countries have also fallen under the logger's axe to meet the banker's deadline. Ecuador loosened logging restrictions to meet international interest payments. In Southern Cameroon, the United Nations' Food and Agriculture Organization is pushing the exploitation of a pristine tropical forest to help retire Cameroon's $4.7 billion debt. In Ghana, the World Bank is asking the forest industry to step up its foreign exchange earnings. To help Ghana comply, Canada's national foreign aid agency donated the forestry equipment Ghana needed to extract the trees. Tropical timbers became so marketable that, by 1990, 14 of the 17 most deeply indebted nations were rapidly losing their rainforests.

The United Nations leads an international effort to increase Third World exports: a controversial 1990 U.N. report exhorted African countries to boost their commodity industries through new exports to Asia and eastern Europe. The World Bank and other institutions encourage countries to boost "non-traditional exports," or exports they have never produced before.

A decade ago, Ecuador boosted shrimp, enough to make shrimp the country's second largest foreign exchange earner after oil, and Ecuador the world's leading shrimp exporter. But shrimp farming has high environmental costs. To create the shallow ponds this industry needs, the coast's mangrove cover was all but destroyed. Meeting no mangrove barriers, storms in

1983 inundated and salinated 80,000 hectares of prime agricultural land. Silt, no longer trapped by the mangroves, now threatens to clog the country's largest port of Guayaquil. Fishing cooperatives blame depleted catches on the loss of the mangroves, which had provided a nursery for commercially important fish species.

The Philippines similarly found prawn farming to be damaging. Because prawns require a mix of fresh and salt water, fresh water is pumped into the ponds and mixed with sea water. Large ponds employ huge turbines pumping 25,000 gallons of water per minute, drying up fresh-water wells and forcing nearby consumers to ration water. After several years, the parched water table sucks in water from the sea, raising salinity levels. Left unchecked, agricultural land becomes salinized and, ironically, the prawn ponds themselves are destroyed. Now, after only a few years of operation, experts believe the prawn farms need to be closed down for a generation to flush out the salinity.

IN 1975, AT THE HEIGHT of the foreign borrowing boom, Philippine President Ferdinand Marcos's government ran an ad in *Fortune* magazine that made it clear where he stood when it came to his country's assets: "to attract companies ... like yours ... we have felled mountains, razed jungles, filled swamps, moved rivers, relocated towns, and in their place built power plants, dams, roads.... All to make it easier for you and your business to do business here." By 1990, the language used by Third World governments to attract foreign businesses, especially those that would produce exports, had become more muted, but remained plunderous none the less.

In glossy brochures distributed to the delegates at the annual meetings of the international development banks every year, Third World governments advertize their countries' resources and new investment opportunities for bankers and manufacturers. At an Inter-American Development Bank meeting, Venezuela waxed eloquent about being the home of the fabled city of El Dorado: it wasn't just a legend, Venezuela said. The jungle region thought to contain the fabled city "does indeed hold vast stores of gold and diamonds." But, the brochure went on to say, there is more to Venezuela's wealth than that: in addition it has oil, iron ore, steel, bauxite and "torrential rivers" providing "abundant and cheap hydroelectric power." Gone was the "inward-looking subsidized economy" in favor of "one propelled by private sector activity and geared towards exports."

Gabon's brochure to the delegates of a World Bank and IMF Annual Meeting bragged about plans to mine new minerals such as barites, niobium, gold, and diamonds; to develop its "almost virgin agricultural sector"; and to take advantage of its new railway into the forests for the "intense exploitation" and "evacuation" of logs and timber.

Chile's exports of choice were copper, fruit, pulpwood and other forestry products, and fish meal. Chile achieved its status as the world's largest fish meal exporter at the expense of its fish stocks, which are now threatened with extinction. For Bolivia, a combination of soybeans, gold, oil, and gas were its exports of choice; for Guatemala, pulpwood; for Burma, oil and tropical timber; for the Sudan, pesticide-dependent cotton monocultures; and for Senegal, Mali, and Mauritania it was rice, sugar, and cotton from the massive Senegal River project. Hundreds of millions of dollars had been borrowed to transform the Senegal's subsistence farmers into cash-crop farmers, and now the millions would have to be repaid.

RESOURCE EXTRACTION CAN BENEFIT an economy without harming the environment, when the extracted resource is controlled by those with an incentive to husband it, and when common resources – air, water, and earth – are intelligently managed to protect the rights of those who might be downwind or downstream.

Traditional societies enforce strong regulations to protect the common environment – anyone poisoning the communal well in an African village will meet swift justice. But traditional societies are in demise, with the traditional rights of individuals and whole communities eroded, even outlawed, by remote central governments prepared to sacrifice individuals and whole communities to the national interest. These rights to property – both private and communal – and to one's health, are now being appropriated by the state in what amounts to another form of asset sale – the exploitation of common resources for export purposes.

In Mexico, 2,000 foreign-owned assembly plants that line the U.S.-Mexican border – *maquiladoras* as they are known – have provided Mexico with an enormous economic benefit. Mexicans assemble U.S.-made parts into finished products, then ship them back to the U.S., helping to reduce the region's unemployment rate from 40 per cent to almost zero and earning more foreign exchange for the nation than anything else save oil. But according to a special report in *The Wall Street Journal*, "their very success is helping turn much of the border region into a sinkhole of abysmal living conditions and environmental degradation.... Old cars on dirt paths raise huge clouds of dust that mingle with exhaust fumes and industrial pollution to cast a poisonous pall of smog over the border towns.... Aquifers shared by both Americans and Mexicans are being sucked dry at an alarming rate, and industrial toxins and untreated sewage are poisoning rivers, streams and other water sources."

Contributing to the poisonous shroud that frequently envelopes the Mexican and U.S. cities of Juarez and El Paso are the U.S. furniture makers who fled Los Angeles' tough new restriction on solvents emissions.

According to *The Wall Street Journal*, "Little is being done about the wholesale environmental destruction, health hazards and poor living conditions that the rush to the border has spawned. Though Mexico's environmental laws were stiffened in 1988, its fiscal crisis has left it with so few inspectors to enforce the laws that they can be evaded with ease; a 1988 survey of *maquiladora* plant managers in Agua Prieta, Mexico, disclosed that none had ever seen such an inspector."

Mexican officials, says *The Wall Street Journal*, are not eager to press the point. "We are not in a position to scare these companies away," says Leobardo Gil Torres, the mayor of one border town. "We are in a crisis, you see. What do we do if these companies leave?"

The trade-offs between economic progress and environmental protection seem irresolvable to this mayor, and to others in the lawless jurisdiction in which Mexicans find themselves. Yet such trade-offs had once been resolved, through traditional laws that enforced respect for property rights. Modern systems cannot cope with the commons they have created, and as long as that remains the case, the asset sale will continue.

5

The Debt Crisis' Silver Lining

"WE'VE ENJOYED THE DEBT CRISIS," said Gustavo Esteva of Mexico, a country burdened with $100 billion in debt it could not repay, and with social and environmental problems as severe as those in any Third World country. Mr. Esteva, a social reformer who describes himself as "a man who works with the peasants," is better known to some Mexicans as a former executive at International Business Machines and a former head of Mexico's General Plan for Public Expenditures.

The debt crisis, said Mr. Esteva, has helped Mexico's

environment: it has given the land and its people a reprieve by shelving unsustainable logging and agricultural schemes, and by delaying Mexico's nuclear program and other environmentally risky projects.

Mr. Esteva was speaking not from theory but from practice. In theory, his government might have been loath to sell off its natural resources, but been forced to do so to satisfy foreign creditors. In practice it had no such loathing, borrowing to its credit limit and beyond precisely to finance rapid resource exploitation. The only brake on that exploitation came from the debt crisis; with a government's capacity to borrow curtailed, so too is its capacity to do environmental harm.

Brazil, the world's largest debtor, piled up 25 per cent of its $111 billion foreign debt on a building binge of unneeded electricity projects that left its creditors dizzy and its environment in tatters. So profligate was the electricity system's expansion that by 1988, one-third of Brazil's national utility system's annual operating revenues went to pay interest on external loans. Consequently, Eletrobrás (the national electric utility) borrowed ever larger amounts – eight dollars out of every ten spent – to finance new projects.

The most spectacular investment ever made by Brazil's electricity moguls involved the Itaipu hydroelectric dam on the Brazil-Paraguay border. Itaipu is the largest dam in the world, so large that the Symphony Orchestra of Brazil held a concert in one of its eighteen turbines. It cost $20.5 billion to build, with incalculable environmental and human costs: Itaipu flooded almost 1,500 square kilometers of tropical forest and farmland; it drowned Sete Quedas, one of South America's most impressive natural cataracts; and it displaced 40,000 people, including the Ava-Guarani Indians, mostly without proper compensation. The dam also destroyed the habitat of 252 species of birds and 70 known species of other animals including armadillos, tapirs, crocodiles, jaguars and deer. For the Brazilian people saddled with paying the $8 billion in foreign debts accumulated by the dam, it was an extravagance they didn't need and couldn't afford. The trade journal, *International Water Power and Dam*

Construction, reports that the investment may never be profitable.

Tucurui, another monster dam built shortly after Itaipu, submerged 2,400 square kilometers of now rotting rainforest and cost Brazil another $5 billion, plus lasting environmental harm. Even the dam building industry called the "whole Tucurui story ... one of incompetence, nepotism and greed."

But the credit available to finance these Third World megaprojects became tighter and tighter, so much so that just a few months after Tucurui's completion Brazil's president decided to suspend the notorious Balbina dam as part of an IMF-induced budget cutting exercise. Brazil was out of money, and Balbina was becoming a rallying point for environmentalists around the world. It took urgent appeals by the governor and other representatives from the state of Amazonas to President Sarney to avert the cutoff of funds.

Armando Ribeiro de Araujo, adviser to the president of Eletronorte, the utility responsible for the Amazon, chided environmentalists for their "hands-off the Amazon" demands. "It is unthinkable that such a rich region as the Amazon might be kept eternally untouched," he said. On the other hand, he acknowledged that foreign funds were the limiting factor. "Right now, in Brazil the problem is money. That's the only limit to what we can do."

By 1987, the credit crunch had accomplished much of what environmentalists had sought. Brazil was defaulting on its debt to commercial banks, very little new money was coming in, and the megaprojects began to fall. Eletrobrás was put on a short financial leash and forced to cut back on five hydroelectric projects, including the second phase of Tucurui.

Brazil's massive nuclear power expansion program, like Mexico's, was also grounded by the debt crisis, its backers bemoaning to *The Wall Street Journal* readers that Brazilian state planners remembered the nuclear industry "only at the time of budget cuts."

Brazil's nuclear program, started in 1969, soon called for nine nuclear reactors by 1990, all but one of which was to be built and financed under an agreement with the West German government. The agreement provided for direct loans and credit facilities and for an extensive program of technology transfer involving some 16 German companies and organizations. By 1990, however, only one of the nine plants, Angra I, had been completed. Its intermittent operation has earned it the nickname, "the firefly." Angra II, with 90 per cent of the work done, was grounded until March of 1990 when the Brazilian National Congress finally authorized $200 million needed for its completion, now scheduled for 1995. Funds to finance the balance of the program have simply dried up – probably a good thing. Brazil's experience with nuclear power has been dismal, with the cost of nuclear electricity approximately five times higher than the government estimated when signing the agreement with the West German government.

In Argentina, the nuclear power program was also slowed by the credit squeeze. In 1988, the National Atomic Energy Commission started to plan the orderly shutdown of the half-completed Atucha 2 nuclear power plant because the $750 million needed to finish it could not be found. "It's not that there has been a conscious decision to postpone nuclear development," said Dr. Pérez Ferreira, the president of the National Atomic Energy Commission, "but that the Government has to postpone everything – teacher's raises, social welfare, pensions and more."

During the 1970s – the decade responsible for the lion's share of the Third World's $1.3 trillion debt – developing countries undertook an estimated 1,614 megaprojects with a total cost of more than $1 trillion. The average size of each project was about $620 million. Nearly a quarter of those megaprojects were in the oil sector, nearly 20 per cent in the mining sector, and over half were for infrastructure projects including electric power, roads, agricultural, and communications projects. Virtually all of these projects required foreign financing to proceed, and virtually none were economic without subsidies. Virtually all of these projects have damaged the environment.

The megaprojects building craze led Brazilian environmentalists like Magda Renner of Friends of the Earth to conclude that "Brazil's environment and the world's financial system would be a lot better off if the international financiers had just kept their money." Like Gustavo Esteva of Mexico, many Third World citizens were suddenly finding they had the unlikeliest of allies – the debt crisis.

Because too much money in the wrong hands so often causes environmental destruction, environmentalists have sometimes found themselves fighting hard to thwart debt-relief measures worked out in Washington and Third World capitals. One such unlikely rallying point for the global environmental movement was the World Bank's Second Power Sector Loan. Like the First Power Sector Loan that helped finish the Balbina dam, the second loan would have both helped Brazil pay back some of its international debts and refueled Brazil's mega-dam plan to build 136 new dams, many of them in the Amazon.

In Peru, exuberant attempts to finance a rapid expansion of hydro dams in the wake of the 1973 oil crisis were dampened by Peru's own credit unworthiness and by the most fundamental handicap for a hydro dam, a lack of water. Construction of the Carhuaquero plant in the north of Peru – designed to generate electricity and to provide water for irrigation – ground to a halt for three years during the 1980s because Peru couldn't raise the money to finish it and because, as *International Water Power and Dam Construction* described it, the dam "would not have sufficient water." Construction of the Charcani V hydro station in the south part of the country was also delayed for exactly the same reasons. While these projects limped along, other large hydro power plants scheduled to be built in Peru's Amazonian areas never got off the drawing boards at all. The debt crisis was the cause: international bankers began insisting that Peruvians finance 50 per cent of each project. Since neither the Peruvian people nor the Peruvian government had this money, the largest schemes were canceled.

Argentina's Yacyretá dam staggers from one financier to another, each financier suspecting that the $5.8 billion dam should be canceled, but each one dedicating an extra few hundred million dollars in the belief that too much money has been sunk into the scheme to turn back now. The current financier, the Inter-American Development Bank, signed a $250 million loan in April 1990, the same day Argentina's President Carlos Menem called the dam a testament to greed and corruption too expensive for the country's treasury. Without fresh money, the Yacyretá cannot be completed.

The debt crisis has been stopping African boondoggles as well, such as the Sudanese government's attempts to finance an increase in the height of the Roseires dam. A ten meter increase would have doubled the dam's storage capacity, increasing its power output and irrigation. But the increased height would have expanded the dam's reservoir and displaced thousands of farming families, many of whom had been previously displaced by the Aswan dam built on the Nile in the 1950s. Sudan's limited access to foreign financing put the $350 million project on hold for at least five years.

Even China, notable for its financial prudence (in limiting its debt servicing payments to between 15 per cent and 20 per cent of its foreign exchange earnings), was forced to shelve projects when foreign funds became scarce. Fiscal constraints slowed China's nuclear power expansion program, and helped postpone the mammoth Three Gorges hydroelectric dam on the Yangtze River, among others.

According to the manager of Asea Brown Boveri China Limited, a Swiss-Swedish company building a hydro project in southwest China, without outside money "we have no chance. They [the Chinese] can't afford to build the project without foreign financing."

All over the world, megaprojects vanished as fast as the money-lenders withdrew their credit lines. In the Cameroon, all that stands between that country's last great standing rainforests and the loggers' chainsaws is an IMF-World Bank austerity program. Thanks to a "restructuring" of Cameroon's forestry sector there are no foresters on staff to carry out a menacing national forestry plan devised by the United Nations Food and Agriculture Organization under the auspices of the Tropical

Forestry Action Plan. Known as TFAP, this plan is a lumbering Frankenstein invented by foreign aid bureaucrats, ostensibly to save tropical forests in dozens of Third World countries. The Cameroon's version of TFAP foresaw the country becoming "the most important African exporter of forestry-based products from the start of the 21st century." To accomplish this it recommended that roads and other infrastructure be built to get the timber out of the rainforest. The 50,000 Pygmy people of the rainforest, who wish that the U.N. experts and their logging entourage would go back to wherever they came from, will have their wish if lending doesn't resume.

While grandiose megaprojects were canceled by the debt crisis, so too were environmentally destructive policies that depended on persistent government subsidies. Agricultural subsidies in Nicaragua cost the country's economy dearly while pumping dangerous chemicals into the Nicaraguan environment. Although the former Sandinista government had, on the face of it, an enlightened pesticides policy – upon taking power the Sandinistas banned a number of dangerous pesticides including DDT, aldrin and endrin – a host of subsidies made pesticides virtually free to most Nicaraguan farmers. All agricultural inputs were brought into the country at a highly favorable exchange rate: pesticides, for example, were imported and marketed through a state-owned agency providing 95 per cent to 98 per cent subsidies on the real price. Another subsidy came in the form of interest rates to farmers at a fraction of inflation rates. In addition, the state-owned bank providing many of the loans periodically forgave them, never foreclosing or punishing producers for not repaying. The consequences of these policies, in the words of an entomologist and foreign aid official, were "easy to predict: the use of agrochemical inputs rose dramatically, as did their waste and misuse." Farmers applied pesticides whenever they had time, since cost was not a consideration.

Cheap pesticides led to irrational use. Although pest infestation did not increase during the periods of subsidies, pesticide use did, doubling in maize in a ten year period.

The irrational use extended beyond any imagined by the

policymakers. Plastic containers were scarce in Nicaragua, and valued as water, gasoline, and diesel storage vessels. Reused pesticide containers filled this demand. During the height of the pesticide subsidies, the containers became more valuable than their contents, leading some entrepreneurs to buy insecticides, dump out the contents, and sell the container.

Pesticides also became lucrative contraband in neighboring Costa Rica and Honduras, which had relatively high pesticide prices. Smuggling sprang up along the borders. Along the Honduras-Nicaraguan border, one gallon of the herbicide Roundup (value U.S. $50) from Nicaragua would be routinely swapped for one pair of U.S. blue jeans coming through Honduras – a good deal for both traders whose profits came courtesy of the Nicaraguan taxpayer.

The Nicaraguan government maintained this costly and environmentally destructive policy for a political purpose: to subsidize the citizenry's basic necessities. For the urban dweller, the government subsidized staple foods and utilities such as electricity, transportation, and water. For the rural dweller, the government subsidized the inputs for agricultural production.

Ironically, despite repeated challenges to the subsidy policy from the Ministry of Agriculture, the Office of the Presidency maintained the subsidies until 1988, when enormous budget deficits and trade deficits (imports cost four times what exports earned) eventually forced an IMF-style austerity package on the government. The currency was subsequently devalued by 3,000 per cent against the U.S. dollar, and cheap credit policies and the preferential exchange rate for imports were abandoned. In a span of a few months, producers found their virtually free agricultural inputs at world-market prices. The effect was dramatic. Producers cut back on many inputs, including pesticides and other agrochemicals, while the Nicaraguan economy and the Nicaraguan environment heaved a sigh of relief.

Oil exploration in Peru, pulp mills in Brazil, railways in Honduras, bauxite mines in Surinam, cheap pesticides in Nicaragua – all disappeared in the absence of the cash to carry out the projects .

Then along came the Brady Plan in 1989, a debt relief plan designed to get new money flowing by having rich countries guarantee the repayment of existing debt. But many throughout the Third World fear that this new money – in the absence of democratic reforms needed to ensure prudent borrowing – will only breathe life into their governments' cash-starved mega-projects.

The Brady Plan's first test case – a rescheduling in Mexico – bore out these concerns. After negotiating a debt management strategy with the IMF and the World Bank, and thus getting back into their good credit books, Mexico borrowed $1.96 billion from the World Bank and $3.6 billion from the IMF. Almost half a billion dollars from the World Bank loan would finance two hydroelectric dams, destroying the environment of at least 3,000 peasants and indigenous people, and foreshadowing a new assault on the Third World's environment. It was the type of agreement that Gustavo Esteva had been dreading: "We are afraid when the debt crisis is over the money will flow again."

PART II

Easy Lenders

INTRODUCTION: PART II

The Queen Comes to Sicartsa

IN FEBRUARY 1983, the *Britannia*, Queen Elizabeth's royal yacht, carried Her Majesty to the port of Lazaro Cardenas on Mexico's west coast. The Queen's mission: to inspect Sicartsa, an integrated steel plant deserving of the Crown's attention, near the remote town of Las Truchas. Phase I of Sicartsa was built and operating, and Phase II's construction was about to begin. One year earlier, the British firm of Davy McKee had won the lion's share of new construction work at Sicartsa: $600 million of the entire $2 billion expansion. But Mexico was now facing a balance-of-payments crisis, and the government of Mexico was considering canceling phase II.

As the *Britannia* docked, Davy McKee agents milled on the pier with those of Lloyds Bank International. Lloyds had done far more than simply arrange private financing: it had helped Davy win the bid in Mexico and win government support back home. Neither the supplier, its banker, nor the U.K. government intended to let Sicartsa slip away. Queen Elizabeth came to silence any murmurings of this possibility in Mexico or elsewhere.

Sicartsa was no ordinary project: not many steel mills in backwaters within the Third World invoked a defense by the British Royal Family. But then neither was Sicartsa that different. The saga of Sicartsa helps explain how developing countries were able to borrow massive amounts of money for projects devoid of economic sense.

THE DREAM OF EXPLOITING Mexico's iron ore deposits goes back half a century. In the early 1940s, President Lazaro Cardenas – who in 1938 had expropriated Mexico's foreign-owned oil installations – conceived the idea of a steel complex at Las Truchas, part of his political base. With his death, the baton was passed to his successors, first to President Diaz Ordaz and then to President Echeverria, who in the early 1970s turned for technical advice to the British Steel Corporation and the world's largest international aid agencies – the World Bank and the Inter-American Development Bank.

By 1973, Mexico had a plan that seemed driven more by politics than by economics.

Sicartsa, or Siderurgica (Steelworks) Lazaro Cardenas-Las Truchas, takes its name from Cardenas. The Mexican government would fashion the massive steel complex – a 'Pacific Pittsburgh' – in four phases, each to be built in the term of a different Mexican president. President Echeverria, who put economic independence from the U.S. atop the national agenda, would preside over creation of the first phase.

Constructing Phase I of Sicartsa alone required a herculean

effort. The site chosen for this modern monument was so isolated – no main roads linked the project to the rest of the country – that an entire infrastructure would need to be created: houses, services, schools, shops, utilities. Not even a method for bringing in the massive amounts of coal required by Sicartsa's blast furnaces existed. A port would have to be built, workers and their families would then have to be brought in, and the population would need to increase almost tenfold, from 7,000 in 1970 to over 60,000 by 1976.

Once the infrastructure for Phase I was in place, the blast furnaces, the rolling mills, and nearly a dozen other major components would be required before the mill produced steel.

Financing a project as large and unlikely as Sicartsa should have strained the credulity of the staid banking world. Yet the financing was remarkably easy to muster. Sicartsa executives, again on the advice of the World Bank and the Inter-American Development Bank, toured the industrial world for financing, and easily found willing lenders. The president of the U.S. Export-Import Bank offered to finance the entire project if Mexico bought only U.S. equipment. Loans were so plentiful, however, that the Mexican government decided instead to diversify its suppliers – creating what some called "a United Nations of suppliers."

The French firm Fives Cail Babcock won the contract for the concentrator; Germany's Lurgi Chemie and the United Kingdom's Head Wrightson won the pelletizer contract; coke production would go to Nippon Kokan Kaisha of Japan; and the blast furnaces to Italimpianti of Italy. Voest-Alpine of Austria won the oxygen converter contract; Schloemann Concast of Germany and Canada the contract for the continuous caster; and Davy Loewy of the United Kingdom would build the rolling mills. Eleven foreign countries in all would work on the Sicartsa steel plant.

A United Nations of suppliers for Sicartsa Phase I brought with it a more than willing United Nations of financiers. Each country with a share of the action made sure money was available.

The European banks offered $180 million, nine governments of industrial nations $170 million, the Inter-American Development Bank $54 million, and the World Bank $70 million. Mexico only needed to provide the remaining $86 million, or 15 per cent of the total.

As with so many mammoth projects, once construction began Sicartsa's cost overruns grew alarmingly. Phase I was supposed to cost $560 million. By New Year's day, 1977, when a completed Phase I began to produce reinforced bars, wire rods, and light steel shapes, its construction cost had almost doubled, to over $1 billion.

Phase I was an economic disaster for everyone except the suppliers. Sicartsa Phase II was consequently shelved while the Mexican steel sector lurched under devaluation, recession, economic restructuring, and eventually a reorganization. Then in 1979, in exchange for access to Mexican oil at market prices for ten years, the Japanese government lent Mexico $150 million to help Japanese suppliers secure Sicartsa Phase II. While the Japanese were confident that they had secured the most lucrative parts of Phase II, competing governments of the U.S., the U.K., France, and Germany prepared to do battle to win those same contracts for their own exporters.

The Mexican negotiators used this competitive atmosphere to manipulate the players in each of these countries, prodding each one's exporters and banks to push their home governments to offer more sweeteners than their competitor nations. As if in orchestrated response, each national alliance of suppliers, banks, and governments from the five countries rolled out its full arsenal of trade support: official export credits, insurance, rediscounting, grants, soft aid loans, and guarantees for commercial bank loans.

The battle ended with the unlikeliest winner: the notoriously inefficient United Kingdom beat out the Japanese, the world's most efficient steel producers, on the prized $596 million plate mill, the key component of the steel plant. The U.K. coalition of suppliers and financiers – Davy McKee, Lloyds Bank International, and the British Department of Trade – had marshaled the necessary public funds to undercut the less heavily subsidized Japanese bid. According to one senior official from Sicartsa, Britain won the plate mill because, politically, it "had its act together."

A recent book from the Harvard Business School interviewed executives from Sicartsa and the major bidding firms and their banks in Britain, France, Germany, Japan, and the U.S. It found that "neither the sellers, the lenders, nor the exporting government officials would assert that the mill made economic sense. They pursued the transaction, not because of Mexico's needs, but because of their own needs at home.... Few players carefully analyzed the economics."

Sicartsa is far from exceptional: Mexico's nuclear expansion program seemed so potentially lucrative to Western salesmen that, as with the Sicartsa steel scheme, heads of state attempted to secure sales. French President François Mitterand, Canadian Prime Minister Pierre Trudeau, and Swedish King Carl Gustav each traveled to Mexico City to present multibillion-dollar financial packages tied to their country's nuclear power technology. Competition between the five nations vying for Mexico's $30 billion nuclear expansion program became intense, with each supplier proffering an array of financial incentives. Canada offered $1.5 billion in export credit loans and another $4 billion from a special pot of money that its Cabinet could tap for loans deemed to be in Canada's "national interest."

The same star-studded international cast prominent in Mexico's development projects are also prominent in many other development projects in many other Third World countries. Together they lent vast sums of money, each for their own reasons, that would eventually shake international financial structures.

6

Bankers to the Third World

THE WORLD BANK is the Third World's single largest creditor. Of the $1.3 trillion the Third World owes to thousands of creditors, $182 billion, or one dollar in seven, came from this one bank.

Along with the International Monetary Fund, the World Bank was created at the Bretton Woods Conference, held in New Hampshire in 1944. The World Bank would first finance the reconstruction of war-ravaged Europe, then turn its attention to developing the Third World. Its most famous founding father was John Maynard Keynes, a giant among men and a legend in his own time. It was said that the Bretton Woods Conference was not a conference among nations, it was a conference of nations with Keynes.

Keynes' extraordinary intellect, oratorical eloquence, and prominence as an economic advisor to governments through four decades of war, peace, and depression made him the greatest economist of his time. He had dedicated his career to steadying the economic ship of nations throughout those tumultuous events, and Bretton Woods was his command performance. After weeks of negotiations, Keynes closed the Bretton Woods Conference with a speech formally moving that the two Bretton Woods institutions, the World Bank and the IMF, be created. For a world torn asunder by war, it was no mean feat:

Finally, we have perhaps accomplished here in Bretton Woods something more significant than what is embodied in this Final Act. We have shown that a concourse of 44 nations are actually able to work together at a constructive task in amity and unbroken concord. Few believed it possible. If we can continue in a larger task as we have begun in this limited task, there is hope for the world. At any rate we shall now disperse to our several homes with new friendships sealed and new intimacies formed. We have been learning to work together. If we can so continue, this nightmare, in which most of us here present have spent too much of our lives, will be over. The brotherhood of man will have become more than a phrase.

Mr. President, I move to accept the Final Act.

Delegates paid tribute by rising and applauding again and again. As he moved towards the door to leave the meeting the delegates rose again, singing "For He's a Jolly Good Fellow."

In his quest to create a world of peace and prosperity, Keynes was driven by a desire to help the public at large. But he had little faith in the public's ability to fashion such a world. "It is most dangerous that the people should, under normal conditions, be in a position to put into effect their transient will and their uncertain judgment on every question of policy that occurs," he wrote. Political parties should have an elitist structure, with decision-making confined to their top echelon. Democracy should be retained, but only as a power of last resort and "until the ambit of men's altruism grows wider." Keynes held views close to Plato's: that society is best governed by a guardian class, unswayed by the venal passions of humanity, exercising power as a byproduct of its own spiritual quest.

So it would be with the World Bank. To place the institution beyond political influence by any one country, the World Bank's founding fathers made it unaccountable to all. According to the bank's Articles of Agreement, management and staff "owe their duty entirely to the Bank and to no other authority." Countries that oppose loans for any but "economic considerations" are chastised for trying to exert political influence, thus violating the bank's charter. Even the accountability of the board of executive directors is ambiguous and unknowable: the bank argues that its executive directors are individuals deriving their authority from and owing their paramount loyalty to the bank, even though they are elected by, and vote on behalf of, member countries.

Steeped in the belief that deficit financing should prime national economies, managed by a guardian class of economic planners, the World Bank would extend the Keynesian revolution to the Third World. While many debate the legacy of Keynesian economics in the industrialized countries – some claim it brought economic stability, others that it brought instability and enormous state debts – the consequences of the Keynesian revolution for the Third World are unmistakable.

SINCE IT COMMENCED BUSINESS in 1946, the World Bank has lent almost $250 billion, some to Western European countries and Japan for their post-war rehabilitation, but most to Third World countries to promote their economic development. Japan, then an underdeveloped nation, borrowed less than one billion, and repaid it. But unlike Japan and the other original borrowers in Western Europe, most Third World countries don't escape debt: new and larger loans replace old ones. Of the quarter trillion dollars borrowed from the World Bank, very little – roughly $55 billion – has been repaid.

The World Bank's role in the debt crisis extends beyond its loans, however. More than any other single institution, the World Bank influences development financing and policy in the Third World.

As the best endowed development agency on earth, with the largest staff and an army of economists, the bank has drawn up investment plans for Third World governments, arranged financing packages for major capital projects, offered financial guarantees to private lenders, provided information about investment opportunities in the Third World, signed special "framework agreements" with the industrialized countries' national aid agencies, managed multimillion-dollar "trust funds" for cash-rich countries, and organized "consultative group" meetings of other aid donors to coordinate tens of billions of dollars' worth of loans. As a result of these efforts, for every dollar the World Bank lent to a Third World project, another $2 to $3 was attracted from other sources, both public and private.

The World Bank did more than organize money for the lending; it created institutions to do the borrowing. To carry out its agenda and its projects, the bank often set up autonomous government authorities, such as development finance banks, agricultural credit institutions, and energy agencies in borrowing nations. Small government agencies and private institutions that thwarted the World Bank's plans were superceded, as occurred in Nepal: when three hydroelectric companies balked at building large and risky dams in the 1960s, they were nationalized, the electricity sector was reorganized, and more pliant institutions emerged.

In Colombia, 36 of the World Bank's first 51 loans went to autonomous agencies that the bank either established or entrenched. In effect, according to Colombian political scientist Fernando Cepeda Ulloa and John Howard from the New York-based International Legal Center, the World Bank acquired the powers of a surrogate government at the international level, while at the national level it became a powerful administrative arm of the Colombian government that "bypassed ... governmental decision-making, including the legislative and judicial branches."

Not only did World Bank-established institutions undermine democratic ones, they also monopolized scarce foreign capital. The World Bank helped set up Colombia's national electricity utility system, and so vigorously financed its expansion program that, said *International Water Power and Dam Construction*, the government found itself with surplus electricity while the rest of the country griped "that most of the foreign exchange income of Colombia had been spent on building large power projects, thus neglecting the other needs of the country such as education, health, transportation, and so on."

The bank sponsored much the same institution-building in its other client states. In Panama, the World Bank thirty years ago financed the then newly created public electric utility – the Institute for Hydraulic Resources and Electrification (IRHE) – to study the hydraulic potential of the country's rivers. Once IRHE had identified the sites, the World Bank would fund feasibility studies for various dam sites, and eventually finance the dams. By 1988 IRHE had become Panama's second-largest public sector borrower after the central government.

The World Bank consciously strove to remove borrowing agencies from the fray of local politics, out of a conviction that "the job of development" would otherwise be botched. This conviction largely reflected the distrust held by Eugene Black, the World Bank's president from 1949 to 1962, of Third World people's "traditionalism," which Black believed would lead them into wrong choices. To save Third World people from themselves, the World Bank hired foreign experts, or "development diplomats," to train local elites. Touted as "apostles of a new life," and as "the politician and the bureaucrat ... [who] are very literally leaders as well as rulers," the local elites would "usher their societies into an age of enlightenment." For Black and the bank, as for the bank's founders, there would be no place for wide popular participation in development decision-making.

The bank's influence with Third World governments came

from its readiness to reward with loans those taking its advice, and from its influence over other donors and financiers. To disregard or disagree with the World Bank's development agenda jeopardized a country's access to foreign capital.

With these tools and this clout the World Bank has helped major capital projects get off the ground, becoming their most frequent financier. In fact, megaprojects – projects costing over $100 million – have received the lion's share of World Bank loans: hydroelectric dams alone received about 20 per cent of them.

When it came to commodities, the World Bank's unbridled optimism in the 1960s and 1970s – it predicted growing world-wide demand – stampeded Third World nations into developing their mineral resources, and into switching their farmers from subsistence and small-scale market crops to monocrop plantations for export. So many Third World nations so quickly expanded production of rubber, cotton, iron ore, tea, and tobacco that these commodities glutted the world's markets, plunging prices and gutting the economies of the producing nations.

The prescriptions in which most of the world's borrowers placed faith had been based on little more than the bank's own economic guesswork, as a World Bank study discovered. A review of 1,015 projects by the bank's Economic Advisory Staff revealed a "striking" degree of uncertainty in predicting its projects' rate of return. A study by the Overseas Development Council found that almost half of the World Bank's loans to revenue-generating projects failed to achieve a desirable rate of return.

In the World Bank's likeness, three other development banks were created, one for each region of the Third World. The Inter-American Development Bank, Asian Development Bank and African Development Bank account for about 5 per cent of the Third World's debt. Together with the World Bank, this group accounts for $250 billion, or nearly 20 per cent of the Third World's total indebtedness. They all have virtually the same Articles of Agreement, structures, and lending patterns, leading to precisely the same dismal results.

Despite their consistent record of failure, the World Bank and its sister banks bask as blue-chip institutions, having no difficulty in borrowing from pension funds, insurance companies, corporations and individuals – all are happy to buy World Bank bonds, yet few would dare lend money directly to the Third World countries that are the ultimate borrowers.

The banks take their blue-chip status as a vote of confidence in their banking prowess, but this status has nothing to do with wise investments: backing all the development bank loans are rich governments who have pledged to repay bondholders should the Third World governments default.

Referring to the Asian Development Bank, First Boston's co-chairman and former head of policy planning at the World Bank, Pedro-Pablo Kuczynski, explained in *Institutional Investor*: "The fact of the matter is that even if all the loans were lousy and in default, the capital structure of the bank is such that it would still have a high credit." The bank, he explained, "could be in the middle of a ship parked off the coast of Vietnam and it wouldn't affect its credit."

When Third World countries began to default on their loans in the early 1980s, the World Bank shifted its lending to keep creditors – including itself – at bay. Instead of funding only specific projects, the World Bank began providing what are known as "structural adjustment loans."

These loans, which now account for approximately one-quarter of all World Bank lending, are supposed to help Third World countries make market-oriented adjustments to their economies. But even the World Bank is unable to explain how these loans help Third World economies "adjust."

Easier to explain, however, is the need to keep cash flowing and old debts serviced, if only at a trickle. Otherwise, the chances of a potentially catastrophic collapse are magnified.

A Third World country receives a structural adjustment loan to pay for its imports, even routine imports such as oil, thus freeing up monies for other uses, including repaying debts. The structural adjustment money thus makes a round trip – from the World Bank in Washington to the Third World country and then

71

back to the West, where much of it repays various creditors.

Through these round-trip loans, however, the Third World country gets deeper in debt; the World Bank holds more of that debt, since it lent more new money than it received; and the private banks – the Chase Manhattans, Lloyds, and Deutsche Banks – are owed less, since old loans were being repaid while new loans weren't extended. Round-trip loans thus transferred the Third World's debt from the private sector to the public sector.

Yet the new loans – though they staved off defaults – did nothing to solve the Third World's debt crisis. Many Third World countries were insolvent, simply incapable of repayment in the house of cards sustained by the World Bank. Not surprisingly, the architect of that house – the World Bank itself – would also be insolvent without continuing bailouts from its rich member countries, which come in the form of regular cash infusions as well as government guarantees.

IF THE WORLD BANK'S SHAREHOLDERS – 155 member countries – tried to privatize it, they would find that no private investor wanted a bank whose assets overwhelmingly consist of loans to Third World countries, most of whom need new loans to pay back their old ones. Without the rich countries' bailouts, a privatized World Bank could not extend the round-trip loans that keep its debtors out of arrears. And without the promise of new and often larger loans, debtor nations might balk at repaying the World Bank first, as they have promised. "If we're not receiving fresh money, we can't pay," said the planning director for the Haitian Ministry of Finance, Claude Grand-Pierre, adding that his government felt no obligation to pay lending agencies that had cut them off. "Normal relations with creditors are our desire," said Brazilian Finance Minister Mailson da Nobrega, in explaining his government's decision in September 1989 to miss a $1.6 billion interest installment to private banks. Referring to some $3 to $4 billion in loans that year that had failed to materialize, he said: "This is a two-way street, in which debt payments should open the way for new resources."

Without the rich country guarantees, the individuals and institutions who now buy World Bank bonds would refuse new offerings. Existing bondholders would find they were holding junk bonds, worth pennies on the dollar, in what would be the world's riskiest loan portfolio.

Far from being blue-chip financial institutions, the World Bank and its sister agencies have become financial albatrosses for the taxpayers in their member countries, largely because these public institutions operate free from either private sector discipline or public oversight and control. The minutes of executive directors' meetings are secret, as are the executive directors' voting records (that of the U.S. director is an exception due to U.S. law); executive directors are subject to no written restrictions prohibiting the use of their positions for personal gain; and no police force is mandated to investigate their wrongdoing, leaving the door wide open for widespread corruption. The public in the member countries has no right to details of World Bank activities, even if the activity is in its own country.

Given the legal no-man's land that international organizations operate in, a private suit by a party hurt by a World Bank project would be very difficult, if not impossible. All governors, executive directors, alternates, officers, and employees are immune from legal process with respect to acts performed by them in their official capacity, unless the bank waives this immunity. The World Bank treats its loans as international agreements, registering them with the United Nations, which further puts them beyond legal challenge by individual citizens.

Reform from within to enforce accountability is possible only in theory. Amending the World Bank's Articles of Agreement requires three-fifths of the members representing 85 per cent of the total voting power, making democratization of the institution unlikely in the extreme: 43 per cent of the votes are controlled by borrowers who shun public scrutiny, the balance by industrialized countries who are reluctant to be seen as diplomatic bullies, and who have their own political interests in seeing World Bank loans finance their countries' exporters.

Proper scrutiny of individual loans suffers from similar problems: one borrowing country will not question a dubious loan to another. While public pressure in a lending nation may prompt an executive director to voice concerns about a particular loan (something that can never be verified), he is quick to remind his critics at home that his minority view cannot swing any vote. Lenders are also loath to line up *en masse* against a borrower, to avoid a diplomatic mêlée. Instead, the World Bank is ruled by consensus decision-making, with the board of executive directors never formally voting on loans, and being hopelessly ill-equipped to do otherwise: it has but two weeks to review multimillion-dollar projects. In an average week the World Bank's board, in this way, nods approval to some $400 million in loans.

7

A Credit Union for Countries

IF EVER THERE WAS an international "villain," it surely must be the IMF. No international institution has been more condemned over the decades for being an enemy of the poor and subjugator of the Third World.

But the power the IMF once wielded has dissipated. On most counts, it has become a paper tiger, increasingly ineffectual and irrelevant. The IMF today is disliked not only by the Third World's populace but also by Western bankers. As a lender, the IMF never carried much weight in any case.

At the end of the 1970s, the Third World owed the IMF only $8 billion. By 1985, at the height of the debt crisis, that sum peaked at $39 billion and today, it is under $32 billion, about a sixth of the $182 billion Third World debtors owe the World Bank, and almost one-fortieth of what they owe all creditors combined.

Another Keynesian inspiration, the IMF was designed to foster free trade and global prosperity by ridding the world of the protectionist, beggar-thy-neighbor policies which had led to the Great Depression. Keynes saw the IMF as an international credit union owned by countries instead of people that would regulate exchange rates to prevent unfair competition and ensure the smooth settling of international accounts. Together, the members made the rules; as in any credit union, members who borrow money are expected to repay it.

When the IMF began operations in Washington, D.C. in May 1946, it had 39 member countries. Today it has 155, rich and poor, all subject to the same rules. As a sort of membership fee, each member deposits into the IMF a certain sum of money, called a quota subscription, based on its wealth and economic performance. Countries pay the quota – which determines their votes in operating the fund and their borrowing limit – 75 per cent in their own currency and 25 per cent in gold or in a convertible currency such as the dollar or deutsche mark.

The IMF functions primarily to ensure that its members pay their international debts. When a member country cannot earn enough foreign currency to meet its obligations to other IMF members – when it has a balance of payments problem – it can borrow from the IMF pool to tide it over. To date, the IMF has lent members some $100 billion for this one purpose – the only purpose for which it lends.

A member can borrow 25 per cent of its quota (the portion in gold or secure currency), no questions asked. To borrow more requires submitting to IMF economic reforms: at this point the borrowing country has become a bad credit risk, and the IMF wants assurances that it, too, will be repaid.

The various assurances are geared to reducing government

deficits and keeping the borrower solvent: a commitment to reduce its spending, a commitment to devalue its currency, and a commitment to encourage exports. Strictly speaking, the details of the reforms – where to apply government spending cuts, how to increase exports – are left to the borrowing government. Fearing accusations of infringing on a member's sovereignty, the IMF has as its only official concern "that the policy changes are sufficient to overcome the member's payments problem and do not cause avoidable harm to other members." Nevertheless, the IMF controls the purse strings. After often months of negotiations and advice from the IMF, borrowing governments well understand which reforms they need to adopt.

The IMF's attempts to impose austerity have earned it a reputation as a heartless interventionist in the Third World's economic sovereignty. What clout the IMF commands stems from its role as regulator and overseer of the Third World's debt.

The IMF applies a borrowing seal of approval for foundering borrowers' economies. Without an IMF-approved austerity package – which once demonstrated a borrower's willingness to right its economy – few private bankers, or even the World Bank and the other regional development banks, would agree to lend more money or reschedule old debts. Third World countries on the brink of bankruptcy were thus held hostage until they agreed to an often-stringent IMF plan. But obtaining the IMF's seal – which has failed to protect lenders even when the austerity package was strict – means less today to lenders, who want more meaningful security, and so less to borrowers, who no longer can be assured of credit by buckling under to this one agency. To most lenders, the IMF has little more influence than a rating agency such as Standard and Poors or Moody's; lenders note the borrower's rating, but need more than a rating agency green light to extend a loan.

Nevertheless, few Third World debtors – if they want to keep borrowing – can avoid the IMF's recommendations, although debtors sometimes do successfully dig in their heels, and not always to the benefit of the populace: "To our distress, but not to our surprise," said IMF Managing Director Michel Camdessus, "we have found that in the end military and security expenditures are those that resist the adjustment effort most strongly."

WHY SOME CREDITORS continue to place faith in the IMF's analysis, and in its prescription for recovery, is a mystery. The IMF has blundered badly, particularly in African countries which have generally sunk deep into debt, and where balance of payment problems have become too chronic for mere IMF quotas.

Even the IMF's role as a credit union for countries has been compromised. Abandoning its traditional conservatism, the IMF has become just one more public bailout body by inventing extraordinary lending mechanisms. To its traditional quota system it layered "special" facilities upon "supplementary" facilities upon "extended" facilities upon "enhanced" facilities, all to allow member countries to borrow up to four times their quotas. Debtors can now take ten years – instead of the usual one to five years – to pay the money back, and at subsidized interest rates. And although the IMF doesn't admit it, it now round-trips its loans, much as the World Bank does.

By relaxing its standards, the IMF's judgment has become tarnished in banking circles. Allowing Third World governments unprecedented overdrafts on their IMF accounts, though providing temporary relief, deepened the debt crisis. The IMF now finds itself with eleven members in arrears in excess of $4 billion.

But the bankers' scorn for the IMF reached new heights in 1989 when the IMF abandoned the sacred banking creed of *pacta sunt servanda* – contracts must be honored – by publicly stating that Third World countries couldn't – and therefore shouldn't – make good on their obligations. Many Third World countries soon stopped or further slowed their payments to the commercial banks: within two years, their interest arrears had tripled, from $7 billion to $22 billion.

The IMF generally targets heavily subsidized activities such as food and energy to bear the brunt of budget cuts. Sometimes these have favorable effects on the economy, environment, or the poor. Ghanaian farmers earned more for their crops, and Ghanaian city dwellers paid less for their rents, with the removal of price controls. But for last-minute lobbying inside Brazil, the IMF almost succeeded in canceling the Balbina dam; similar IMF pressure to remove electricity subsidies to large industries did diminish the demand for more hydrodams, saving the Brazilian economy billions. A 1991 IMF-induced austerity program in Egypt removed subsidies from fuel – protecting the environment by discouraging wasteful vehicular use.

Sometimes these budget cuts hold promise, but only in theory, of benefiting the poor. Egypt imports most of its wheat – 5.2 million of the 8.1 million tonnes it consumes – because it keeps the price of baladi (its local bread) so low. At 5 piastres, or 1.8 cents, a loaf – only enough to cover the costs of shipping the wheat from the port to the flour mills – the policy has become ludicrous: bread sells for less than wheat, leading farmers to feed it to cattle instead of feed, and making Egypt the world's third largest wheat importer, after the USSR and China. Egypt's IMF austerity policy will remove bread subsidies – necessary if the country is to regain its self-reliance and avoid sinking further into debt, but beneficial to the poor only if the subsidies saved on the poor's bread consumption are redistributed to them – an unlikely occurrence, given the history of IMF adjustment programs.

IMF policies tend to be counterproductive, especially for the Third World's poor, justifying the poor's near-universal reluctance to accept IMF medicine for their economy's ailments.

In a 1988 report analyzing the effect of its adjustment programs on seven Third World countries, the IMF admitted that its miscalculations affected large groups of the urban poor in Chile, the Dominican Republic, and the Philippines following currency devaluations. In the Philippines, for example, spending on health and schools was cut, import restrictions raised prices sharply, and restrictions on the money supply cost jobs and lowered wages. In the Dominican Republic, its policies led to "major social unrest" in which 50 people died in rioting.

"Although many of the major policy instruments improved the position of the dominant poverty groups in the sample countries, other poverty groups were made worse off in the short run," the report said, adding elsewhere that in Kenya and Sri Lanka its policies may have hurt the poor in the long run as well as the short run.

IMF policies are fed through its Washington computer models, which recommend devaluations and tax hikes to fight the Third World's rampant inflation and hunger for imports. These macroeconomic measures – utterly divorced from the actual workings of Third World economies – routinely increase inflation and lower tax revenues, as the Third World's citizenry devise defenses against policies that attempt to manipulate them.

The IMF's poor record, concludes Hernando de Soto, the celebrated author of the *The Other Path* and president of the Lima-based Institute for Liberty and Democracy, stems from its top-down approach.

De Soto lauds IMF goals such as privatization and liberalizing foreign trade, noting that they coincide with policies supported by a public groundswell. Peru's informal transportation operators – 300,000 taxi drivers, truckers, and other private entrepreneurs – demonstrated their distaste for protectionism by successfully lobbying the government to remove tire import duties which, by inflating tire prices 250 per cent, protected only Goodyear of Peru and its local workforce of 1,258. The duties raised the public transportation costs of 5 million riders, and cost the economy over $100 million.

Such "bottom-up structural adjustment" works, de Soto says, when the citizenry's views can be incorporated into the enactment of rules and policies. But generally, in Peru as in other places,

> *the state receives no input from those affected by its decisions. Thus, the state does not govern in accordance with the interests of the majority. As a result, structural adjustment "from the bottom up" is impossible. This*

makes the IMF and foreign governments appear "impe-rialistic" and causes the poor undue hardship because they do not realize who the proposed adjustments are affecting.

Chastened by its findings, the IMF has come to recognize the shortcomings of top-down structural adjustment. "Adjustment does not have to lower basic human standards," said Camdessus in the introduction to the IMF's 1988 report. "The more [that] adjustment efforts give proper weight to social realities – especially the implications for the poorest – the more successful they are likely to be." Yet the IMF keeps its operations strictly off-limits to the public, determining structural adjustment packages, austerity measures, taxes, and government expenditures, behind closed doors. IMF plans – being centrally and remotely designed, without the benefit of public input and public debate, away from the homes and markets of the Third World – become prone to serious miscalculations.

The hurdle impeding a successful IMF – how to "give proper weight to social realities" in countries around the globe from its vantage point in Washington, D.C. – is almost certainly insurmountable, and does much to explain the IMF's abject failure.

Like other public lenders, the IMF now needs a bigger pipeline to move ever larger sums of money to the Third World. Also like other public lenders, to do this the IMF has convinced its members to raise its capital base, in its case by 50 per cent to $180 billion.

But the IMF alone cannot be blamed for the failure of its economic reform packages. While it preached prudence, other lenders practiced profligacy.

8

The New Mercantilists

ONE YEAR BEFORE MEXICO touched off the Third World's debt crisis by suspending payments to foreign creditors, British Prime Minister Margaret Thatcher rose proudly to announce in the House of Commons that her government had just committed millions to the Mexican government to build the $2 billion Sicartsa steel plant:

> *We were delighted to get [the Sicartsa contract, which] will contribute about 28,000 man years of work. It will help a great deal with Davy's ... main manufacturing*

centre in Sheffield. It will also mean the provision of about 80,000 tonnes of British Steel Corporation steel ... and a good deal of electrical work through GEC.... It is a very welcome contract and was won in the teeth of French, German and Japanese competition. We won it on price.

Mrs. Thatcher's "win" came at the expense of the taxpayer. British exporters won the $596 million contract courtesy of $500 million in loan guarantees and an outright $57 million grant from the British government. "It was a gift that Mexico had neither to service nor to repay," said Harvard Professor Philip Wellons in describing Sicartsa. The deal – more favorable than those offered Mexico by the French and the Japanese – could hardly be refused.

The only competition evident in the Sicartsa bidding war was between the Japanese, French and British governments to see who would dig deepest into its treasury to subsidize its exporters. In the end, Mrs. Thatcher dug deepest. Adam Smith may have turned in his grave.

Adam Smith, the father of economic liberalism, had two centuries earlier attacked the era's dominant economic theory – mercantilism – which held that a country would get rich by subsidizing exports, restricting imports, and hence amassing gold, which was a currency of the day. Mercantilism operated through a web of decrees, tariffs, regulations, and royal patronage plums to shipyards and porcelain factories, tapestry works and arsenals; industrial growth under the mercantilists depended upon a politically administered national economic policy. Adam Smith's landmark treatise, *An Inquiry into the Wealth of Nations*, flayed mercantilism for favoring a few industrialists at the expense of the working class and the economy as a whole.

Though utterly discredited in theory, mercantilism has never been stamped out. Today government agencies – called export credit agencies – promote mercantilism. Britain's is called the Export Credits Guarantee Department, the U.S. has its Export-Import Bank, Canada has the Export Development Corporation, France the Banque de France and Coface, and Japan the Export-Import Bank of Japan. All industrialized countries have them.

The export credit agencies subsidize exports by using public funds to finance, insure, and otherwise guarantee payment to their country's exporters – even when the purchaser is all but bankrupt. They have been so successful at promoting the Third World's purchases of the industrialized countries' exports that 15 per cent of the Third World's outstanding debt is now owed to these agencies.

For decades, private commercial banks have serviced their exporting clients, and imposed on them the cold discipline of the private sector. But once the export credit agencies started guaranteeing commercial trade, prudent lending by the private sector gave way to a free-for-all.

The Pearson Commission, struck by the World Bank in the late 1960s to investigate Third World poverty, first noticed the problem. The private banks were becoming "less concerned about the borrowing country's credit worthiness because of the facility of export credit insurance," the Pearson Commission warned, explaining that imprudent use of export credits "involves very real dangers." It found export credits to be an expensive form of external finance. Though the interest rates offered the borrower were favorable, the exported product would usually be marked up, by as much as 100 per cent.

To its horror, the Pearson Commission also discovered that export credits often financed projects whose only "feasibility study available is one prepared by the equipment supplier," and that borrowing countries pushing reckless development schemes often favored export credit agencies because they enforced less "rigorous tests of economic desirability."

More than one project rejected for financing by the World Bank Group on economic grounds has been promptly financed by an export credit. This is the most unfortunate aspect of export credit finance: it provides a temporarily painless way of financing projects conceived by over-optimistic civil servants, by politicians more concerned with immediate political advantage than with potential future economic problems, and by unscrupulous salesman for the manufacturers of capital equipment in developed countries.

All this, according to the Pearson Commission, created an excessive use of short-term export credits to finance long-term investments and a serious balance of payments problem for developing countries: "Since the mid-1950s, [this] has been a major reason for the need to reschedule the debts of a number of countries, notably Argentina, Brazil, Chile, Ghana, Indonesia, and Turkey."

"This rescheduling will be more difficult in the future if export credits are imprudently used," predicted the Pearson Commission in 1969.

Imprudently used they were: export credit programs continued at full throttle throughout the 1970s. With the debt crisis of the 1980s frightening away commercial banks, export credits became an even more important source of external financing to the Third World and to Western exporters. While commercial banks abandoned the field after the Mexican debt crisis of 1982, the export credit agencies did not. Today, according to estimates by the National Foreign Trade Council, an American export industry association, one-third of the $30 billion a year in capital goods traded worldwide is financed through tied aid and export financing packages.

That support was not necessarily conditioned upon economic viability. British law, for example, permitted the Export Credits Guarantee Department to provide financial support for vote-getting and other political purposes; and its Aid and Trade Program permitted increasingly reckless governments to support exports to what one British trade official called "dodgy markets." The Thatcher government even silenced an internal Treasury report arguing against export subsidies. A French study reached similar conclusions: "Export-credit subsidization wastes France's scarce public resources in promotion of the wrong industries exporting the wrong products to the wrong markets." As an industrial subsidy, export credits are unparalleled failures, creating coddled and uncompetitive enterprises that depend for their survival on continuing state subsidies.

Though harmful to the economy as a whole, export credits are boons to favored businesses. About two-thirds of Boeing Aircraft's commercial jet sales abroad, mostly to the Third World, were guaranteed under the U.S. Export-Import Bank's financing programs. In the business, the Ex-Im Bank became known as "Boeing's Bank." Boeing Chairman T.A. Wilson claimed these programs essential when testifying before the U.S. Congress in 1981: "Without the involvement of Ex-Im, commercial banks will not participate in loans to emerging nations."

The export credit agencies' analysis of the environmental viability of their projects showed even less concern than their economic analysis. Little wonder, then, that the environmental consequences of projects like Sicartsa were ignored. By 1980, raw sewage from the town and industrial effluents from the steel plant, which was using the nearby Balsas River as a sedimentation pit for its waste, had destroyed the river's once rich estuary. Meanwhile toxic gases from the steel plant and dust particles blanketed the town of Lazaro Cardenas.

The U.S. Ex-Im Bank is the only agency to have anything that could remotely be considered an environmental review process. Yet even it doesn't require that environmental factors be considered for all loans; projects found to be environmentally damaging need not be rejected; and the entire process can be modified in order to meet bid dates and "the pressures of competition." Canada's Export Development Corporation has never bothered to consider the environmental consequences of its loans. A former Minister for International Trade explained that "if EDC were required to apply environmental standards that other export credit agencies were not, or that the foreign buyer was unprepared to accept, the Canadian exporter would not be in a position to bid on a given transaction, and he would therefore lose the deal. Moreover, there would be no net benefit to the world environment. The same projects would still go ahead, but the successful bidders would be from countries other than Canada."

Rather than scrutinizing their projects' economic or environmental viability, the export credit agencies have instead concentrated on marketing their export promotion funds, designing a dazzling array of loan packages, credit lines, insurance programs, and loan guarantee schemes to make sure Third World purchasers have the necessary money to buy their countries' goods and services.

For the markets that they consider "spoiled" – those already accustomed to receiving low-cost financing – the export credit agencies usually draw on more heavily subsidized funds to create what is known as "credit mixte" – a mix of greatly discounted financing with conventional export financing to produce what the Export Development Corporation calls "low blended interest rates." The purpose, says EDC, is "to match ... subsidized financing offered by competitors." In Canada this greatly discounted financing is disbursed from a $13 billion fund known as the Canada Account when export contracts deemed to be in the "national interest" involve too much risk for even the Export Development Corporation.

Governments hand out export credits to create jobs in particular constituencies while patronizing their favorite firms. Mrs. Thatcher seized upon the opportunity to trumpet the jobs created by the Sicartsa deal in the British Parliament with great fanfare. The Canadian Export Development Corporation rarely announces a new deal without estimating the number of "person-years" of employment created.

But beyond these job-creation claims, just about no one will defend the use of export credits, even those in charge of them. Robert Richardson, president and chief executive officer of Canada's Export Development Corporation, in an article in the Canadian *Financial Post*, agreed that concessionary financing is not economical. "If other countries didn't do it, we wouldn't either," he said. "Our approach is merely to match others."

U.S. Ex-Im Bank officials agree. Citing trade warfare reasons, the Bush administration in 1990 launched a $500-million program to combine subsidized export credits with aid money. "We think it's a lousy and costly way to do business," said Eugene Lawson, vice-chairman of the Export-Import Bank, who announced the initiative. The purpose, he went on to explain, was to "attract the attention of our allies." The initiative was designed to serve notice to America's competitors – principally Japan and France – that the U.S. would use subsidized export and aid credits to fight for foreign markets, until everyone gave up the costly practice. According to one commercial banking lawyer, "trade has become akin to modern warfare, an all-out national effort in which the taxpayer is as much in the fray as the forces in the field."

Only now are taxpayers in the industrialized countries beginning to recognize the scope of casualties from years of lending subsidized money to "dodgy markets."

In 1990, the U.S. Export-Import Bank admitted that $3.5 billion, or more than one-third of its loan portfolio, was "delinquent." To cover possible losses on those delinquent Third World debts, Congress forced the Ex-Im Bank to establish a $4.8 billion reserve, knocking Ex-Im's equity position to a negative $4 billion. "It has gone into technical insolvency," said former National Security Council member and debt consultant Norman Bailey. "Not that anybody gives a damn."

As long as the bank has the full faith and credit of the United States Treasury, something that shows no signs of changing, it will be able to continue lending. Ex-Im's chairman, John Macomber, tried to put a happy face on the bad debts, insisting that the accounting change "is not a write-off.... We continue to expect that all loans and guarantees will be paid in full." The Ex-Im Bank is most exposed in Mexico, where it has issued $2.2 billion of loans and loan guarantees; next comes Brazil with $1.9 billion in outstanding debts; the Philippines with $1.25 billion; and Colombia with $952 million.

The U.S. Ex-Im Bank was following the lead of Britain's Export Credits Guarantee Department, whose Third World loan losses had earlier forced it to set aside reserves against delinquent debts. The Export Credits Guarantee Department, whose successful efforts in winning the Sicartsa deal brought such exultation from Mrs. Thatcher in 1981, fell from her favor and was almost dismantled entirely in 1990. An angry riposte from the House of Commons trade and industry committee – which had been deluged with submissions by bankers and industrialists defending the Export Credits Guarantee Department's services to exporters – saved the day for the mercantilists.

Canada's auditor general – Parliament's watchdog over the government's financial management – recommended that Canada's Export Development Corporation follow the practice of the U.S. Export-Import Bank and Britain's Export Credits Guarantee Department. In his 1989 annual report to Parliament, Auditor General Kenneth Dye called the Export Development Corporation's financial statements "misleading," explaining that "loans receivable are overvalued because the Corporation's estimate of the allowance for losses on loans is significantly understated." The Export Development Corporation's financial statement therefore, concluded Mr. Dye, "does not conform to generally accepted accounting principles." A year later, Mr. Dye was still warning the Canadian Parliament that the EDC's major asset – sovereign loans receivable to the tune of nearly $5 billion – was "overvalued" and the EDC's accounts in need of "prompt remedial action." As for the Canada Account, Mr. Dye could not identify an arm of the Canadian government that was responsible for it, even though it was costing the Canadian taxpayer millions.

The export credit agencies have their own way of pretending that their bad loans aren't bad after all. Where the international development institutions "roundtrip" money, the export credit agencies "reschedule" debts. Through what is known as the Paris Club, a rendezvous of lending and borrowing nations formed in Paris in 1954 after Argentina asked its official creditors to discuss relief, the French finance ministry hosts regular sessions to renegotiate Third World debts to official lenders, including the export credit agencies. Under rescheduling, if a debtor falls behind on interest, a creditor may convert the interest to principal. If a debtor falls behind on principal, the government may adjust repayment dates or provide a repayment holiday.

Eugene Rotberg, a former treasurer of the World Bank,

considers loan rescheduling to be a "financial charade."

If someone owes you money and you say "You don't have to pay it for ten years," then ten years go by, and you don't collect, and another ten years – well you may not wish to call that forgiveness for bookkeeping or political purposes, but you're not getting paid. "Forgiveness" is a legal term that says, "You owed me the money – you no longer owe it." The Paris Club says, "You owe me the money, you haven't paid me, and I agree that you don't have to pay me, but you still owe it." Now I'm not going to talk about how many angels can dance on the head of a pin, but that is de facto forgiveness.

"The problem," explains Canadian Auditor General Dye, "is that rescheduling is used as a shield to hide from public scrutiny losses the government has suffered or is likely to suffer on its sovereign loans. Paperwork disguises reality."

But the public is beginning to grow wiser to reality, thanks to auditors general like Mr. Dye who now insist that more of these rescheduled export promotion loans be written down as bad loans, unlikely to be repaid. As such, bad loans are now showing up in the national debts of countries. Taxpayers, realizing they must now pay for the ill-considered loans of their export credit agencies, are losing their ardor for export subsidies.

The combined activities of the export credit agencies, the World Bank, the regional development banks, and the IMF – all instruments of public policy – are responsible for creating 40 per cent of the Third World's debt. Add to them the national aid agencies and the figure for governments amounts to more than half.

9

Givers and Takers

MOST TAXPAYERS in the rich industrialized countries believe, as the Pearson Commission inquiry into foreign aid believed, that "it is only right for those who have to share with those who have not." Much of the Western World's sharing, though, has been in the form of loans, not gifts. The Third World has borrowed about one-third of the $400 billion in foreign aid that it has received from the rich countries' national aid agencies.

Though national foreign aid loans were cheap – provided at well below commercial rates – they have nevertheless proven to be unrepayable. Over the years these loans have accumulated, fallen into arrears, and been rescheduled so often that by 1989 the Third World owed the rich countries $180 billion, or 14 per cent of their $1.3 trillion debt, for national foreign aid – as much as they owed the World Bank.

Not only have Third World countries needed to borrow much of their aid money, they have also been forced to spend it on the donor's products, even when the price and the product were not right. According to the Pearson Commission and to a Canadian Treasury Board study, the goods and services bought with foreign aid funds have been inflated by 20 to 25 per cent as a result. That extra 25 per cent could well have made profitable investments unprofitable, and payable debts unpayable. The only beneficiaries of rules tying aid are the few favored companies that supply this captive market, and the political parties able to boast of the jobs created.

In the same way the British government used aid to secure the Sicartsa contract, the Canadian government has cofinanced at least two massive projects a year over the last decade through the Canadian International Development Agency and Canada's Export Development Corporation. One of these projects is the Chamera dam in India, which $650 million in loans locked up for Canadian firms. In a speech to the Canadian Exporters Association, Peter Haines, a former CIDA vice-president, explained: "The best way to be competitive is, of course, to avoid the competition altogether and that is essentially what ... we did on the Chamera Hydro Project in India." Haines noted that "there are immense front-end costs in taking a project off the market," but made clear that these were well worth bearing to win the contracts for Canadians.

Throwing these foreign aid projects at Third World countries has exacerbated their debt. With their repayment difficulties extreme, national aid agencies agreed in 1988 to provide debt relief, especially for the low-income countries of Africa.

The Paris Club, where sovereign debts are more likely to be rescheduled than forgiven, began considering ways to reduce interest rates, to cancel some of the debt related to foreign aid, and to reschedule, or stretch out, debt repayment.

Within two years, the Paris Club members had canceled over $5 billion in foreign aid debts. Canada forgave $400 million in debts to Francophone and Anglophone Africa and the Caribbean; Denmark promised to write off repayments of earlier development loans to all least-developed countries and other low-income countries with serious balance of payments problems; France wrote off $2.7 billion in debt owed by 35 poor African countries; Germany provided some $1.5 billion in debt relief to six African countries; Italy converted the outstanding debts of a number of African countries to long-term low-interest loans; Japan forgave $1 billion worth of interest and principal on past foreign aid debts for some 20 countries; the U.S. announced $1.3 billion in write-offs for low-income African countries with World Bank or IMF-assisted economic restructuring programs; and the Netherlands canceled all foreign aid debt due from the least developed countries.

Paris Club members, several years earlier realizing that the debt crisis was as much their doing as their debtors', had already begun to lend less and give more: foreign aid delivered through loans was halved to 20 per cent, with some countries – Australia, Canada, Ireland, New Zealand and Switzerland among them – providing all their aid in the form of grants.

To help cash-starved Third World countries, national aid agencies also started making World Bank-type "round-trip" loans, but these failed to lift Third World nations out of their debt quagmire. So some aid donors – the Netherlands and Switzerland among them – went further, providing foreign aid to pay off commercial bank debts.

In spite of, and possibly because of, these recent debt relief measures – the endless restructuring, stretching out, and granting of grace periods – Third World countries have remained deep in debt. For Africa's nations and others, says Jeffrey Sachs, Harvard economist and advisor to the Bolivian and Polish governments, the Paris Club's willingness to reschedule *ad infinitum*, and even to provide new loans, casts a cold financial shower over whole economies. "It stops investment.... It creates expectations of instability. It absorbs enormous waste of time in negotiations. There's always the possibility that creditors might get tough."

Expectations of debt relief have one other inevitable effect – a willingness to spend recklessly, as illustrated by the remarks of Gabon's President Omar Bongo, upon learning in 1987 that Canada had forgiven all of Gabon's foreign debts: "I even regretted not having had more debts with Canada," Mr. Bongo said, adding that "One country has to go first, perhaps the others will follow."

NATIONAL FOREIGN AID officials cannot claim that the debt crisis took them by surprise. The Pearson Commission had warned about more than export credits; it warned about the national aid agencies' role in expanding the Third World's debt. During the 1960s, the proportion of foreign aid which was lent instead of given had tripled, and the grace period for repayment was quickly running out.

Pearson concluded that several factors were conspiring to create catastrophe: the debt guaranteed by Third World governments was increasing by an alarming 14 per cent per year, capital was becoming more expensive with interest rates having risen from 4.25 per cent in the late 1940s to 7 per cent in 1969, and the Third World would soon be paying more to service old debts than its export earnings and new loans would be bringing in. Pearson asked the rich countries to curb their export credits, to give more aid in the form of grants, to untie aid, and to extend the payback period for foreign aid debts.

Pearson predicted a debt crisis caused primarily by governments: Third World governments were borrowing more from First World governments than they could pay back. What Pearson could not have foreseen was the chaos of the coming decade, in which the commercial banks would take over as the Third World's main lenders.

10

The Petrodollar Recyclers

IN 1969, WHEN THE PEARSON Commission warned of the
Third World's looming debt crisis, it feared loose purse strings
at government agencies, and paid scant attention to the private
commercial banks, who accounted for 15 per cent of the Third
World's borrowing. Within five years the commercial banks had
abandoned their back seat role to overtake international development agencies as the Third World's most important source of
credit. By 1980, through what could only be described as
feverish lending, the banks were providing nearly two-thirds of

the Third World's foreign financing.

The banks' lending binge flowed from the OPEC oil crisis of 1973, which saw oil prices double, then double and double again, within a decade selling for 20 times their former price. Arab sheiks and other oil producers, suddenly swamped with billions of dollars in unexpected earnings and unable to otherwise invest them, deposited them in Western banks. The banks, unable to say no to these windfall deposits, eagerly accepted them, then set about lending these billions to any and all borrowers to earn the interest needed to pay the oil sheiks.

Many of those borrowers were in the West – often in the booming energy business, much of it nuclear and tar sand megaprojects that would later go bust. But the West had too many constraints on unbridled expansion. Most of the commercial banks had to go further afield to place their cash.

They came to the Third World, over one thousand of them from Chase Manhattan, Lloyds Bank, and the other big names in international banking circles, to the small banks of rural USA, all desperate to place their cash and gluttonous for profits in an unprecedented banking bonanza.

They weren't disappointed: million and even billion-dollar bank deals were settled in a matter of days. A Salomon Brothers report showed the thirteen largest U.S. banks had quintupled their earnings from $177 million to $836 million during the first half of the 1970s, with the most spectacular part of the increase coming from the Third World loans. By 1976, Chase Manhattan Bank was earning 78 per cent of its income abroad, Citibank 72 per cent, Bank of America 40 per cent, First Boston 68 per cent, Morgan Guaranty 53 per cent, and Manufacturers Hanover 56 per cent. The Banque Nationale de Paris (BNP), one of the world's largest banking houses, was thought to be profiting more from its various affiliates in Africa than from its extensive branch network in France. In absolute terms, Nigeria alone came to account for up to 20 per cent of BNP's after-tax earnings in the late 1970s. A 1982 bank survey reported that international lending had been more profitable than domestic lending for two out of three banks.

As the petrodollar deposits accumulated in Western banks, so did the pressure to lend. The competition between banks for Third World business became intense. With so much money to be lent and so much money to be made, Mexico's Minister of Finance David Ibarra recalled the days when "I had many bankers chasing me trying to lend me more money." Ibarra wasn't complaining: during his tenure Mexico added $30 billion to its debt, almost doubling it.

To lend such vast sums, the banks needed to innovate. International trade finance had always been the meat and potatoes of the banks' international lending. A bank would finance an exporter until the importer paid for the goods, upon their receipt. These loans were short-term, with the goods themselves serving as collateral in the event of non-payment. But only a limited amount of money could be moved in this way. So the banks entered the uncharted world of balance of payments finance in which there was no collateral, in which loans were long-term, and in which borrowers were governments with persistent balance of payments deficits. The banks' only security became "sovereign guarantees," or government promises to pay the money back.

At the same time the Western governments – fearing unemployment at home if the Third World couldn't afford Western goods – were pressing the banks to lend money to the Third World's oil importing nations to help them pay their oil bills and to finance their ambitious development programs. By going along with the Western governments' requests, the commercial banks were making a virtue of recycling the petrodollars, crediting themselves with helping to carry the world economy through the trauma of dramatic oil price increases.

Not only did the Third World come to account for so much of the world's banking business, but this business seemed to be less risky too. The loss rate on international loan portfolios tended to be low: Citibank's foreign losses were half that of its domestic losses throughout the 1970s, for example.

Minimizing the risk further, the commercial banks believed, were quiet understandings between them and the governments of the industrialized countries. Since the banks had come to the rescue of the global economy, they expected the governments to return the favor.

The overwhelming majority of loans carried sovereign guarantees. According to Pedro-Pablo Kuczynski, a former World Bank official, Peruvian cabinet minister, and later an investment banker with First Boston Corporation, "banks preferred to lend to the public sector, not for ideological reasons but because government guarantees eliminated commercial risk." Credit judgments, explained Mr. Kuczynski, "were much simpler to make than for a corporation, which might disappear in a bankruptcy."

This view was epitomized by the leading international banker of the time, the man described as "the intellectual author of overlending to developing countries," Walter Wriston, chairman of Citicorp. "The country," Wriston explained in his now famous statement one month after the Mexican debt collapse in 1982, "does not go bankrupt.... Any country, however badly off, will 'own' more than it 'owes.'"

To maintain the illusion of security, banks heaped rationale upon rationale to keep away any sober second thoughts. Rather than evaluating the investment quality of loans, they based their lending decisions on statistical theory and political guarantees.

For example, the banks used what Mr. Kuczynski called the "pseudo-science" of "country risk analysis" to determine how much to lend to each Third World country. This analysis assumed that risk could be measured by probability, the way insurance companies determine the chance of someone dying. But while insurance companies base their probability calculations on historical information from millions of unrelated cases, banks applied these statistical tools to about one hundred countries, all dependent upon the same international financial circumstances. The result was statistical rubbish.

Banks also comforted themselves by "herding" together: as long as all the banks were making loans to the Third World, they thought, any crisis would be system-wide and would force governments to bail out those countries in trouble.

98

Helping the banks to herd, and to simultaneously recycle huge sums of petrodollars, was the joint loan, or syndicated loan – the vehicle for a massive expansion in world credit that fueled economic growth after the oil shocks of the 1970s. Hundreds of billions of dollars in loans were syndicated between 1970 and 1982. Mexico's syndicated loans marshaled credit from a record 1,400 banks. At the high point of the recycling phase, when the financial needs of Latin America as a whole seemed insatiable, $1 billion syndicated loans were commonplace.

Syndicated loans work like this: A lead bank negotiates the terms of the loan with a state corporation or other borrowers, invites 50 or more other participating banks to join it, and manages the paper work. One or two dozen banks would normally agree to take part with contributions of $1 million to $10 million each. For the participating banks, it was an efficient way to lend money – they avoided preparing the credit analysis and legal documents while diversifying their loan portfolios, scattering their loans among a wide variety of clients in a large number of countries, instead of putting all their eggs in one basket. And, the argument went, syndications allowed the small banks to take part in the boon, without knowing anything about the Third World, since they could rely on the judgment of the big banks in New York and London.

But the wide variety of clients did nothing to diversify the risk. The diversity of borrowers disguised the fact that there was really only one ultimate borrower – the central government. By 1983 the nine largest U.S. banks were owed nearly $39 billion, by just four borrowers – the governments of Mexico, Brazil, Venezuela, and Argentina.

IN THE EARLY 1980s, when the banks came to realize that their Third World clients were all but bankrupt, they began taking measures to protect themselves. New loans covered shorter periods of time in the belief that, if widespread problems emerged, the banks could reduce their exposure by simply not renewing expired loans. This logic turned out to be hopelessly flawed. A bank could only be repaid if another lender extended a new loan to the troubled country. The commercial banks did not expect all lenders to simultaneously cut off funds to Third World borrowers. They didn't expect a run on Third World treasuries.

It all ended on Thursday, August 12, 1982, with Mexican Finance Minister Jesus Silva Herzog telephoning U.S. Treasury Secretary Donald Regan, U.S. Federal Reserve Chairman Paul Volcker, and the Managing Director of the International Monetary Fund, Jacques de Larosière, to tell them Mexico was broke. Within 24 hours, as the sums were tallied, the international banking system's vulnerability became evident.

August 13, the Mexicans were in Washington to begin negotiations. Brazil followed in November. Within twelve months, 27 Third World debtor countries had begun rescheduling their debts; more did so thereafter.

Unable to collect on their outstanding loans, some of the biggest banks faced the unthinkable prospect of default. If the banks couldn't get their money back from their Third World debtors, they could not repay their own depositors and the other banks from which they had borrowed, who in turn couldn't pay off their own debts. Nor was there much security behind the banks themselves: they had broken a cardinal rule by lending an inordinate proportion of their capital to such risky borrowers. It soon became apparent that three of the four largest U.S. banks – Chase Manhattan, Citibank and Manufacturers Hanover – were particularly vulnerable. To the richest countries of the world who were home to the world's big commercial banks, the world banking order suddenly seemed precarious. A string of bank collapses could set off chaos in trading relations and bring on recession, if not an all-out depression.

To stop Mexico from triggering this doomsday chain reaction, the world's banking officials sprang into action. The safety of the major international banks, especially in the U.S. and Britain where banks were deeply steeped in Mexican debt, depended upon a regular inflow of interest payments. Without the inflow the banks' billions in Mexican loans would become "non-performing," leading to huge losses on their earning statements, and plummeting share prices as shareholders dumped bank stocks.

The U.S., major European, and Japanese central banks committed money to a massive emergency loan package. Then the IMF's de Larosière made the commercial banks an offer they could not refuse: lend Mexico another $5 billion, or there would be no IMF funding. The message was unmistakable: without the IMF funds, the entire rescue operation could fail and Mexico would default, taking some banks down with it. The stunned bankers, coerced into throwing good money after bad, did what they were told. To the commercial banks' $5 billion, the IMF added $1.3 billion and governments $2 billion.

For the next eight years the same scene would be replayed. Endless negotiations, or "debt workouts," among Third World governments, the banks and the banks' home governments, and the World Bank, International Monetary Fund, and other international institutions would take place. Debts would be refinanced and rescheduled, new loans would be extended to make interest payments on old loans, old loans that could not be paid back would be extended into the future. In many cases the money never left New York.

To cut their losses, some banks started to sell off their Third World debts, getting, for example, 58 cents for a dollar's worth of Mexican debt or 11 cents for a dollar's worth of Bolivian debt, or swapping their debts for minerals or other assets in the debtor countries. By 1989, after a decade of defaults and much hand wringing, they had written down hundreds of billions in doubtful Third World debts. At the same time, like the person who prepares for disaster, the commercial banks were stashing away cash reserves to cover further losses.

At the 1989 annual meeting of the World Bank and the International Monetary Fund, a gathering considered a rite of passage for budding international bankers, J.P. Morgan Bank stunned the thousands of delegates by announcing that it had set aside enough loan-loss reserves to cover 100 per cent of its troubled medium and long-term Third World debts. By the end of 1989, most big Western banks had moved to put the nagging issue of troubled loans to developing countries behind them.

By 1990, they were safely out of danger of financial collapse, and with this new-found financial security they also bought freedom from the latest debt workout – the Brady Plan, endorsed by the U.S., the World Bank, and the International Monetary Fund. Under the Brady Plan, the banks would write down a portion of their existing loans in exchange for taxpayer guarantees for the remainder. To many bankers, this rang of the IMF's extortion over Mexico.

The banks' mistrust of government assurances would persist. Bank of Nova Scotia President Cedric Ritchie, reacting to later government appeals to provide Eastern Europe with huge amounts of investment capital, dismissed the requests, saying they had "a familiar ring. Not so long ago, the analogous responsibility was to recycle petro-dollar surpluses to finance the development of Latin America." This time around, Ritchie said, his bank would do nothing of the sort "on the faith that public policy might be standing behind us this time. Today, we require assurances that are more tangible than simply a wink and a nod."

PART III

Eager Borrowers

INTRODUCTION: PART III

Ponzi Writ Large

CHARLES PONZI attained immortality in the 1920s through a financing concept now known as the Ponzi Scheme, in which the Boston financier attracted millions of dollars by promising investors a 50 per cent profit in 90 days.

"Widows, orphans and even staid financiers, rushed to press their money into his eager palm," according to *Life* magazine. Ponzi, who kept his investors' money in wastepaper baskets, paid off his investors promptly – sometimes in 45 days instead of the promised 90 days. "In a few months he took in $15 million and became the best-known financier in the country. Then the bubble burst. It was discovered that Ponzi was not making a fortune by juggling International Postal Union reply coupons, as he said, but was simply paying off his early investors with money collected from late-comers." When Ponzi was arrested, he owed approximately $7 million to gullible investors but had only $4 million in assets. No one knew the exact numbers because Ponzi never kept any books.

Ponzi died destitute in 1949 in a Rio de Janeiro charity ward, but his technique – also known as borrowing from Peter to pay Paul – did not die with him. This technique has been alive and well, reaching unheard-of heights in Third World financial markets.

Third World governments have been close to default on their foreign loans since capital transfers began after World War II, with new loans being used to pay back old loans. In 1965, a senior vice president at First National City Bank castigated Argentina, Bolivia, Brazil, Chile, and Uruguay for playing fast and loose with their treasuries, leading them to "year after year [come] back to Washington for bailout loans and foreign debt stretch-outs." In 1969, the Pearson Commission, pointing to a series of debt crises throughout the late 1950s and the 1960s, warned the world the day of reckoning was fast approaching.

FOR EVERY EASY LENDER from the rich countries, there was an eager borrower in the Third World, dreaming up ways to raid the treasure trove of easy money.

Once the dust settled from the whirlwind of lending and borrowing, it became embarrassingly clear that no one really knew where all the money had gone. Money is notoriously difficult to trace, especially when lent to what one banker called the "big pot" – the treasuries of borrowing governments – from whence it can be stolen or stirred up and dished out in an infinite number of ways.

But this much is clear: through borrowing and loan guarantees, Third World governments are responsible for over 80 per cent of the Third World's debt. The remaining 20 per cent is made up of private debts, incurred by private individuals or corporations in the Third World, for which the Third World's citizenry is not liable.

Throughout the 1970s, most of Latin America's debt stemmed from the rapidly expanding role of the state, whose external debt grew almost ten times from 1973 to 1983, two and a half times that of the private sector. The same lopsided growth in public sector debts occurred in Africa and Asia as well.

Sharing the lenders' view of them as good credit risks, Third World governments had unconstrained visions of cornucopia. Commodity prices were at an all-time high and the Club of Rome, an influential think-tank, had come out with its widely publicized report, *Limits to Growth*, predicting that the world would soon run out of resources. Believing the Club of Rome's world computer projections, the resource-rich Third World talked of OPEC-like cartels for coffee, bauxite, and other commodities.

Their natural riches aside, borrowing Third World governments were often offered money at interest rates too low to refuse. By the late 1970s, real interest rates had become negative, with inflation exceeding interest rates, allowing borrowing countries to pay back less in real terms than they actually borrowed.

Many borrowing governments decided to capitalize on the glut of petrodollars to propel their countries into the ranks of industrial giants. Brazil's President-General, Ernesto Geisel, brought state companies together with European and Japanese groups to draw up an ambitious development plan for basic industries: aluminum refineries in the Amazon, a copper refinery in the northeast, steel mills, hydroelectric power stations, railways, capital goods factories, petrochemical complexes and a vast comprehensive nuclear power program, from uranium mines to refineries to nine large nuclear plants.

With abundant foreign finance, Brazilian thinking went, Brazil would grow rapidly, precisely when almost every other country was facing recession. The thinking was similar in Africa, where new capital cities were rising out of nowhere,

where elaborately equipped airports with almost no traffic were being built, and where steel plants without a source of raw material were being constructed. And in Asia, where roads were being built for people who owned neither cars nor shoes to protect their feet from the burning tarmac.

As documented in the *Journal of Economic Growth*, after 30 years, and almost $2 trillion of capital that has been given or lent, many Third World countries now look – on paper – more industrialized than many industrialized countries. Using World Bank measures of industry's share of the nation's output, Zimbabwe, Botswana, and the People's Republic of the Congo look more industrialized than Japan; Zaire looks more industrialized than the United States; and Argentina more industrialized than every country in the European community.

By the same token, Third World countries look less agricultural than many Western countries. In Zimbabwe, agriculture's share of the country's 1985 national output was smaller than Finland's in 1965. In 1986, agriculture contributed more proportionately to output in Portugal than in Gabon; more to Spain's output than to Botswana's; more to Greece's than Peru's; more to Denmark's than to Trinidad and Tobago's.

The statistics also defy common sense and a century of research that show the poor spend a higher percentage of their incomes and invest less than the rich. Yet West Germany invested relatively less than Togo, Nepal, Egypt, or Costa Rica; France less than Mali; and Britain less than Sri Lanka. All Western countries have investment ratios lower than that of tiny Lesotho in Southern Africa.

Looking only at the share of industry and investment in national output, Mexico seems more developed than the United States, Peru more developed than Sweden, and India more developed than Denmark.

Development, it turns out, could not be bought. In the 1960s Nicaragua, Bolivia, the Central African Republic, Zambia and Jamaica each had higher ratios of gross domestic investment to national output than the United States, but all experienced declining per capita incomes for the two decades that followed.

The investment ratio for Africa as a whole has matched or exceeded that of the United States virtually every year since 1965. Yet Africa today is in tatters, its industry in steep decline, its agriculture unable to keep up with population growth. Only its debt and disease are on the increase.

Industrialization without prosperity and investment without economic growth have been a recipe for debt. Borrowed money – although at bargain-basement interest rates – went to marginal if not outright disastrous investments that would never generate the wealth needed to repay the loans.

The investment ratios of Third World countries have not been determined by how much and in what the public wanted to invest, and by what it could afford. Instead, a Third World nation's investment ratio has been determined by unrepresentative leaders, by the political goals of foreign aid and export credit, and by the historical blip called the oil crisis.

Though called investments, the borrowings more closely resembled expenditures, and the magnitude of these expenditures shocked the Third World's public, which had rarely been informed, let alone consulted, about the debts incurred by their governments. By 1990, the Third World's people would discover that they owed about $1 trillion to creditors in the rich countries.

Citizens groups and government bodies throughout the Third World are now trying to find out what their governments did with the money. They are discovering many patterns, and a wealth of anecdotal evidence. But many pieces of the puzzle remain to be found.

Brazilian congressional attempts to track the money and identify the signatories to loan contracts have been thwarted by elusive documents. Everywhere, the absence of good records hampers a thorough review of the decade of debt buildup. Latin America, whose state enterprises received about $80 to $100 billion in foreign loans over the 1970s – the equivalent of one-quarter of the region's external debt – yields remarkably little public information: even records of such things as sales, profits, subsidies, and expenditures on investment are generally hidden or – as with Ponzi – nonexistent. On the other side of the world, the Philippine Commission on Good Government, aided in part by American courts and Swiss laws, has been tracing some $10 billion that the Marcos family allegedly moved out of the Philippines into New York real estate and Swiss bank accounts.

Through investigative efforts such as these, through the self-analysis of the borrowers and the post-mortems of now repentant bankers, much is now known about where the money went.

11

The Business of the State

"NOBODY KNOWS WITH CERTAINTY how the universe came into being but if God had said 'let there be light' while in Colombia, He would not have had enough money left for the rest of creation. Because the truth is that in a country where there are projects which have cost a lot, few have cost as much as the expansion of the electric sector during the last ten years."

So began an article entitled "The Black Hole," in *Semana*, Colombia's *Time* magazine. Electricity expansion plans accounted for close to 30 per cent of Colombia's debt. As the

Minister of Mines, Oscar Meija, put it, "the electric sector became a kilowatt carnival." All over the Third World, kilowatt carnivals were sucking in billions of dollars of foreign loans.

The conduits for these electricity investments, as with most other Third World investments, were state enterprises. Treating development as a product to be assembled, Third World governments set up a myriad of state corporations to invest in the component parts: energy projects; the steel industry; bauxite mines and aluminum plants; agricultural marketing boards; railways, airlines, roads, and bridges; paper plants; textile companies; computer companies; marble and tinted glass operations. Next to governments themselves, state enterprises became the Third World's largest accumulators of foreign debt.

Of these, the state electricity companies throughout the Third World borrowed the most. The electric companies favored huge plants, but these took decades to build, piling up enormous financing costs before generating any revenue. Assuming that a growing economy required a growing energy supply, and knowing no bounds, Latin American countries planned to double their electricity supply every eight years.

The most costly light in Colombia's kilowatt carnival was the Guavio dam. Delays due to collapsing tunnels and other technical problems, and stubborn landowners who refused to evacuate their homes to make way for the dam, doubled Guavio's cost to over $2 billion. The cost overruns equaled the cost of building a subway system for the capital city of Bogota, half of the country's annual coffee exports, or half of the country's social spending.

In Brazil the story was much the same. A fabulously expensive electricity expansion program contributed over $25 billion to the country's foreign debt. Record-breaking dams – the world's largest and the first in the rainforest – proved unnecessary. By 1983, electricity capacity exceeded demand and Brazilians were admitting that they had over-indulged. While "many countries over-consumed," they said, "Brazil over-invested."

Despite shaky financial estimates touting many of Brazil's dams, electric power utilities had little trouble raising construction money. One syndicated loan for the Itaipu dam aimed to raise $50 million. The Western banks offered $103 million, and the Brazilians took it. In the end, Itaipu's cost overruns came close to 400 per cent.

Zaire's equivalent of Itaipu was the Inga-Shaba hydroelectric project and power transmission line, the longest in the world. Originally estimated at $450 million, it ended up costing over $1 billion – equal to 20 per cent of Zaire's debt. U.S. Export-Import Bank loans and guarantees to commercial banks covered the initial bill, while commercial banks covered cost overruns, as the project fell further behind. "It's taking so long that a lot of the equipment they're putting at the two ends is deteriorating," one U.S. embassy official noted. When the project was finally completed, the power – destined for Zaire's rich copper mines – was no longer needed: the Belgians, who were running the mines for the Zaire government, had tapped their own sources of external finance as well as locally available hydroelectric power to keep themselves afloat.

Nuclear power investments, like more conventional electricity investments, also turned into financial quicksand.

Brazil's nuclear power program was eviscerated, with only two of nine reactors likely to be completed. Mexico's only experience with nuclear power – two reactors at Laguna Verde near the ancient port city of Veracruz – were finished in 1990 after an on-again, off-again construction schedule that stretched over two decades. Laguna Verde's costs, originally projected at $1 billion, eventually amounted to almost $4 billion.

Vying in popularity with state electricity utilities in attracting loans were other state energy companies, particularly oil companies, which lenders viewed as blue-chip borrowers. Next to the Mexican government itself, Pemex, the country's state oil monopoly, was considered Mexico's best credit risk, despite its notorious inefficiency, with production costs nearly twice the industry average. (The Mexican government even used Pemex to borrow money for general government purposes.) By 1982, Pemex accounted for about one-third of Mexico's public sector medium-term debt.

Like Pemex, other national oil companies, such as Pertamina in Indonesia and Petrobrás in Brazil, frequently went to international capital markets, racking up debts the government would eventually assume, and political obligations that destined financial disaster.

Petrobrás was created in the 1950s, when "public sector" became an economic catch-phrase and state-run enterprises promised industrial growth without pain. It became Latin America's largest corporation, and one of Brazil's largest losers, politically obliged to charge low prices for its oil, one-third of which is imported.

Compounding its woes, Petrobrás became an infirmary for sick ventures of various kinds and a development agency for government programs. In addition to petroleum, Petrobrás counts among its products sugar-cane alcohol (at a cumulative investment cost of about $650 million), naphtha (at an annual loss of about $500 million), and even lobster exports to the U.S. (at an unknown cost). Unpaid oil bills by other state entities come to about $600 million.

Taken together, oil and electricity state enterprises often accounted for half of a nation's foreign debts. Close behind were the national steel companies.

No country, according to conventional wisdom, could be modern without a steel industry. The Pearson Commission considered steel consumption "one of the basic indicators of industrialization." Third World governments and their financiers, in an attempt to assemble developed economies, created Sicartsas everywhere.

Like other state enterprises around the world, in Mexico Sicartsa became a metaphor for nationalism, touted to the public as a protector from self-serving private interests, whether foreign or national. Yet Sicartsa, again like other state enterprises, became another state vanity project and a costly folly for all Mexicans. The Sicartsa complex remains unfinished: Mexico can no longer pay to put it in place. Completion would cost billions more, and the completed plant would then only lose money. Mothballing the complex for a more propitious time

113

would cost $2.1 billion. Shutting down for good would cost $1.4 billion. Sicartsa's functioning Phase I has debt obligations that consume more than 30 per cent of its revenues, preventing it from showing a profit. To keep up with the debt, the government replaces old loans with new. The government would like to privatize it, but negotiations with buyers have been difficult – Sicartsa's production costs are twice those of South Korean steel mills.

The Sicartsa experience occurred in other Third World countries. In Brazil, Siderbrás's Açominas steel plant in Minas Gerais, built in the late 1970s at a cost of more than $2.5 billion, was financed almost entirely with external borrowing. Within a few years that cost had escalated to $5 billion and the plant was idle.

Siderbrás, "once the jewel in the caps of ruling generals," according to *Euromoney*, "has fallen deepest into the mire." With estimated debts of $13.5 billion, the group of steel-making companies posted losses of over $7 billion in 1988 to make it the Third World's heaviest-losing company, with almost nine times the losses of British Coal, also state-owned. Companhia Siderurgica Nacional, one of the group, lost $7 billion during the 1970s by selling its product to Brazilian industry at 40 per cent below world steel prices. Brazil's state steel companies share responsibility with the nation's state electricity and oil companies, Eletrobrás and Petrobrás, for the bulk of Brazil's public indebtedness.

Venezuela's state steel company, SIDOR, is in similar dire straits. Estimated to have cost more than $6.5 billion, by the end of the 1980s SIDOR was reckoned to be "technically bankrupt": it had a market value of $600 million and debts amounting to $1.5 billion.

In Togo, after the state steel company built a mill with West German financing, the Togolese government realized that no iron ore was available to start up production. It ordered the German technicians to dismantle an iron pier located at the port – a pier that had been constructed by Germany prior to World War I and still functioned well. Once the steel mill had exhausted

114

the pier as a feedstock, it closed down.

Nigeria also purchased an integrated steel complex from Germany, financed by a combination of export credits and a $350 million term loan syndicated by German commercial banks. According to former banker Richard Lombardi of the First National Bank of Chicago: "The steel plant was originally conceived to utilize on-site, relatively low grade iron ore deposits. But Nigeria typically was sold – and bought – at the top of the line. With subsequent add-ons, the steel plant became increasingly sophisticated." In fact, so sophisticated that the Nigerian government was forced to import higher quality ore. Even ignoring the cost of having to purchase the higher grade ore, the cost of the steel complex will exceed $1 billion. That works out to be approximately $12 for every Nigerian man, woman and child, the equivalent of one-tenth of their average income for a steel mill. And this amount covers only the loan principal – not interest, commissions, nor front-end fees, nor the cost of refinancing.

The iron and steel complex and copper refinery for which Zaire's Inga-Shaba power line was built met the same ill fate. The Maluku steel plant, as it was known, never operated at more than 10 per cent of its capacity; its steel is of poor quality and costs three or four times as much as imported steel; it employs 1,000 people instead of the 10,000 promised.

Throughout all these financial debacles in country after country, foreign financiers showed no interest in avoiding bad projects. One study found an unusual number of boondoggles in countries which, having enjoyed large and sudden windfalls from sharp commodity price increases, subsequently enjoyed another windfall in the form of abundant loans from "impressionable and over-enthusiastic international bankers." A study sampling 1,600 state vanity projects in seven oil-exporting countries found them to have been plagued with frequent cost escalations, completion delays, and postponements or suspensions: almost half of the projects over $1 billion went wrong in one way or another, with the average cost escalation being 109 per cent. In general, the larger the project, the greater the waste.

Even those that were completed as expected often turned out to be economic albatrosses. A sugar project in Trinidad completed in 1983 was saddled with production costs five times above those of efficient world-scale producers, even though the latter sometimes had far higher labor costs.

To Argentineans, the country's state-owned enterprises – which first started under the government of Juan Perón – are the culprits of Argentina's economic collapse. One former secretary for growth promotion from the 1980s explains the problem: "The largest 12 of them account for 80 per cent of the fiscal deficit. National railroads lose about $5 million a day. Aerolineas Argentinas loses close to $1 million daily." The losses are not difficult to explain, according to Hector Zanelli, Executive Vice President of Ferrocarriles Argentinos, a state-owned railway company with a bloated payroll of 95,000. "Our salaries cost us about $500 million, and our sales are about $300 million, so you can see where our problems start." One consultant involved in the discussions over possible privatization of the state-owned railway estimated that half of Ferrocarriles' employees could be cut from the payroll without a diminution of service.

State enterprises throughout Latin America borrowed so much from foreign sources that they soon accounted for an unprecedented proportion of the country's total investment. With enormous debt repayment commitments exacerbated by outdated, inefficient production methods and a requirement that state enterprises sell goods at below cost, they drove public sector deficits. In the mid-1970s, state enterprises in the seven largest Latin American economies accounted for one-quarter of the public sector deficit. That rose to about one-half by the early 1980s. Brazil's state enterprises by 1990 accounted for roughly half of its foreign debt. In Mexico, where public expenditures accounted for almost half of the nation's economic activity, state enterprises were responsible for half of that.

Most large enterprises touched by state hands suffered from incredible cost overruns, excessive foreign borrowing, and levels of economic inefficiency so great that they have often assumed comical proportions.

In the Republic of the Ivory Coast, a $60 million sugar plantation and mill, discouraged by the World Bank, was later financed, along with five other complexes, by the export credit agencies of Belgium, Canada, Holland, the U.S., and France, for an overall cost exceeding $1 billion. When the plants started producing sugar in the late 1970s, production costs for a pound of sugar averaged nearly 300 per cent of the world price. In all six cases, investment expenditures surpassed original estimates by more than 200 per cent. According to former banker Lombardi, "The entire sugar program, including original feasibility studies, down payments, front-end fees, and early interest payments, were funded on borrowed money, that is, through a combination of export credits and associated commercial bank loans." The vignette ends, Lombardi explains, "with the picture of an Ivory Coast farmhand spraying unwanted molasses on a dirt road in order to keep the dust down."

State enterprises depended on state guarantees to finance their expansion. They then depended on other state subsidies to make their operations seem viable.

So numerous were the subsidies, so twisted were the tasks assigned them, so unrealistic were the prices set by fiat, that centrally planned economic chaos was inevitable. Ghana's State Fishing Corporation was forced to sell fish at the same price everywhere in the country, regardless of costs. Brazil's regional utilities were prohibited from making more than a 10 per cent profit – anything over that figure was to be handed over to Eletrobrás, the national utility. The regional utilities, to keep profits in their own enterprise, built more electricity plants regardless of need. Egypt's electricity utilities subsidized 87 per cent of industry's electricity cost, accounting for 70 per cent of the government's budget deficit.

State enterprises dominate the debt landscape in countries large and small, in governments of all political stripes. When Malawi became independent in 1964, its unabashedly capitalist president Hastings Kamuzu Banda announced a development policy based on the "acquisitive instincts of the people." But driven in part by fears of domination by foreign companies,

Banda set up three state firms to promote agriculture, industry, and local entrepreneurs, which came to account for one-third of the country's GDP.

12

Money for the Military

DURING THE DECADE of the debt buildup, dictatorships outnumbered democracies in the Third World five to one, arms expenditures amounted to 40 per cent of the debt increase, and Third World arms sales more than doubled. In the mid-1980s, the Stockholm International Peace Research Institute (SIPRI) attributed 15 per cent of the non-oil-exporting Third World's accumulated debt directly to arms purchases. The German Institute for Peace Research attributed 20 per cent of the Third World's accumulated debt to weapons imports. And in 1989,

World Bank President Barber Conable put the figure at one-third for some Third World countries.

In the 1970s the superpowers, wincing under their own budget deficits and trade imbalances, stopped giving away arms and started selling them. To pay for their arms, Third World countries borrowed heavily. Without the OPEC oil crisis – which squeezed military budgets to purchase oil – the arms build-up would have been even more dramatic, according to SIPRI.

Dictatorships, be they military or not, tend to purchase military hardware to wage wars against their neighbors: of the 180-odd wars waged since the Second World War, virtually all have been fought in the Third World, generally between Third World combatants with the blessings, and the arms, of the Cold War powers. But dictatorships also need arms to wage war against their own people. In Argentina's so-called "dirty war," 9,000 innocent citizens disappeared for disagreeing with their government. The Chilean junta's list of the disappeared is over 2,000 long. The Ethiopian rulers killed at least 60,000 by forcibly resettling between 700,000 and 800,000 of their citizens from areas of rebel activity. "In the ultimate mockery of 'defense'," says *World Military and Social Expenditures*, "military power wedded to political control turns inward to terrorize the people it is intended to protect."

Unrestricted access to their countries' treasuries made these internal and external wars possible. Operating above the law and beyond public scrutiny, dictatorships are notoriously undisciplined spenders, acquiring exotic missiles, tanks, and fighter aircraft in much the same way other despots acquire hydro dams and other vanity projects. In Argentina under the generals, no one body oversaw the accounts. For several years of military rule, no records of foreign borrowing were kept – for military expenditures or otherwise – breeding unchecked borrowing. A subsequent central bank investigation discovered that about $10 billion in debt derived from arms purchases, much of it through Argentina's state oil company. The oil company – which was run by one of the generals – ran up a debt of some $4.5

billion but kept only $300 million of it, turning over the balance to the military government for still unknown purposes.

In many Third World countries, military personnel dominate the official bureaucracy and the military budget dominates the central government's budget. The poorest countries typically spend the most: Africa as a whole spends proportionately more on its military than does any other developing region except the Middle East – about 4.3 per cent of GNP in 1987. Africa's poorest country, Ethiopia, spent nearly nine per cent of its GNP on arms – more than twice that spent on education and eight times that spent on health care. Other war-torn African countries such as Angola and Mozambique spent up to half the public budget on the war effort.

Compared to the Middle Eastern countries, whose militaries spent a feverish 10 per cent to 20 per cent of their GNPs, to the former Warsaw Pact countries, which spent 10 per cent, and to NATO countries, which spent 5 per cent, most Third World nations don't seem profligate militarily. Latin America, in particular, spends only 2 per cent of its GNP for military expenses. Yet compared to their people's state of health and education, and to the state of their economies, Third World military expenditures are exorbitant.

In the early 1980s, the Third World's military expenditures grew faster than other government expenditures, with two of three governments spending more on their military than on health care, or on social security and welfare.

The combination of military expenses and debt payments soon starved governments of the revenues required to run their countries. By the mid-1980s, Third World governments found themselves spending up to 85 per cent of their total revenues for these two items combined: 50 per cent in the case of Chile, 64 per cent for the Philippines, 46 per cent for Zimbabwe, over 60 per cent for Pakistan, and 85 per cent for Jordan. It could not continue for long.

As the debt crisis became worse, military budgets tended to be the casualties. Apart from five countries especially involved in conflicts or arms races, the Third World's arms imports declined by over 25 per cent. In Latin America, said SIPRI, this spending decline reflected a decline in militarization, a return to civilian rule, and a shortage of foreign exchange. In Africa, less money – even with more conflicts – squeezed arms imports.

The World Bank and the IMF have also been turning the screws on the military, increasingly pressing Third World governments to reduce their military expenditures. Both institutions insisted in the mid-1980s that Peru reduce its military expenditures by one-third from 6 per cent to 4 per cent of the country's GDP. A 1989 World Bank plan to restore growth in Africa criticized military spending for having "diverted enormous resources from southern Africa's development, and [consuming] nearly 50 per cent of government expenditures in the countries experiencing the worst destabilization." World Bank President Barber Conable – echoing the IMF – announced that defence costs would in future be a factor in loan discussions with African countries.

With the Cold War thawing, the USSR (the leading Third World arms supplier, with $236 billion in sales from 1969 to 1988) and Western governments such as the U.S. ($149 billion), France ($43 billion), and the U.K. ($23 billion) are less determined to arm their client states, and more concerned with how their monies are spent. Zaire, the African bulwark against communism in Africa, now receives tough messages from its long-time donors – the Americans and the Belgians – to combat official corruption and start respecting its citizens' civil rights. The World Bank excoriated the Third World for allowing military expenditures to increase "more than twice as fast as ... income in the developing world since 1960," and called on other donors to ensure their assistance is not squandered on military spending.

SIPRI sees reason for hope: "The combination of high military spending and debt repayment creates an untenable and explosive situation for Third World governments, as they fail to meet the most basic welfare needs of their citizens," leading to a new preference in many countries for social programs over arms expenditures.

Although in most countries the military has lost ground because of the debt crisis, it has gained strength in Guyana, India, Malaysia, Sri Lanka, Gabon, Sudan, Uganda, and Zaire, where health clinics and school budgets were cut to spare the military.

Third World countries still have eight soldiers for every physician, two and a half times the proportion in industrialized countries, and the rich countries still have attractive arms promotion packages in place.

13

Despots on the Dole

IN 1990, THE *FORBES* annual hunt for the world's billionaires tracked down 271 individuals and families worldwide. Yoshiaki Tsutsumi, a Japanese developer whose vast holdings include railroads, ski slopes, hotels and golf courses, had the world's largest empire at $16 billion. Another Japanese developer was worth $14.6 billion, largely through inheriting land near the Parliament in Tokyo, which he transformed into a great commercial center. Thirteen others – 12 from developed countries, and a lone Korean from the Third World – have wealth estimated at between $5 and $10 billion. *Forbes'* list of "The World's Billionaires" included all who had made their fortunes in private sector business activities, and excluded royal families and heads of state because their wealth "derives more from political heritage than from economic effort."

Had *Forbes* included political leaders and royalty, the Third World would have found itself well represented. Topping the list would be the Sultan of Brunei, with his estimated $25 billion, followed by King Fahd of Saudi Arabia, for whom "no line separates his fortune from his nation's, and his visitation rights to the Saudi treasury are generous." King Fahd's personal fortune is estimated at $18 billion. (By comparison, the Queen of England has a personal fortune estimated at $11.7 billion.) Following the sultan and the king come various less royal leaders, who made their fortunes while serving in public office. To do so, they stole from their people.

Philippines' President Ferdinand Marcos and his wife Imelda probably surpassed all other politicians at fiscal manipulation, economic favoritism, and "cooking the books" to enable themselves, their friends and their relatives to steal from the Filipino people.

The extent of their theft cannot be easily estimated because the Marcoses deposited their takings in countries with strong secrecy laws, but few dispute the $10 billion estimate of President Aquino's Commission on Good Government, which was established to recover Marcos-family assets around the world. When Marcos came to power in 1966, the Philippine debt stood at under $1 billion; when he left in 1986 the debt stood at $28 billion. Almost one-third of the increase can be accounted for by the wealth this one couple accumulated so assiduously.

One venture from which the Marcoses skimmed a little off the top was the nuclear reactor project on the Bataan peninsula. This Westinghouse plant, originally estimated at $500 million for two reactors, ended up costing $2.8 billion for a single reactor: it is today the single largest item on the Philippines' debt rolls, accounting for 10 per cent of the country's debt.

From the beginning the project was rife with commercial

irregularities and safety concerns. A panel appointed by Marcos and the head of the Philippine National Power Corporation recommended purchase of a General Electric reactor. But Marcos overruled the panel's choice in favor of the much more expensive reactor from Westinghouse before the latter had even submitted a detailed bid. The Filipino Secretary of Industry wrote angrily to Marcos that he had bought "one reactor for the price of two."

Westinghouse, the dark horse in the race, won the contract with the help of Herminio Disini, a Marcos aide who received $80 million for what Westinghouse called "assistance in obtaining the contract and for implementation services." According to evidence later presented in a government lawsuit against Westinghouse, Disini, a regular golfing partner of Marcos, had openly "flaunted his close relationship with President Marcos" and claimed "he had the authority to arrange the entire nuclear power plant project in any way he wished." Disini received the $80 million only to later pass on the bulk of it to the president. According to the lawyer and a banker who negotiated the deal, Disini received payments through a variety of channels.

When construction began in 1977 the best contracts went to Disini's companies, many of them new and inexperienced in the nuclear reactor business. According to documents left behind in the presidential palace, President Marcos also had an interest in Disini's companies.

In one case, Westinghouse helped Disini acquire Asian Industries, its distributorship in the Philippines, with commissions paid to the company for Disini's benefit. In another contract Disini set up a construction company which was soon named the chief contractor for building the reactor. In a third instance a small insurance company owned by Disini was awarded a $688 million policy on the nuclear plant, the largest ever written in the Philippines. And finally, Disini received most of his money through a Swiss subsidiary of Westinghouse which had set up another entity – Westinghouse International Projects Company – solely to handle the Philippine reactor.

According to a *New York Times* investigation, "The reason

for the complex arrangement with the Swiss concern ... was that Westinghouse couldn't pay fees directly to Disini without risking charges of bribery under various United States fraud laws or laws requiring corporate disclosure. But there were no similar restrictions in Switzerland."

The banker who represented Disini in the transaction explained that a special Swiss fund dispensed the money to Disini, President Marcos, and one or two of Disini's employees, and that Marcos was to receive 95 per cent of the fee. "After all, it was Marcos's deal; Disini was just a conduit."

To see the project through, Westinghouse and Marcos had to deflect growing concerns about the safety of the plant, which was sited at the foot of a volcano, in the middle of the Pacific "fire rim" earthquake zone of high seismic activity. The International Atomic Energy Agency, the international promoter for the nuclear power industry, termed the site "unique to the nuclear industry," and considered the risk of a future volcanic eruption "credible." The Philippine Atomic Energy Commission, who refused to give the plant – already under construction – a construction permit, was also nervous. Finally, after much wining and dining by Westinghouse and pressure plied by the energy minister, and just one week after the Three Mile Island nuclear accident in Harrisburg, Pennsylvania, USA, Librado Ibe, the head of the commission, issued the permit and then moved to the United States. As he explained to *Fortune* magazine, it was unsafe to resist Marcos's lieutenants for too long.

President Marcos could not have accumulated his offshore estate had he restricted his means. Hardly any government institutions were beyond his power: where none existed to serve his interest, he created them. "Corruption was centralized as never before and was thus carried on more efficiently," an independent Filipino research team discovered. "Vast legislative powers Marcos accorded himself through Proclamation 1081 placed him in a vantage position to spot lucrative deals, then wheel and deal through his cronies who also held important government posts."

The government-owned Philippine National Oil Company

127

(PNOC) was also placed at the service of Marcos and of his energy minister and chairman of PNOC, Geronimo Velasco, who is believed to have siphoned off millions of dollars in illegal kickbacks and rebates from the company.

Velasco, according to the head of the Commission on Audit set up by the government of Cory Aquino, "took a staggering amount.... We really don't know how much it was, or how much went to Marcos, because for all these years PNOC was never audited." PNOC – the country's largest business enterprise – was set up by President Marcos during the oil crisis in 1973 and was specifically exempted from normal auditing controls by presidential decree.

The absence of regulatory and public oversight allowed Velasco to defraud the enterprise he ran. Whenever he chartered tankers to bring crude oil to the Philippines, Velasco would add a 5 per cent commission to be kicked back and paid through the treasurer of a shadowy Filipino firm who would deposit the money in banks in Hong Kong and the United States.

Velasco would use a similar scheme when PNOC bought insurance for each tanker voyage from an insurance company owned by another notorious Marcos crony. The PNOC routinely paid more for its tanker insurance than its competitors.

PNOC also paid 10 per cent more than the going price for three oil tankers the company bought from Japan in 1974 and 1975. This purchase was believed to have come from a $400 million discretionary fund, called the Oil Industry Special Fund, over which only Velasco and Marcos had authority. Tariffs on imported oil kept the fund full.

So pervasive was corruption that First Lady Imelda Marcos was nicknamed "Mrs. 10%" for the cut she allegedly took off the top of large government contracts, of which many were within her reach: Mrs. Marcos ran the Greater Manila Area, in which the bulk of foreign investment occurred. As the minister of human settlements, Mrs. Marcos administered vast sums of money, including foreign aid from the U.S. Agency for International Development. Her ministry built convention centers and luxury hotels; 40 corporations that she controlled, like the national oil company, were exempt from audit.

One Filipino businesswoman who ran against the Marcos incumbent in the powerful business district of Makati in the 1984 elections, argued that: "Instead of funneling money through the Marcos government, the U.S. might as well drop all pretenses and hand it over to him personally."

While the Marcoses' assets climbed nearer and nearer to those of Tsutsumi of Japan, so too did the Philippines' foreign debt. As national looters go, the Marcoses were rivaled by few others. President Mobutu Sese Seko of Zaire comes closest.

Premeditated theft and systematic fraud is the only explanation for the near coincidence of Mobutu's personal wealth and his country's national debt – the former approaching $6 billion, the latter $9 billion. The most influential factor in Zaire's economic crisis is corruption, which "reaches an intensity in Mobutu's Zaire that goes beyond shame and almost beyond imagination," according to one Africa specialist.

President Mobutu Sese Seko – self-designated as Zaire's "savior guide" – has put the state machinery, the military, and the nation's rich mineral resources at the service of his family and his associates. His country is also in hock to international agencies, primarily the World Bank and the IMF, to the tune of $1.6 billion. *The Wall Street Journal* calls him a "despot on the dole."

Mobutu and friends shifted funds abroad through manipulation of the exchange rate – purchasing zaires at the dirt-cheap black-market rate and reselling them to the Mobutu-controlled national savings bank at the artificially high official rate. Mobutu is also alleged to have routinely diverted diamonds from the state mining monopoly for private sale in London, to have smuggled gold to Europe, and to have sold strategic minerals through South Africa, with the proceeds sent to his foreign, mainly Swiss, bank accounts.

Until it was dismantled under duress from the IMF, the major source of foreign funds for the "savior guide" and his cronies was Sozacom, the state enterprise responsible for marketing the country's copper and cobalt. The Zairean elite used

Sozacom's access to foreign exchange to make an estimated $1 billion on the black market.

Now and then a few brave souls objected. In 1980, thirteen members of the Zaire parliament wrote to Mobutu, noting that Zaire's debts could be paid off if only a quarter of the elite's illicit earnings were returned from foreign bank accounts. All thirteen were arrested.

The IMF also objected. Mobutu's failure to live up to two agreements with the IMF in the late 1970s led the IMF to insist that an IMF team – headed by West German Erwin Blumenthal, a retired Bundesbank official – run the Zaire Central Bank as a precondition for more aid.

As the IMF team tried to curb foreign-exchange plundering by the president and his relatives, and to force Zairean companies to repatriate capital shifted abroad, the team was relentlessly threatened and intimidated by Mobutu and his aristocrats. On one occasion soldiers under the command of General Tukuzu, Mobutu's father-in-law, threatened Blumenthal with sub-machine guns because they could not get access to foreign exchange for their general. By the end of his stay in Zaire, Blumenthal was sleeping with a shotgun under his bed and a two-way radio to keep him in constant touch with the West German and U.S. embassies. In a reflection on his stay in Zaire, he found it

alarmingly clear that the corruptive system in Zaire with all its wicked and ugly manifestations, its misman-agement and fraud, will destroy all endeavours of institutions, of friendly governments, and of the com-mercial banks towards recovery and rehabilitation of Zaire's economy. Sure, there will be new promises by Mobutu, by members of his government, rescheduling, and rescheduling again of a growing external public debt, but no (repeat: no) prospect for Zaire's creditors to get their money back in any foreseeable future.

One who was close to Mobutu, former Prime Minister Nguza-Karl-I-Nond, estimated that by 1982 Mobutu had stashed between $4 and $5 billion in Swiss, Belgian, and French bank accounts. In addition, Mobutu was reputed to have eight houses and two chateaux in Europe, as well as a Swiss estate, a Paris apartment, three hotels in Dakar, villas scattered across Africa, a Versailles-like palace in northern Zaire, numerous ships, jet planes (including a Boeing 747), and at least 51 Mercedes.

That Mobutu and his extended family pillaged billions from the Zairean people is subject to little debate, except from Mobutu himself. A recent book about Zaire contains an interview with the man. "Clearly, I would be lying if I said I do not have a bank account in Europe; I do," Mobutu said. "I would be lying if I said I do not have considerable money in my account; I do. Yes, I have a fair amount of money. However, I would estimate it to total less than $50 million. What is that after 22 years as head of state of such a big country?" On another occasion, a slighted Mobutu publicly complained when not described as the world's seventh-richest man.

Despite attempts from the IMF and others to curb Mobutu's corruption, little has changed over the duration of his regime. In 1989, exiled Zairean critics charged their country's government with corruption and gross mishandling of World Bank funds. "The World Bank has no way of monitoring what Mobutu does with the central bank's funds," charged exiled Zairean political scientist Nzongola Ntalja. "There shouldn't be any World Bank lending as long as there is no mechanism for control and oversight to see that the government is using the money the way it is supposed to be used." The U.S. Agency for International Development confirmed that the World Bank unsuccessfully sought an explanation from Mobutu concerning more than $400 million in unreported 1988 export earnings.

Mexican President Lopez Portillo is believed to have retired in Rome with some $1 billion. His successor, Miguel de la Madrid, a Harvard-bred technocrat, was exposed for accumulating $162 million in a Swiss bank account, not enough to earn him a spot in *Forbes'* list of "The World's Billionaires" but a tidy sum nonetheless.

131

14

Corruption in High and Not-So High Places

A YEAR AFTER PHILIPPINE President Marcos and his first lady were forced from office, the U.S. Public Broadcasting System interviewed Jose Mari Velez, a governor of the Development Bank of the Philippines, for a program called "In Search of the Marcos Millions." During the interview, Velez described how his bank – a state-owned bank which borrowed from foreign banks and aid agencies to relend to Filipino entrepreneurs – made decisions: "Persons seeking the loan would just come around here and say that we need $100 to $200 million for this project which looks viable. It's not viable but Marcos says it is viable. When he says that then it better be viable."

These loans were known as "behest loans" or loans issued at the behest of Mr. and Mrs. Marcos.

State-owned development finance banks also issued behest guarantees. Because foreign lenders considered the Philippines a very high risk country, they would not lend to Filipino entrepreneurs unless the government guaranteed repayment. So the state-owned development banks issued guarantees at the express instructions of the ruling couple. Those of the Development Bank of the Philippines alone totaled $2.54 billion.

To illustrate behest accounting, Velez described a $65 million loan guarantee his bank provided for a steel mill. When the mill failed to repay its loan his bank was asked to honor its guarantee. "[The bank] asked to see where the factory is, and to this day, after several months, nobody has found it," Velez said. "In short, this factory does not exist." But the $65 million loan, unlike the steel mill it supposedly financed, wasn't a phantom, and still had to be paid back.

The Marcos system of crony capitalism pervaded his government. Many of the country's 500 state enterprises were first formed as private ventures by Marcos's friends, who used them to accumulate large personal gains. After they had been drained of their state-guaranteed financing, and defaulted on their debts, they would then be taken over by the state.

In this way Herminio Disini, who helped Marcos collect $80 million in kickbacks from the Bataan nuclear power contract, was himself helped by Marcos. Without the president, Disini, an accountant in a cigarette factory, could never have acquired his empire of 52 companies with assets of roughly $400 million. When a number of his companies finally went bankrupt in 1982, Disini left for his castle near Vienna, leaving the government banks to pay off his creditors.

Crony capitalism amounted to a parallel economy run by and for the president and his close associates. Typically, the foreign loans aided selected entrepreneurs in gaining control of specific sectors, which would also be favored by presidential decrees. Many loans exceeded business requirements, with the difference – less the presidential tithe – diverted into the pockets of the borrowers. A senior Central Bank official explained crony capitalism's logic in describing why sugar mills were built in areas unsuitable for sugar production, or in places where adequate milling capacity already existed: "The profit was not in the operation of the mill – it was in the procurement of the milling equipment."

The development banks of other countries, too, became renowned for their corruption and monumental losses.

In Bangladesh the Asian Development Bank investigated $300 million in defaults on loans it and two other banks had provided to two nationalized Bangladeshi banks. It found that local businessmen had borrowed cash for projects "without any serious intention of pursuing such projects." Although the businessmen were only required to put down 5 per cent to 7.5 per cent of a project's cost themselves, even the down payment could be borrowed. The Asian Development Bank found a "lack of motivation and indifference to successful operation" because fund-raising was so easy. Repayments by companies were extremely rare, with 90 per cent of industrial loans rescheduled.

Similarly, the Inter-American Development Bank now admits that government-distributed development funds are too susceptible to political influence, and too immune from the principles of economy and efficiency.

Government finance is also prone to misappropriation. Late in 1986, Argentina's Central Bank announced that it had been defrauded of $110 million in export credits by Banco Alas, the thirteenth-largest private bank in the country. With seven senior Banco Alas officials under arrest, including the president and vice-president, the Central Bank informed Argentineans that of Banco Alas's $110 million in export credits, only $300,000 could be verified. An investigation found that 16 of the 20 exporters receiving Banco Alas credits did not exist, and that the other four denied doing business with the bank. The police did find $750,000 in cash in the bank vice-president's Mercedes-Benz, and several Swiss and American bank accounts in the names of bank officials. Suspicions that the scam required the collaboration of high government officials led to the arrest of three senior Argentine Central Bank officials. The Central Bank admitted "deficiencies" in its internal control structure, adding "corruption continues to exist in the financial system."

The Banco Alas scandal was just the tip of the iceberg: a month after it broke the state prosecutor accused the entire former board of the Central Bank of fraud.

Nigeria may top all countries for corruption. With about $30 billion in debt, it is also Africa's most indebted nation, thanks to a succession of military and civilian regimes that have governed the country and its enormous oil wealth inefficiently and corruptly. Corrupt politicians used a variety of conduits to hijack the proceeds of the "national patrimony," with invoicing fraud a common method.

Over-invoicing is especially favored in countries which inflate the value of their currency, creating a large gap between the currency's worth and its official exchange rate. To prevent their citizens from changing their currency for dollars or another convertible currency, the government attempts to control all transactions, allowing only a favored few to purchase convertible currencies at an artificial exchange rate. The right to buy foreign currencies – or foreign exchange as such currencies are called in a country that manipulates its currency – thus becomes something of value, and those who control access to foreign exchange become powerful bureaucrats.

With over-invoicing, an importer asks a foreign supplier to inflate the price of his product, allowing the importer to ask his government for an inflated amount of foreign exchange, the difference going into the importer's own foreign bank account. Sometimes the importer doesn't even import the goods. The government official who grants permission for the inflated foreign exchange request, meanwhile, receives something for his trouble too.

Import licenses – because they provided access to foreign currencies – were so valuable in themselves that Nigerian government officials treated them as patronage to reward political service, with the recipients then selling them to genuine importers of goods. By 1983, estimates of the foreign exchange siphoned out of the country ran as high as $7.5 billion, or about 40 per cent of the Nigerian foreign debt. In Ghana, a government investigation in the early 1980s revealed that the country was losing at least $60 million a year through over-invoicing imports. And in Asia, according to Morgan Guaranty Trust Company, the value of Malaysia's reported exports between 1976 and 1984 fell roughly $10 billion short of their value as recorded by Malaysia's trading partners.

While importers over-invoiced, exporters under-invoiced. An exporter would bill foreign purchasers less than the agreed price, with the difference being deposited in the exporter's foreign bank account.

Under- or over-invoicing aside, many of the "exports" vanished without arriving at their destination. Nigeria became the world's most frequent victim of maritime fraud, with oil cargoes hijacked and sold, the proceeds laundered through Swiss and Hong Kong bank accounts. For the privilege, oil traders routinely put kick-backs into the foreign bank accounts of government officials.

One of Nigeria's most profligate projects involved a new national capital at Abuja, estimated to cost $24 billion, or the equivalent of the country's total sovereign foreign debt. Between 1980 and 1983, the government spent over $2 billion on the new capital without the completion of any road, building, or other construction project. Corruption became so rife that at the fall of the country's second republic in 1984, several of the buildings, including the tallest building in Africa and the Accounts section of the federal Capital Development Authority in Abuja, were all burnt, apparently to conceal widespread fraud.

Nigeria's administrations became so flagrant that a country with a healthy flow of oil earnings – $25 billion per year throughout the 1970s – by 1983 had only enough foreign exchange to cover one month's imports. A Nigerian government investigation estimated that, at the height of the oil boom in 1978, corrupt politicians were transferring $25 million abroad every day, or $10 billion a year – almost 40 per cent of the nation's foreign exchange earnings.

In Venezuela, the aluminum industry served as a vehicle for the appropriation of public funds. Polished up with subsidies to provide a luster of efficiency, Venezuela's aluminum industry in reality has administrative costs double the world-wide average. According to the *Wall Street Journal*, "payoffs are allegedly built into every construction project." The country's controller general has complained about numerous examples of irregular practices of the government's huge Venezuelan Guayana Corporation (CVG) and its subsidiaries (including aluminum, bauxite and hydroelectricity companies). An investigation of CVG by the opposition party found: "There are no controls. Everybody participates in the corruption.... In each of the 10 cases we looked at there was a payoff." Multinationals bidding for CVG projects complain of protracted delays during which CVG executives allegedly fight among themselves over who will receive the bribes. "Telexes get stolen and contracts get copied by rival groups within the CVG."

In Argentina, corruption reached a peak under the generals, coinciding with the astronomical rise in debt. While everyone had his hand in the till, no one had his hand on the controls. By the end of 1982 no one really knew for sure what the total debt was. The economy minister, Jorge Wehbe, declared a $43 billion debt. The air force insisted it was no more than $37.8 billion. In 1983 AmEx Bank estimated it at $43.7 billion, adding that of the $63 billion of debt "missing" among the twenty-four largest debtor countries, Argentina had "lost" a quarter of the total.

Debts were "lost" because they had been contracted by the government, state-controlled companies, and the military on their own authority, bypassing the notice of government departments that normally would track them. Determining after the fact the volume and purpose of the loans, the interest rates charged, and the dates the loans matured proved to be difficult.

Argentina's military was particularly lax with public funds, running up a $9 billion arms bill in a bout of words with Chile over the disputed Beagle Channel. The $6 billion nuclear program, also under military control, was mainly financed by foreign borrowing. After the Malvinas (or Falklands) War, more military expenditures for replacement equipment added another $1.5 billion to the military component of the debt. This "military" component, however, functioned mainly to create sinecures for officers. In other cases, suspicions ran high that the military had run up debts without the money ever entering the country. As an investigating judge put it, "It is not clear whether we are dealing with the results of massive looting or chaos or both."

The opportunity to appropriate funds became an incentive to the powerful to approve unneeded and ill-considered projects, creating a system in which decisions on public expenditure were based not on their value to taxpayers but on payoffs to decision-makers. The coincidence of large debts, political corruption, and the absence of democratic institutions in countries with decreasing standards of living is therefore unsurprising. Business and economic theorists construct elaborate models to explain what is common sense: civilian and military elites unchecked by legislative rules and the ballot box, and free of personal financial liability for their actions, know no limits when borrowing money in their peoples' name.

The constellation of ruinous economic policies can hardly be attributed to well-meaning, perhaps naive, and possibly incompetent Third World leaders. Instead, these policies generally represented deliberate acts by those in power to aggrandize or enrich themselves. The upper classes in developing countries controlled not only the borrowing and spending of foreign loans, most of them publicly guaranteed, but also the economic policies and financial regulations that made it lucrative, and possible, for them to pillage their national treasuries for their personal gain.

"Local elites do not just react passively to the local governments. In many cases they *are* the local governments, or at least the executive committees," explained James Henry, an American economist and expert in capital flight. In Mexico, for example, "a basic method of taking money out ... has been to exploit overvalued official exchange rates with the help of foreign banks. The preservation of this exchange rate system even in the face of massive capital flight is very hard to understand unless we take into account the profits made from it by people in positions to influence policy."

In Argentina, swapping pesos for foreign currencies was not only legal, it was subsidized by the state and aptly called "the bicycle" by Argentineans. The public sector would borrow money from foreign banks, then sell the foreign currency to private individuals and companies who deposited it abroad.

In Nigeria, only the elite had access to central bank-issued exchange forms. With them they would buy heavily subsidized dollars from the Nigerian central bank and export the dollars to neighboring countries in which a black market in foreign currencies existed to serve the hundreds of thousands of immigrant workers who were traveling back and forth. There they would purchase nairas with dollars at the real market rate (dollars were worth much more than the Nigerian central bank recognized), deposit their left-over dollars in foreign bank accounts, then smuggle enough nairas into Nigeria so they could pay back the Nigerian central bank.

The ways to get capital out of a country are as diverse as human beings are ingenious. The degree of foreign exchange restrictions would determine the method.

Money would be smuggled out in suitcases with false bottoms, and even in poultry, as a Filipino customs officer discovered when he found a frozen duck stuffed with $29,000 bound for Hong Kong. In 1981 Venezuelans entering Miami reported – on treasury forms handed entrants to the U.S. – that they were carrying over two billion dollars in cash. In other cases, the commercial banks themselves would engineer an exit route via the bank accounts of intermediaries in tax havens, making a paper trail impossible to follow.

For those in positions of power – those who award public contracts, issue import licenses, and set government regulations – the possibilities for misappropriating borrowed funds and then sending them abroad have been endless: phony intermediary companies would recontract with foreign suppliers and take a hefty spread in the transaction; developers would get public loans for projects that didn't exist; local "consultants" would be paid by foreign suppliers in foreign accounts, and outright smuggling of goods. Diamond smuggling from Angola – 75 per cent of which is done through the VIP lounge at the Luanda airport – cost the Marxist government some $70 million a year in lost foreign exchange.

Corruption in undemocratic governments has few checks and generally spreads to the institutions with which they deal, and from which they draw support. In Mexico, corruption in this periphery reached extraordinary heights in the person of Joaquín Hernández Galicia, for three decades the union boss of the 170,000 workers in Mexico's nationalized oil industry. With the complicity of five successive Mexican administrations who dared not take him on, La Quina, as the union leader was known, was allowed to run the oil-rich Gulf coast almost as a private fief, enjoying a power that rivaled that of government leaders. Through control of jobs in Pemex, the hugely overmanned state oil monopoly, and kickbacks from the oil giant's construction contracts, La Quina probably controlled over a billion dollars. The La Quina empire encompassed everything from farms to subsidized food outlets to funeral parlors, enabling him to create a cradle to grave existence for "his" workers.

La Quina's right-hand man, Sergio Bolaños, fronted a 27-company industrial empire for the union, and profited enough from running La Quina's businesses to make the highest offer – in cold cash – for the Government's stake in Mexicana de Aviación, one of the two flagship airlines being privatized. Mexican authorities have found Bolaños to hold foreign real-estate worth about $84 million, including a castle in France and a lavish compound in Vail, Colorado. When an elite Mexico City school denied his daughter entry, Bolaños bought it.

La Quina did not tolerate dissidents, rivals usually meeting their fate in a hail of bullets. One government attempt to rein him in was followed by a chain of 13 explosions in oil installations across Mexico. Always fearful of the consequences should

140

Pemex workers go on strike – Pemex is Mexico's major foreign exchange earner – successive governments treated La Quina with kid gloves, until January 10, 1989. On that morning, the army forced entry into La Quina's Gulf Coast headquarters with a bazooka round, found 200 Uzi submachine guns and 40,000 cartridges in the raid, and arrested 45 close associates, including Bolaños. La Quina and his henchmen have been charged with illegal arms possession, murder, conspiracy against the state, and, through Bolaños, tax evasion.

THE ONLY LIMIT to unchecked governments can come from the lenders themselves, yet they are as unreliable as any corrupt leader: financiers didn't just tolerate irregularities in foreign-financed public projects, they were ready participants. Canada's Atomic Energy of Canada Limited, a crown corporation that markets the country's CANDU nuclear reactor, paid $18 million to an "agent" to clinch the sale of reactors to South Korea and Argentina. An investigation by Canada's auditor general discovered payments that had all the characteristics of a bribe. In response to the public furor that followed, the Canadian government stated that not only was it legal for a Canadian to bribe a foreign official, but that bribes could also be deducted as an expense from his taxable income, provided the briber receives a receipt. Then Trade Minister Jean Chrétien explained: "Commercial practices in other countries sometimes are different from ours. I am not about to condemn the morals of anybody. It would be very presumptuous for Canadians to tell other people how to conduct their morals." Chrétien urged Canadians not to put their "head in the sand" and pass up overseas sales by being rigidly moralistic.

The World Bank and Inter-American Development Bank have also turned deaf ears to tales of corruption involving an Argentine project to which they have both lent millions of dollars. The Yacyretá hydro dam on the Paraná River between Argentina and Paraguay, one of the largest public works projects under way in the world, was conceived under the government of Juan Perón. But only under the military government of the late

1970s did money start to really flow. Within a few years, more than \$1 billion had been spent without land being broken for the main project. Most of the money went to build two towns to house 7,000 workers and for other preliminary work. The dam is now expected to cost \$12 billion, 800 per cent of its original cost estimate. Although the Inter-American Development Bank and the World Bank sometimes raised questions about accounting and record-keeping procedures, they eschewed extensive oversight. Nor was the Inter-American Bank deterred in 1990 when, just minutes before its officials were about to sign a new \$250 million loan to the dam, Argentinean President Menem called for the dam to be canceled, saying, "Here's a monument to corruption." The bank decided to overlook the presidential gaffe and went ahead with the signing ceremony anyway.

Corruption in the Third World required complicity from those in the West who, one way or the other, benefited from the Third World's status quo. Thanks to secrecy and a public perception in France that "power gives you the right to accept certain things," it may never be known whether the Giscard d'Estaing family's extensive overseas business interests received favors from kin who occupied the nation's most important public posts. In late 1975, President Valery Giscard d'Estaing paid a state visit to Zaire's President Mobutu Sese Seko. In a country in which few have electricity and a third of the populace live close to starvation levels, work soon began on a new national telecommunications system, complete with TV studios, at a cost of \$500 million. The French president's first cousin headed the company that received most of the contracts to build the microwave system, and another cousin headed the state-owned export credit agency, Banque Française du Commerce Exterieur, that provided much of the scheme's financing.

"Gossip or not," reported the *Wall Street Journal* in a front-page exposé of France's most enterprising family, "public records indicate that companies in which members of the Giscard d'Estaing family hold high positions have had extensive business dealings in Gabon, Morocco, Chad, the Central African Republic, the Cameroons, the Ivory Coast, Mauritania, Niger and Upper Volta. In many of these countries, the existing regimes are heavily obligated to President Valery Giscard d'Estaing's government for the French military support that keeps them in power."

With such obliging financiers, it can hardly come as a surprise that borrowing country officials should treat public borrowings as private assets. Mobutu rewarded loyal lieutenants with spectacular gifts, such as Mercedes cars and houses, and allowed them "to misappropriate state funds at will." He nationalized various foreign-owned enterprises only to hand them over to his cronies – not the state – who swiftly set about stripping them of their assets. Before too long, they could pay neither taxes nor the debts of their newly-acquired enterprises. Yet "every time Mobutu stole money, [Western donors] gave him more. It was like supporting a junkie," says Stephen Lewis, editor of London-based *Africa Confidential.*

Foreign financiers coddled Third World corruption willingly and knowingly, fueling what Octavio Paz, the Mexican poet and Nobel prize winner, described as the typical Latin American "patrimonial state" in which "the Prince governs with his servants, his slaves and his family – in other words, where he regards the realm as his personal property."

15

The Nether Borrowers

"NOTHING HAS SO MUCH cowardice as money," Argentina's Juan Perón once observed. Perón spoke with authority. In the 1950s he and his second wife, Evita, fearing for their money's security, sent an estimated $700 million out of the country they governed into the refuge of numbered Swiss bank accounts. The Peróns' successors perpetuated the practice. In the last decade, Argentineans, from the wealthiest in the land to their chamber-maids, sent 65 per cent of the country's incoming loans right back out again. Such flights of capital became a prime cause and a prime effect of the debt crisis. Some consider capital flight the single largest obstacle to resolving the Third World debt crisis.

The flight of valuables, generally foreign exchange, to countries safe from revolution, confiscation and economic disarray, or to countries that provide a better return on investment or escape from high taxes, has always occurred.

In sound economies, people routinely transfer their money across borders to finance trade deals, to earn higher interest rates in foreign bank accounts, to buy foreign securities, or to invest in real estate and other business endeavors. Money leaves a country in millions of transactions, large and small, in debt and in equity, but money comes in too, with the net effects generally being unalarming.

The routine transfers which were occurring in the Third World, however, were different: mainly cash was going out, and – in large part to replace that cash – mainly loans were coming in.

According to Morgan Guaranty Trust Company, the flight of capital has been so large that without it Argentina, Venezuela, Malaysia, and Mexico would have been almost debt-free, and Nigeria and the Philippines would have had their external debt halved. By the end of 1987 the foreign wealth held by the citizens of the 15 largest Third World debtors amounted to $300 billion – more than half of the foreign debts owed by their countries.

In Mexico, the revolving door's rotations reached a peak under President Lopez Portillo – a former law professor whose administration became synonymous with profligate spending, corruption, and capital flight. During his presidency, the country's foreign debt more than doubled to $85 billion, as Mexicans sent roughly $90 billion abroad. The more foreign exchange became available, the more left the country.

A Mexico City newspaper published a list of 575 names of Mexican nationals, each of whom had at least $1 million deposited with foreign banks. The exposure of these *sacadolares* – people who take out dollars – caused an uproar as it coincided with Mexico's pleading for $10 billion in new foreign loans to avert bankruptcy. "The problem is not that Latin Americans don't have assets," commented one U.S. Federal Reserve Board member. "They do. The problem is, they're all in Miami."

The simultaneous accumulation of foreign debt and flight capital is no coincidence: foreign loans provided foreign currency to ship abroad. As explained by James Henry, an expert on capital flight: "More than half of the money borrowed by Mexico, Venezuela, and Argentina during the last decade has effectively flowed right back out the door, often the same year or even month it flowed in." Oil-rich Venezuelans sent back some $27 billion between 1979 and 1984, $4 billion more than the country borrowed.

Ironically, while foreign borrowing fueled capital flight, capital flight caused foreign exchange shortages that drove several debtor countries back to the banks.

A year after borrowing a billion dollars in 1978, the Nigerian government went back for a second billion dollars – naked looting and capital flight had swallowed the first billion as fast as it came in. (Later, the billion was traced to Swiss bank accounts, but by then the military government of the day had retired with political immunity.)

While easily available foreign loans made capital flight possible, economic mismanagement made it inevitable.

To foster local investments, Third World governments put caps on interest rates often below the inflation rate, but caps instead chased money to countries providing higher rates of return. High fixed exchange rates for national currencies, designed to make imports look cheap and keep inflation down, also made foreign investments look like bargains. People converted their local cash and businesses into dollars as fast as they could and sent them abroad. The artificial exchange rates encouraged imported luxury goods, all of which were available for pesos on the dollar. In countries like Mexico and Argentina, where the citizenry was free to purchase foreign currency until 1982, these policies combined to drain national treasuries of their foreign currencies in a matter of years, sometimes months.

Inflation rates, meanwhile, skyrocketed out of this world. Governments across Latin America, in particular, were printing more and more money to help cover the costs of extravagant investment schemes, subsidies to industries, and the salaries of teachers and health care workers. But the more money they printed the less it was worth. Their citizens watched with horror as their savings dwindled overnight. Inflation became so bad in Bolivia, for example, that the Banco Boliviano Americano didn't bother to check the number of notes deposited with it, but merely weighed them by the sackful to assess their value. According to the *Wall Street Journal*, "To buy an average-sized television set with 1,000 peso bills takes more than 68 pounds of money." One commentator called the spiraling inflation and capital flight the "fever blisters of sick economies in conflict."

The public could see the writing on the wall: the high inflation, persistent trade deficits, and uncontrollable foreign borrowing would inevitably force steep devaluations, wiping out their savings. Millions of Latin Americans – even cab drivers and waitresses – cashed in their pesos for dollars, often banking the proceeds offshore. The Asian public responded similarly. The first finance minister in the new Philippines government of Corazon Aquino remarked that "every successful businessman, lawyer, accountant, doctor, and dentist I know has some form of cash or assets which he began to squirrel abroad after Marcos declared martial law in 1972 and, in the process, frightened every Filipino who had anything to lose."

When they weren't sending their assets abroad, Third World citizens were safeguarding their assets by hoarding "Yanqui" dollars in their own countries. By the mid-1980s, U.S. monetary officials noted that three $100 bills were in circulation for each man, woman, and child in the United States. The U.S. Treasury estimated that as many as $20 billion in $100 bills (or 200 million $100 bills) were offshore.

Eventual devaluations and foreign exchange controls didn't stop the hemorrhage. In 1986 Morgan Guaranty Trust Company appraised capital flight from the big ten Latin American debtors (Brazil, Mexico, Venezuela, Peru, Colombia, Ecuador, Bolivia, Uruguay, Argentina, and Chile) at fully 70 per cent of all their new loans from 1983 to 1985, with Mexico sending out almost twice the amount being received in new loans.

Brazil, whose realistic exchange rates had always kept its citizens' cash at home, joined the ranks of the capital flight countries as the public voted non-confidence in the worsening economy of the late 1980s: almost $20 billion left the country in just 1988 and 1989. Brazil's flown assets are now estimated at over one-third of its external debt.

Monies spirited out of the Third World were parked in everything from real estate to time deposits to car dealerships and bank accounts abroad. "Many parts of California don't realize how much of their prosperity they owe to Mexico's crisis," said David Todd, a partner in the accounting firm of Price Waterhouse in Newport Beach.

Mexicans sank as much as two-thirds of their flight capital into bank time deposits. Along with U.S. government treasury bills, these deposits were safe, highly liquid, untaxed, and simple. When some large Mexican depositors began to worry about the health of the U.S. banks that loaned too much to places like Mexico, they shifted their holdings into U.S. government securities. "What's indisputable," said Henry, "is that when wealthy Mexicans invest their own capital abroad, they are much more cautious than the foreign bankers who financed all their country's debt."

The wiser the big commercial banks became, the more aggressive became their efforts to attract deposits from wealthy Third World citizens. With their Third World sovereign loan business on the wane, the big commercial banks moved on to "IPB" or international private banking, a fiercely competitive, but necessarily low profile, growth field for the world's largest banks.

Mexican depositors were especially wooed. Citibank, Morgan Guaranty, Bank of America, and Chase Manhattan, plus several large regional banks in Texas and California, all served a key client list of at least several hundred wealthy Mexican customers. According to Henry:

They all have very active calling programs designed to recruit new clients. They all play an active role in helping wealthy Mexicans get their money out of the country. They all help such customers design sophisticated offshore trusts and investment companies to shelter income from taxes and political exposure. They all try very hard to keep the identity of their customers a secret. They are all more or less actively involved in lobbying U.S. authorities to preserve policies toward taxation, bank regulation, and bank secrecy that are favorable to their clients.

One IPB agent, a Mexican graduate of the University of California, was hired by Merrill Lynch, Pierce, Fenner & Smith to recruit Mexican clients. According to the *Wall Street Journal*, "His technique was simple: Open the Mexico City Yellow Pages and call up the presidents of the companies that had the biggest ads. 'If you didn't come back from Mexico with $1 million in investments, the trip was considered a failure,' the Mexican graduate explained. 'But the competition was very rough.'"

In 1986 Citibank, the most aggressive American bank in international private banking, had over 1,500 people dedicated to IPB worldwide (although to maintain discretion, they were usually connected with other parts of the bank). About half of its $26 billion in IPB assets probably belonged to Latin Americans. The "Big Four" – Brazil, Mexico, Argentina, and Venezuela – owed Citibank only about $10 billion. All told, Citibank may owe more money to Latin Americans than Latin American countries owe it.

As U.S. tax laws exempt non-residents from paying taxes on portfolio interest, and disclosure laws do not require U.S. banks to report the countries of origin of private banking assets, the U.S. became one of the world's more attractive tax havens for flight capital. U.S. banks came to manage international private banking assets of roughly $100 to $120 billion, 60 to 70 per cent of which came from Latin American private banking assets, while U.S. banks had outstanding Latin America loans of about $83 billion. Not only was the U.S economy as a whole probably a net debtor of Latin America: U.S. commercial banks were close to being net debtors of Latin America.

The banks' real role, said Henry, "has been to take funds that Third World elites have stolen from their governments and to loan them back, earning a nice spread each way." The banks had to realize they were playing the role of the go-between: just as surely as they lent the money to governments, deposits from individuals in those same countries would come right back to them. "Sometimes the money never even leaves the United States. The entire cycle is completed with a few bookkeeping entries in New York."

The result, according to the late economist Carlos Diaz-Alejandro, was the accumulation of "private assets and public debt."

Economist George B.N. Ayittey, a native of Ghana, blames both parties to the transaction. "It takes very little common sense to realize that pouring water into a bucket full of holes is pointless. Similarly, without genuine efforts by the [poor countries] to address the domestic side of the debt crisis, an international rescue package of loans will flow right back out of the debtor nations in the form of capital flight and booty."

After years of propelling the revolving door with billion-dollar loans to Third World governments and billion-dollar deposits from Third World private citizens, Walter Wriston, then chairman of Citicorp, spoke to the nub of the issue in early 1986, after $3 billion had left Mexico in one month alone: "If your own people don't trust you, why should anybody else?"

16

Unchecked Governments

WHEN GOVERNMENTS WEREN'T borrowing on behalf of their state enterprises or their military, or to compensate for monies draining the country through corruption and capital flight, they were borrowing on their own account.

Soaring oil bills after the OPEC oil crisis come in for the most blame in indebting Third World governments. Yet, of the ten most indebted developing countries, three export oil and only three – Brazil, India, and South Korea – depended heavily on imported oil. Of those three, only Brazil could not manage its

151

debt. Among the next 25 most heavily indebted countries, only four more – the Philippines, Pakistan, the Sudan, and Uruguay – suffered seriously. Uruguay, for example, spent 44 per cent of its export earnings on imported oil in 1975.

Others – Argentina, Peru, and Chile among them – depended far less on imported oil. Despite a threefold increase in oil prices by 1975, these countries spent only about 15 per cent of their export earnings on imported oil.

In fact, the oil crisis most crushed those that it enriched – Mexico and Venezuela, two of the world's biggest oil producers. Being rich in oil, and hungry for funds to develop their oil reserves, Mexico and Venezuela borrowed heavily against their natural assets.

The oil crisis disproved Pearson's dire warnings that Third World nations would soon run out of credit. Awash with petrodollars, the private banks – until then minor lenders – stepped in to fill the financial breach, allowing Third World countries to blissfully borrow more to pay off old debts. But Pearson's prediction had only been postponed: the Ponzi game continued on inexorably toward a conclusion one decade later.

The borrowers' luck finally ran out. Worldwide interest rates, but especially those in the United States to which most Third World loans were tied, went sky high, forcing Third World countries to pay more. At the same time, commodity prices fell through the floor, giving them less with which to do so. Meanwhile, like Mr. Ponzi, Third World governments had failed to put their money in income-generating investments, squandering it instead on ill-considered megaplans and more.

Contributing to the spending deficits of oil exporting and importing nations alike were all manner of subsidies. For the oil exporting countries, subsidized domestic fuel encouraged wastefulness and – since less was left to sell – represented foreign exchange forgone. For all countries, energy subsidies encouraged consumption at the expense of the environment and the economy.

Next to energy subsidies were food and agricultural subsidies, which especially wreaked havoc on Third World economies by undermining local agriculture.

African governments have provided cheap food to the politically important urban populations by forcing state grain boards to sell their stocks below market prices. As a result, most governments have run up large deficits for decades. In Zambia, corn subsidies for the urban population alone accounted for 16 per cent of the government's 1986 budget deficit.

To help pay for the low consumer prices, farmers have in turn been expected to hand over their crops for a pittance, driving them out of business or into the black market, out of the marketing board's reach. For export crops, says the Heritage Foundation, a conservative think-tank based in Washington, the marketing board's "rule has been: buy low, sell high and pocket the difference." Farmers in Ghana, Nigeria and Tanzania – among Africa's main coffee-, cocoa- and cotton-exporting countries – received only about 50 per cent of the export price of their crops in 1984. Cameroon's coffee farmers received 29 per cent for their Arabica beans in 1986 – $1,400 a ton against a world market price of $4,800 a ton.

"Price-conscious African farmers," reports the Heritage Foundation, "responded by selling their production in black markets, smuggling it across the border, shifting into livestock, reverting to subsistence agriculture or leaving the land entirely to join the urban swell." By so grossly underpaying their farmers in an attempt to squeeze the maximum profit for the state, African governments eventually drove an important source of revenue away.

Mismanaging agriculture has generally been very costly for governments and farmers alike. In El Salvador, the Coffee Growers' Association railed against the state monopoly marketing board for costing the nation $400 million from blundered speculations and inexperience, for paying coffee growers less than their own costs of production, and for delaying payment, thereby adding to the growers' own debts on production loans.

State-subsidized agriculture has also drained many Third World treasuries of scarce resources. In Mexico and Brazil, government-subsidized credits had low, if not negative, interest rates, with the well connected borrowing state money at low interest rates, only to invest it in government bonds that were indexed to the much higher inflation rate. In 1975, Brazil lent farmers more than the net value of their crops, as the loans became too cheap to refuse. Depending on the loan's use, interest ranged from 13 per cent to 21 per cent, much less than inflation. Farmers could put their borrowed money in banks and earn three or four times as much. According to *The Economist*: "That is the only way to explain how the acreage receiving credit for favored crops like wheat and soybeans regularly exceeded the acreage harvested – depending on the crop – by between 30 per cent and 100 per cent in 1976."

The biggest farmers were the quickest to take advantage of the credit windfall. In 1976, 4 per cent of the loans accounted for 52 per cent of all the money, widening the already cavernous gap between rich and poor farmers: 10 per cent of the farmers control three-quarters of the country's farmland. Brazilians called this form of arbitrage *ciranda financeira*, or "financial ring around the rosy." One Brazilian economist called it "perverted," explaining that the government was issuing credit that was being used to finance not development but speculation.

Bloated state payrolls have also drained Third World treasuries.

Brazilian governments at all levels kept an estimated seven million people "paid, and sometimes employed," according to the financial magazine, *Euromoney*, with payroll padding rife throughout the system: the agrarian reform agency had 600 doormen on the payroll, but occupied buildings with only 10 entrances.

In his six years in office, President Sarney increased real spending on personnel by 71 per cent with over 50,000 hirings. By the time he passed on the presidential sash to Collor de Mello in 1990, federal and state government payrolls exceeded the federal government's entire tax revenues. The new Brazilian president decided to fire between 20 and 25 per cent of the federal payroll, including several dead civil servants. Eleven thousand federal employees holding two or more government jobs were told to quit their extra employment.

To meet an IMF budget-cutting requirement in 1983, Zaire fired a third of its teachers and civil servants, including several thousand fictitious people on the state payrolls. Some school headmasters kept the fictitious staff on the payroll to appropriate the salaries, while dismissing their real staff.

The Third World governments' reaction to their highly vulnerable position only made matters worse. Zambia's President Kaunda, seeing his country's export earnings slashed in half upon the collapse of copper, its main export, decided to "carry on as before, namely to keep importing and hope for the best."

The borrowers' luck got worse. The major banks, questioning the credit-worthiness of their clients, began to bail out, raising interest rates on new loans, avoiding the jumbo syndicated loans, and shortening the length of their loans.

Needing new loans to pay back older debts, Third World nations took the shorter-term, much more expensive loans, but found the foreign exchange relief short-lived: these loans were expensive and had to be paid back in very short order, with interest. Latin American debt, especially, began to snowball. Short-term debt as a proportion of all external debts almost tripled, rising from 15 per cent in 1973, when the OPEC oil crisis occurred, to 43 per cent in 1981.

Zaire's debt servicing payments shot up from 10 per cent of the national budget in 1982 to 44 per cent in 1985. By the last year of the Marcos reign in the Philippines, the country's interest payments had climbed to almost half of the government's annual budget, making it the single largest budget component, larger than education and defense combined.

Government deficits accumulated into national debts so large that they sometimes exceeded the value of all the things the country could produce in a year. The more a government borrowed, and the more its interest payments climbed, the more it needed to borrow to keep the country functioning and its creditors at bay.

Third World countries borrowed from their own citizens

too. Mexico nationalized the banking system a few weeks after its August 1982 bankruptcy announcement, then installed its own hand-picked bank executives who raided the bank reserves to finance the public sector deficit, leaving virtually no bank credit available to the private sector. Prospective homebuyers couldn't even secure modest mortgages.

To pay back their citizens, many governments simply printed money, effectively repudiating their domestic debt by repaying with near-worthless paper. Early in 1990 the Brazilian rate of inflation reached 19,000 per cent a year, unimaginable to most Westerners. Brazilian economist Carlos Langoni described the uncertainty that comes from living with rapidly rising prices: "Hyperinflation," he said, "is when you discover that it's a better deal to pay for lunch before the first course than after dessert."

To pay off foreigners, Third World governments can't repudiate their debts by printing money: debts must be repaid in what are called "hard currencies" – dollars, marks, yen, and francs. Pesos, cruzados, and nairas will not do.

The more anxious Third World debtors were to borrow from foreign bankers, the more anxious these bankers became about lending to the Third World. New lending began to slump. By 1981 new loans to Latin America barely covered the interest payments flowing back to the lenders. By 1983, what the Pearson Commission had predicted more than a decade earlier finally happened: the Third World was paying more to the First World than it was receiving in new loans and foreign aid. The Ponzi scheme had collapsed. But unlike Mr. Ponzi, Third World governments couldn't be thrown in jail. So they – or, more to the point, their people – had to come up with the foreign currency to pay off their creditors.

PART IV

The Third World's Tax Revolt

INTRODUCTION: PART IV

Illegitimate Debts

THE HUT IS SINKING in the mud near the bridge over the River Guaibe in Porto Alegre, Brazil. A woman social worker is welcomed by five children, the oldest about 8 years old. The parents have gone out foraging in the garbage heaps. Noticing how poorly the children look, the social worker asks them whether they have eaten recently. 'Yes, miss, yesterday Mummy made little cakes from wet newspapers.' 'What? Little cakes from what?' asks the woman. 'Mummy takes a sheet of newspaper, makes it into a ball and soaks it in water and when it is nice and soft kneads it into little cakes. We eat them, drink some water and feel nice and full inside.'

This story was told in the "Information Newsletter" of the Brazilian Evangelical Lutheran Church; millions of similar stories remain untold. From the shantytowns of Porto Alegre to Brazil's poor north-east, starvation is endemic. So bad are nutrition levels in the north-east today that IBASE, the Brazilian Institute for Social and Economic Analysis, claims the situation has produced a sub-race of people, or, in the terminology of nutritionists, that the region suffers from an epidemic of dwarfism.

The situation seems to be getting worse rather than better. In the early 1960s, an extensive household survey conducted by the Brazilian Institute of Economics and the U.S. Department of Agriculture concluded that one-third of the Brazilian population suffered from malnutrition. More than 20 years later, another survey found that two-thirds of the country's population suffered from malnutrition.

The boom days of the debt build-up – full of high-flying bankers doing deals with generals building monuments in the rainforest – had benefited Brazil's poor not a whit: development projects brought disease along with the disruption of economies and environments. The debt crisis has only added salt to their wounds: bystanders as the debts were incurred, they are now expected to do their part to pay off their nations' creditors.

Like Brazilians, other Latin Americans saw the desperate living conditions created by the borrowing binge become more desperate once the bankers pulled the plug on the spendthrift generals that called themselves governments. Often, the new and indiscriminate austerity measures spurred the decline of health conditions: while nutrition levels fell the incidence of disease rose.

By the end of the 1980s, the Third World's poor had lost so much ground that UNICEF, the United Nations Children's Fund, called it the "decade of despair." The burden of cutbacks in public expenditures was falling not only on megaprojects and military expenditures but also on the world's most vulnerable – hundreds of millions of children. "It can be estimated that at least half a million young children have died in the last twelve months as a result of the slowing down or the reversal of progress in the developing world," UNICEF estimated in its *1989 Annual Report*, laying the blame for that reversal squarely on the debt.

Calling the debt "an economic stain on the second half of the twentieth century," UNICEF condemned both those who incurred the debt and those who extended it. "It is hardly too brutal an oversimplification to say that the rich got the loans and the poor got the debts," the report says. "The fact that so much of today's staggering debt was irresponsibly lent and irresponsibly borrowed would matter less if the consequences of such folly were falling on its perpetrators.... When the impact becomes visible in rising death rates among children ... then it is essential to strip away the niceties of economic parlance and say that what has happened is simply an outrage against a large section of humanity." UNICEF laid out the facts: throughout most of Africa and much of Latin America, average incomes had fallen by 10 per cent to 25 per cent in the 1980s; the average weight-for-age of young children, a vital indicator of normal growth, had fallen in many of the countries for which figures were available; in the 37 poorest nations, spending per head on health had been reduced by 50 per cent, and on education by 25 per cent over the last few years of the 1980s; in most of the 103 developing countries from which recent information was available, the proportion of children from 6 to 11 years old enrolled in primary school was falling.

Now that the party is over and the bills are coming in, UNICEF stated, "it is the poor who are being asked to pay.... The heaviest burden of a decade of frenzied borrowing is falling not on the military or on those with foreign bank accounts or on those who conceived the years of waste, but on the poor."

SOME WESTERN COUNTRIES have a debt comparable to Brazil's: Canada's foreign debt in 1988 was about twice as large in an economy twice the size. Servicing Canada's federal government debt alone consumes over one-quarter of every tax dollar collected. Because Canada borrows just to make its interest payments, its debt grows every day, and has become the source of heated debate. Yet Canadians don't suggest repudiating their debts. They were accumulated with everyone's full knowledge, with the majority's consent, and Canadians enjoyed the use of the loans. Canadians acknowledge that Canadians must repay their debts, and to do so, Canada's federal government has dedicated the proceeds of an existing sales tax, and the proceeds of future privatizations of crown corporations. Both the tax and privatizations are controversial subjects in Canada, yet Canadians generally approve of paying down the debt from their proceeds.

Most Third World nations, poor though they are in relative terms, could easily repay their debts through taxation and privatization of their assets – a Japanese consortium led by Bishimetal Corporation Limited, a subsidiary of Japanese conglomerate Mitsubishi Metal Corporation, for example, offered to assume all of Brazil's foreign debts in exchange for the gold mining rights to the Amazon. All countries have minerals, agricultural lands, state corporations, and other assets whose title – if the public were willing – could be transferred to foreigners. Through taxation of the Third World's rich and middle class, and through a wholesale asset sale, the entire Third World debt could likely be liquidated in a matter of years.

But no one in the Third World talks of this option because, unlike Canadians, the Third World's public does not recognize the legitimacy of its debt. It revolts at the notion of being taxed to repay it, and for good reason: generally, the debts were not accumulated with public knowledge and consent, and the public did not enjoy the use of the funds. Such debts are odious to one and all alike. Odious debts, moreover, have special status in law.

17

The Doctrine of Odious Debts

IN THE LATE 1800s, with the Spanish empire on the wane and American influence in its ascendancy, the Cuban people – then under Spanish rule – yearned for self-government. But democratic reforms, though promised, never came. Then Cuba's sugar exporting economy foundered: competition from sugar beet producers in Europe and elsewhere, combined with U.S. protectionism, devastated sugar markets, driving down the world price of sugar from eight to two cents a pound. As deprivation and hardship grew, Cubans took to guerrilla warfare, burning loyalists' plantations by night and hiding in the hills by day. The exasperated Spanish, to restore order, incarcerated suspects in concentration camps.

Sympathizing with the Cubans, Americans armed the guerrillas and talked of intervention. Then on February 15, 1898, an explosion – believed to have been caused by the Spanish – sank the American battleship *Maine* in Havana harbor, taking with it 260 lives. War followed, and the Spanish were soon routed.

In the subsequent peace negotiations, the Spanish argued that the U.S. – which now held Cuba's sovereignty – should assume Cuba's debts. The Spanish asserted a principle of international law: that state obligations belong to a land and its people, not to a regime:

> *It would be contrary to the most elementary notions of justice and inconsistent with the dictates of the universal conscience of mankind for a sovereign to lose all his rights over a territory and the inhabitants thereof, and despite this to continue bound by the obligations he had contracted exclusively for their regime and government.*
>
> *These maxims seem to be observed by all cultured nations that are unwilling to trample upon the eternal principles of justice, including those in which such cessions were made by force of arms and as a reward for victories through treaties relating to territorial cessions. Rare is the treaty in which, together with the territory ceded to the new sovereign, there is not conveyed a proportional part of the general obligations of the ceding state, which in the majority of cases have been in the form of a public debt.*

To bolster their argument, the Spanish cited historical precedents.

The Americans replied that the cases cited by Spain were inapplicable, legally and morally, to the so-called "Cuban debt," the burden of which, "imposed upon the people of Cuba without their consent and by force of arms, was one of the principal wrongs for the termination of which the struggles for Cuban independence were undertaken." Furthermore, the Americans added, much of the borrowing was designed to crush attempts by the Cuban population to revolt against Spanish domination, and so was expended in a manner contrary to Cuba's interest. "They are debts created by the Government of Spain, for its own purposes and through its own agents, in whose creation Cuba had no voice." As such, the Americans argued, these debts could not be considered local (Cuban) debts, nor could they be binding on a successor state.

As for the lenders, the Americans replied that "the creditors, from the beginning, took the chances of the investment. The very pledge of the national credit, while it demonstrates on the one hand the national character of the debt, on the other hand proclaims the notorious risk that attended the debt in its origin, and has attended it ever since."

In the end, the United States never acknowledged any liability for the Cuban debt, nor were any Spanish debts assumed by Cuba or by the United States, nor did the holders of the so-called Cuban debt collect fully on their claims.

The dispute over the "Cuban debts" became one of the most contentious cases of debt repudiation – repudiation caused not because the debts imposed an excessive burden on the successor, but because they were contracted for illegitimate purposes by illegitimate parties. Such debts became known in law as "odious debts."

The legal doctrine of odious debts was given shape by Alexander Nahum Sack a quarter of a century after the settlement of the Spanish-American War. Sack, a former minister of Tsarist Russia and, after the Russian Revolution, a professor of law in Paris, authored two major works on the obligations of successor systems: *The Effects of State Transformations on Their Public Debts and Other Financial Obligations* and *The Succession of the Public Debts of the State*. With colonial territories becoming independent nation states and colonies changing hands, with monarchies being replaced by republics and military rule by civilian, with constantly changing borders throughout Europe, and with the ascendant new ideologies of socialism, communism and fascism overthrowing old orders,

Sack's debt theories dealt with the practical problems created by such transformations of state. Like many others, Sack believed that liability for public debts should remain intact, for these debts represent obligations of the state – the state being the territory, rather than a specific governmental structure. This he based not on some strict dictate of natural justice, but on the exigencies of international commerce. Without strong rules, he believed, chaos would reign in relations between nations, and international trade and finance would break down.

But Sack believed that debts not created in the interests of the state should not be bound to this general rule. Some debts, he said, were *"dettes odieuses."*

If a despotic power incurs a debt not for the needs or in the interest of the State, but to strengthen its despotic regime, to repress the population that fights against it, etc., this debt is odious for the population of all the State.

This debt is not an obligation for the nation; it is a regime's debt, a personal *debt of the power that has incurred it, consequently it falls with the fall of this power.*

The reason these "odious" debts cannot be considered to encumber the territory of the State, is that such debts do not fulfill one of the conditions that determine the legality *of the debts of the State, that is:* the debts of the State must be incurred and the funds from it employed for the needs and in the interests of the State.

"Odious" debts, incurred and used for ends which, to the knowledge of the creditors, *are contrary to the interests of the nation, do not compromise the latter – in the case that the nation succeeds in getting rid of the government which incurs them – except to the extent that real advantages were obtained from these debts. The creditors have committed a hostile act with regard to the people; they can't therefore expect that a nation freed from a despotic power assume the "odious" debts, which are personal debts of that power.*

Even when a despotic power is replaced by another,

*no less despotic or any more responsive to the will of the
people, the "odious" debts of the eliminated power are
not any less their personal debts and are not obligations
for the new power....*

*One could also include in this category of debts the
loans incurred by members of the government or by
persons or groups associated with the government to
serve interests manifestly personal – interests that are
unrelated to the interests of the State.*

For creditors to expect any protection in their loans to
foreign states, their loans must be utilized for the needs and
interests of the state, otherwise the loans belonged to the power
which contracted them, and were therefore, *"dettes de régime."*

Sack was no stranger to odious debts. He had watched as the
Tsarist debts were first honored by the Provisional Government
and then promptly repudiated once the Bolsheviks were in
power. In 1918, the new Soviet government decreed: "All
foreign loans are hereby annulled without reserve or exception
of any kind whatsoever." When creditor countries protested, the
Soviets maintained that "governments and systems that spring
from revolution are not bound to respect the obligations of fallen
governments." According to the Institute of Soviet Law, the
debts were personal debts of the Tsarist government and therefore could not be transferred to the new Soviet government.

The Bolshevik debt repudiation challenged international
law, which rarely countenanced the repudiation of state debts,
and then only when sovereignty changed hands. But here, in
Russia, was a change in government so dramatic that the
distinction between a change in government and a change in
sovereignty was meaningless.

Although the doctrine of odious debts had become recognized in international law, it was open to abuse by self-serving
interpretation. To avoid arbitrarily repudiated debts, Sack proposed that a new government be required to prove that the debt
ill-served the public interest and that the creditors were aware of
this. Following these proofs, the onus would be upon the
creditors to show that the funds were utilized for the benefit of

the territory. If the creditors could not do so, before an international tribunal, the debt would be unenforceable.

For a while, during the 19th century especially, international tribunals held that states were not bound by *ultra vires* contracts (contracts made by someone without proper authority) with foreigners. So, when the Venezuelan President Páez had his New York consul improperly enter into contracts that fell within the legislature's authority, the contracts were later declared *ultra vires* and claims under the contracts were rejected.

Perhaps the best known case absolving states of responsibility for debts involved the governments of Costa Rica and Great Britain. In that case, President Tinoco, a Costa Rican dictator, had made a sweetheart deal with a British oil company, granting it a concession through a contract authorized by him and approved by the Chamber of Deputies, a Costa Rican House of Congress. But under the Costa Rican constitution, a contract involving a tax provision, as that one did, required the approval of both Houses of Congress. After the Tinoco government fell, the new government repudiated the contract on the grounds that those who had entered into it acted *ultra vires*.

The new Costa Rican government also challenged odious debts entered into between the Tinoco government and the Royal Bank of Canada. The law Costa Rica passed to renounce both of these dealings, the Costa Rican Law of Nullities, was challenged in *Great Britain vs Costa Rica*, heard before Chief Justice Taft of the U.S. Supreme Court, sitting as an arbitrator. But the challenge failed, and the law was upheld in Justice Taft's 1923 ruling that decided:

The transactions in question, which in themselves did not constitute transactions of an ordinary nature and which were "full of irregularities," were made at a time when the popularity of the Tinoco Government had disappeared, and when the political and military movement aiming at the overthrow of that Government was gaining strength. The payments made by the bank were either in favor of Frederico Tinoco himself "for expenses of representation of the Chief of the State in his approaching trip abroad," or to his brother as salary and expenses in respect of a diplomatic post to which the latter was appointed by Tinoco. "The case of the Royal Bank depends not on the mere form of the transaction but upon the good faith of the bank in the payment of money for the real use of the Costa Rican Government under the Tinoco régime. It must make out its case of actual furnishing of money to the government for its legitimate use. It has not done so. The bank knew that this money was to be used by the retiring president, F. Tinoco, for his personal support after he had taken refuge in a foreign country. It could not hold his own government for the money paid to him for this purpose." The position was essentially the same in respect to the payments made to Tinoco's brother. The Royal Bank of Canada cannot be deemed to have proved that the payments were made for legitimate governmental use. Its claim must fail. [The matter quoted within the above passage refers to evidence presented by the parties.]

Because of the international significance of *Great Britain vs Costa Rica*, Chief Justice Taft accepted no payment for adjudicating the case:

So far as the payment of the expenses of the arbitration is concerned, I know of none for me to fix. Personally, it gives me pleasure to contribute my service in the consideration, discussion and decision of the questions presented. I am glad to have the opportunity of manifesting my intense interest in the promotion of the judicial settlement of international disputes, and accept as full reward for any service I may have rendered, the honor of being chosen to decide these important issues between the high contracting parties.

In the twentieth century, legal thinking swung away from these principles and toward pragmatism. Coincident with the rise of Keynesian economics, concern grew for the hardship of lenders, and for the difficulty of fostering international trade and investment without lenders feeling secure. States were increasingly made responsible for those who acted with apparent, not real, authority. This bias toward international financial intercourse persists to this day. To this same end, international legal thinking also favors recognizing *de facto* governments, and supports their power to bind their people even in the absence of a social contract with them.

But this new legal thinking could be short-lived: more traditional principles, still firmly rooted in law and precedent, needing only to be tested anew to determine their worth and relevance, could reemerge.

For this reason, lawyers at The First National Bank of Chicago wrote in a professional journal article in 1982: "The consequences of a change of sovereignty for loan agreements may depend in part on the use of the loan proceeds by the predecessor state. If the debt of the predecessor is deemed to be "odious," i.e. the debt proceeds are used against the interests of the local populace, then the debt may not be chargeable to the successor." Although the intended use of proceeds is usually spelled out in bank loan agreements, the lawyers went on to say, the use described is often too general to ensure that the loan benefited the people and so to guarantee loan enforcement. Moreover, the loan documents rarely restrict the money's use.

"Commercial banks should be alert to the dangers of such doctrines," the bank lawyers warned. "Because successor governments have invoked doctrines based on an 'odious' or 'hostile' use of proceeds, lenders should describe with specificity the uses of the loan proceeds and, if possible, bind the borrower by representation, warranty, and covenant to those uses." For years bankers have not exercised the vigilance that would make state debts lawful. The consequences could be breathtaking: the Chase Manhattans, Lloyds and Ex-Im banks might find that their Third World loans were uncollectable, except from the personal estates of the Marcoses and the Mobutus who contracted them.

Lenders who finance the arming or enrichment of despotic rulers and the suppression of popular insurrections – as the Spaniards discovered with their Cuban debts – have no guaran-

tees of protection from international law. Financing the colonization of the Amazon and its peoples by Brazil, or of Indonesia's
outer islands, would also be odious, according to Sack: "When
a government incurs debts to subjugate the population of a part
of its territory or to colonize it with members of the dominant
nationality, etc., these debts are odious to the indigenous population of that part of the territory of the debtor State."

Even those loans extended for purposes that are broadly
governmental – to an electric utility or for balance of payments'
support – are subject to challenge. When government officials
treat state investments as vehicles for political favors, graft, and
capital flight, and are prepared to turn a blind eye to the technical
and economic viability of such projects, foreign bank loans
become grease in wheels that turn against state interests. Foreign
bankers who fail to recognize or to act upon pricing irregularities, slipshod plans, and suspect contracts soon become parties
to hostile acts against a populace.

18

Mercantile Law Versus The People

GOD WORKS IN STRANGE WAYS in Indonesia. He annuls property rights on whim, seizes the lands of indigenous peoples to place them at the disposal of modern conglomerates, and disbands traditional economies.

In Indonesia, God is a mercantilist, or so the central government believes. In 1967 it decided that "gifts from God," such as minerals, belonged to the state. Through its Basic Mining Act, all natural deposits found in Indonesia's mining areas thus became a national asset, to be controlled and utilized by the state to maximize the people's welfare. With a government permit, local people could still mine their land – which was sometimes privately held, sometimes communally held – unless the state required the lands to be carved into concessions for large-scale exploitation.

Indonesia also passed the Agrarian Basic Act and the Forestry Basic Act, again to turn local assets into national ones, again for the presumed benefit of the people, again regulated nationally. But the benefits have been distributed unevenly, according to the governor of one of Indonesia's remote islands.

"I am confused," Governor H.M. Said of South Kalimantan told WALHI, a prominent Indonesian environmental group in 1987, two decades after the passing of the Forestry Basic Act. "I have to round up illegal loggers throughout Kalimantan. But I realize that many of them are local businessmen who have been producing lumber for the last 40 years. When the new regulation for forest exploitation required that all permits for timber exploitation be submitted to the Ministry of Forestry in the capital, they had no access to the bureaucrats in Jakarta. That is why they couldn't get concession rights. Now they are considered illegal loggers. It's very difficult for me to implement this order. They are my people, I have to protect them. The concessionaires are from Jakarta. So I am in a dilemma."

Governor Said's dilemma is shared by millions of his compatriots who have been deprived of their livelihoods through arbitrary government regulation. A parliamentarian who visited Central Kalimantan in 1990 found almost 2,000 Dayak craftspeople starving following a federal ban on the export of raw rattan, including webbing, which the government deems to be only half processed. The Dayaks – who before the ban exported their rattan products directly to Japan and other countries – now must sell their wares, literally for starvation wages, through the Indonesian Association of Furniture Producers.

According to WALHI:

The rattan ban is just one aspect of sacrificing grassroots people in attempt to raise national income by shifting exports from raw materials to finished products. The trend began in 1980, with a plan to gradually ban raw log exports and to build a plywood industry in Indonesia. First the log export tax was raised so that the trade was no longer profitable for small concessions. Then concessions were legally required to establish a wood processing factory to make plywood, veneer, or sawnwood. Small companies which were unable to build their own factories because of limited capital or expertise were urged to merge with bigger concessions or with several smaller concessions to establish a processing plant.

The latest policy bans sawnwood exports. In an attempt to stimulate the production and export of finished sawnwood products such as furniture and molding, the export tax for unfinished sawnwood has risen from $150 to $750-$1200 per cubic meter. Small-scale sawmills, unable to afford the export tax, will be forced to set up processing industries. Most, however, do not have the necessary capital, political support, skilled labor pool, and expertise to create a furniture industry that will be competitive in the international market, and are therefore forced to join conglomerates.

The Dayaks of North Kalimantan began their lumber trade with Chinese and Egyptian merchants 1,000 years ago. This trade, and the Dayaks' low-impact *kuda-kuda* method of sustainable logging, are ending with the advent of the conglomerates, some 50 business groups that now control logging over one-third of the Indonesian land mass through their ability to convince the central government of the wisdom of one policy over another, or of the need for this regulation over that.

To accomplish such sweeping redistribution of logging rights in the fifth most populous country on earth required more than the favor of the ruling politicians; this feat required nothing less than the destruction of property rights, which had been upheld through Indonesia's traditional *adat* laws until the 1960s.

Usurping the *adat* laws, which remain today mainly as an appendage, was new mercantilist legislation that imposed national policies over community or individual values. Property rights provide the best protection for indigenous people – or any people – to maintain their resource base, their economy, and their culture. For this reason, whenever newcomers have wanted to change the status quo, be it in Indonesia's remote islands in the 1960s or in the USSR in 1917, in North America in the 17th and 18th century or in Latin America in the 16th century, indigenous property rights must be denied to impose a new order.

What WALHI describes in Asia for a rural setting, Hernando de Soto details for urban life in Latin America, where the legal system denies the poor or ill-connected access to the economy.

To demonstrate the hurdles involved in establishing a typical small business – a simple garment factory – de Soto's researchers rented the premises of an existing factory on the outskirts of Lima, Peru, installed sewing machines and other equipment, and recruited four university students to comply with the Peruvian bureaucracy. Although an administrative lawyer guided them, the students handled all the necessary red tape themselves, going from government office to government office, filling out form after form, as would a person of humble origin.

To comply with the law took 289 days and 11 permits. Ten bribes were solicited by bureaucrats, eight were avoided and two paid to prevent the experiment from failing. The cost of the entire procedure amounted to $1,231, or 32 times the minimum monthly living wage.

In a different study, de Soto discovered that 83 months were required to deal with the red tape involved in acquiring an urban lot and obtaining permission to build a house. And in yet another, that 14½ years are required to establish an outdoor market – little wonder that people in Latin America operate illegally as street vendors, and build informal housing for themselves. Being "illegals," with no security should some "legal" want their land or their business, little wonder they will not invest in their properties.

Mercantilism, whether in left- or right-wing regimes, whether in in democracies or dictatorships, seeks to "regulate every issue, every transaction, every property," says de Soto, and only impoverishes the nation by excluding the average person from the economy.

The powers which tradition and the legal system vest in our rulers, even if they are democratically elected, give them absolute authority over economic and social activities and make it illusory to think that there might be some property right or transaction which cannot be arbitrarily harmed by the state. The state has virtually all the legal instruments it needs to interfere in the institutions which are supposed to lend stability to business activities: it runs an administrative apparatus which expropriates or freezes private resources, has unrestricted rights over any property which has not been assigned to private individuals, and has central control of import and export tariffs and licenses, currency exchange, and prices, and most savings and credit. It also controls virtually all the imaginable – and apparently harmless – means of discriminating and redistributing the country's resources according to arbitrary political criteria. All these powers are generally hidden behind the magic words "planning," "promotion," "regulation," and "participation." For all practical purposes, most of the people do not have rights that can be effectively defended against the state.

Access to the economy, in which the state routinely and arbitrarily intervenes, is soon restricted to those skilled in politicking and red tape. This grassroot view from WALHI and de Soto – that unchecked state intervention favors special interests at the expense of the general interests of society and the economy – has percolated up to the United Nations, which now rejects central planning and "the 'platonic' theory ... that government would be an essentially benevolent guardian of the public welfare, acting in a disinterested manner." In its *Human Development Report 1991*, the United Nations acknowledges: "Citizens use political influence to get access to government services.

Politicians ensure that government resources are directed toward their supporters. And public officials exploit their official positions for personal reward."

Dictatorships, even benign ones, don't work, but yet neither do democracies when a vast voting commons results in a tyranny of the majority, a process that ultimately discriminates against the poor, as the U.N. illustrates through a simple example:

If everyone in a democracy voted exclusively in their self-interest, the poorest 49 per cent of voters would always lose out. The top 49 per cent need only bribe the middle 2 per cent to gain a majority. No group is ever so calculating, but there nevertheless is some evidence of a tendency for democracies to redistribute benefits to the middle-income groups rather than the poor.

The answer lies in entrenching minority rights within democracies, to ensure that the middle and upper classes cannot appropriate the poor's resources, or deny them full access to the economy.

The state's prime role, says the U.N., should be "to provide an enabling framework rather than try to do development itself, through public sector enterprises or the direct provision of social services." While the state still needs to assure a social safety net, most decisions should be left "to the 'invisible hand' of the market place. The reason is that when political pressure groups intervene, they are liable to be an 'invisible foot' trampling on the finely wrought work of the other limb."

The pressure groups' interventions have been quantified in Peru. Of the country's half-million laws only 1 per cent emanated from the body created to make them: the Parliament. The rest came from the executive branch of government without debate or criticism, and often without the knowledge of those affected by them.

People want deregulation, the U.N. is saying, leaving the state to administer justice rather than resources; and they want a decentralized system that transfers much lawmaking and decision-making to the local level, where governments can be better watched, and where feedback between the governed and the government isn't hampered by distance and diluted by national constituencies.

Most existing laws and regulations – being self-serving, remote, and impediments to feedback – could simply be abolished. Without foreign exchange controls, for example, most private enrichment at public expense would cease while the day-to-day fluctuations in exchange rates would provide governments, corporations, and individuals with feedback to better conduct their affairs. Without tampered prices, sometimes to inflate the cost of products, sometimes to subsidize them, prices would rise and fall with demand and supply, continually informing people of purchases to make or to postpone, businesses to start up or to close down, services to sell or to seek. Without the World Bank and other international institutions in the business of converting dynamic economies into mercantile bureaucracies, most of the environmental and economic damage slated by these behemoths to occur would vanish.

Paralleling these calls for a shrunken, more responsible state are calls for environmental accountability. Environmentally damaging development projects usually cannot proceed without government financing or guarantees for foreign loans, and other subsidies which give them a façade of economic viability. These subsidies, being hidden from the people who pay for them, allow these projects to proceed at everyone's expense but the proponent's.

To empower those affected, 300 citizens groups in Asia have drafted a *Charter on Environmental Rights and Obligations of Individuals, Groups and Organisations* – a modern-day environmental version of the Bill of Rights. Their charter spells out broad rights and obligations of man and the state based on secure property rights, access to information, due process in law, and user fees to attack the environmental commons. "While information, education, and regulations are important, appropriate market signals are necessary to bring about structural adjustment all across. Governments should change their tax, excise and levy systems to secure the 'polluter pays principle,'" they said, and cease state subsidies to industry, agriculture, forestry, mining, and transport that have promoted the wasteful use of natural resources.

Good laws improve accountability by eliminating unmanageable commons and impediments to feedback. Laws that govern public finance, the Third World's public is saying, should do likewise.

19

The Virtues of Taxation

IN THE SPRING OF 1989, astrophysicist Fang Lizhi, China's most prominent dissident, asked the world's leaders to withdraw foreign capital from China, starting with a suspension of World Bank loans and credits. "We must make our government realize that it is economically dependent on its citizens," he said. Less than two months later, Fang sought asylum in the U.S. embassy after being accused of fueling the student democracy movement that ended in the bloody massacre at Tiananmen Square.

Many view taxation as little more than a means of redistributing income or, more cynically, as a means of supporting government in the style to which it is accustomed. The indiscriminate nature of taxation – politicians draw taxes from the national economy as if from a public commons, without a clear connection between the tax and the service it provides – robs taxation of legitimacy in many taxpayers' minds. When politicians enlarge the commons beyond the national economy by borrowing to further boost tax revenues, the cynicism grows. Unlike borrowing, however, taxation – because it is quickly felt by the public – limits politicians and constituents in raiding the public commons. Taxation forces a confrontation, or an accommodation, between the taxer and the taxed, making the act of taxation an important accountability mechanism.

Fang recognizes the discipline imposed by taxation to be far more profound in an undemocratic setting such as China's. By going outside the country for its money, the Chinese government could avoid accountability and divorce itself from its citizenry.

In Guyana, former Prime Minister Cheddi Jagan concurs. He blames Guyana's woes – among them annual debt payments totaling 73 per cent of the government's total revenues – on lavish foreign financing that allowed the government to be unencumbered by the rules of democracy. "Ironically it is money – more and more borrowed money – which is at the root of our problem," he explains, since these funds fuel an "administrative dictatorship" that perpetuates a system of racial and political discrimination, nepotism, extravagance, and corruption.

From Guatemala, lawyers, professors, and businessmen repeat the same refrain: seemingly endless foreign borrowing can only "relieve the government from having to use taxpayers' money for infrastructure and allow the government to continue spending without having to curtail the deficit."

Analyses such as these call for a cessation of foreign lending until governments are fiscally accountable to their people. Lending by outsiders, they say, will only free governments from their citizenry and undermine local efforts to establish good governance.

THROUGHOUT HISTORY, governments have had to exercise caution in taxing their subjects, who have tolerated it to a point; beyond that point looms revolt and revolution.

The Ptolemies in ancient Egypt devised all manner of levies upon their productive citizenry to finance their great engineering works and expensive wars. As corruption grew, the government's exactions grew, leading to industrial and agricultural decay as producers lost financial incentives, to revolts, and ultimately to the ruin of the civilization.

Two millennia later the question of taxes, and how best to extract them without invoking insurrection, remained vexatious. Sir William Petty, a 17th-century British economist, noted that people believed that their sovereign was taxing the wrong people too much for unnecessary purposes. The 18th century found Adam Smith arguing that all taxes should conform to standards of justice, certainty, convenience, and economy. Absentee landlords with more land than they needed for their subsistence, Smith explained by way of example, should be more heavily taxed than owner-occupants. At the same time, the issue of taxation without representation inflamed the American colonies, triggering the Boston Tea Party and the American War of Independence. Governments around the world have since recognized the risk in taxing a hostage public.

But exorbitantly taxing a represented public is risky as well. Government leaders know that public approval flows from expenditures, not from taxation. The difference between government spending and its tax revenues comes from borrowing money, or from printing it. But printing money has immediate repercussions: inflation, the debasement of the nation's money supply and of the public's savings. Borrowing delays the repercussions, allowing governments to shower the public with gifts while deflecting into the future the day of repayment.

Most governments try to circumvent tax revolts through deficit financing – a dangerous and dishonest invention of the 20th century which obscures the costs to the public of its government's activities. Deficit financing – which amounts to future taxation since future taxpayers will be saddled with repayment – thus gives governments and their expenditures a degree of anonymity unimaginable were governments forced to confront taxpayers for every expenditure.

The economic function of deficit financing first advocated and popularized by John Maynard Keynes – to stimulate and fine tune economies to maximize employment and output – while attractive in theory has generally proved to be uncontrollable in practice. Governments, whether democratic or not, have no built-in incentives to stop borrowing in order to satisfy those who would throw them out of office: the benefits of borrowing come quickly and can be directly attributable to the government while the costs, which are difficult to attribute to any particular cause, come much later, making them a future government's worry.

FOREIGN AID, like borrowing, also provides anonymity and removes the need for governments to be accountable to their people.

Had foreign aid been successful in developing the Third World, the anonymity it provides governments might have been justified as a necessary evil. But foreign aid has been an abject failure, particularly in those countries – such as Sub-Saharan Africa – which most received it. Africa's share of world trade is now half what it was a generation ago, before the aid money started flowing. With aid to Africa increasing more than tenfold between 1970 and 1988 – from $1 billion to $13.4 billion per year – per capita incomes have decreased and private investment has all but dried up. In the last decade, with cash infusions of $100 billion, Africa's economy has shrunk by 20 per cent. Africa's GNP compares to that of Belgium, which has a population 2 per cent and a land mass 1 per cent that of Africa.

"Aid is not the answer," concludes Nigeria's Claude Ake, a Fellow at the Brookings Institution and an advisor to the World Bank on African affairs. If aid disappeared – something he would not oppose – Africa would "have to take the idea of self-reliance more seriously ... and when you take the idea of self-reliance more seriously, you cannot ignore democracy."

Aid programs, because they assume that Western donors and Third World government officials are better problem-solvers than individuals or private organizations, are often at odds with the priorities of their recipients. Anonymous aid allows governments to finance vanity projects – such as the Ivory Coast's $100 million neoclassical basilica inspired by Rome's St. Peter's – or simply to line the pockets of leaders and influential officials.

Nepal provides a perfect picture of foreign aid run amok. That country's best-known water resource specialist, Dipak Gyawali, is highly critical of aid agency consultants and engineers who run the country's water department, implementing policies as an arm of the government without any public debate or legislative oversight. In the name of providing clean water to the capital city of Katmandu, the U.N. and the World Bank are proposing to divert the waters from the nearby Melamchi River catchment area, depriving thousands of the water they need for their irrigation systems and their *ghattas*, or water mills. To do so, the foreign aid agencies, on the advice of their Western consultants, propose to build a 27 kilometer long tunnel through an unexplored area of geologically fragile Himalayan mountains as well as an area known as the main Central Thrust – the most active of Himalayan faults. The project will cost an estimated $118 million – all to divert water to Katmandu's municipal water supply system, which has a wastage and leakage rate of about 70 per cent. "Adding a costly supply scheme to a sieve is ludicrous," says Gyawali, who objects to a foreign aid bureaucracy so pervasive that "every vegetable has a foreign aid project behind it."

Gyawali's view of foreign aid is widely shared. The *Manila Declaration on People's Participation and Sustainable Development,* signed by citizens' groups from every continent, claims that the international development institutions and their financial transfers have been damaging to the cause of democracy. Where governments and their foreign financiers do not recognize that "people must control their own resources, have access to relevant information, and have the means to hold the officials of government accountable, (development) often becomes a conspiracy between the donor or the lender and government against the people."

To enable Third World citizens to establish responsible government, state-to-state development aid – whether through foreign aid agencies, export credit agencies, or the international agencies like the World Bank – should end, and these institutions – neither reformable nor worth reforming – should be closed down. (Emergency relief, being humanitarian and short-term, should continue, as should the only foreign aid efforts exhibiting any success – those carried out by independent private groups working with like groups in the Third World.)

THIRD WORLD STATES, spending unaccountably, have failed thoroughly to enrich the lives of their citizenry or to entrench just laws that would allow the citizenry to create the wealth to enrich themselves.

States should live within their means, balancing their expenditures with their revenues. Balanced budgets are of such importance to the economy, to the environment, and to responsible government that they should be entrenched in state constitutions.

With constitutionally mandated balanced budgets, legislators and their constituents would be forced to weigh government services against higher taxes, creating a continual debate about government priorities and keeping the government in touch with its people. A government claiming to need more money would have to deal with its own taxpayers – the ultimate test of legitimacy.

CONCLUSION

Tragic Commons No More

THIRTY WOMEN CROWDED into the parlor of the tiny, concrete block home typical of the neighborhood. Chairs were scarce and babies howled but soon the commotion died down for the meeting to begin. "I pledge to strive to increase my income, to use the profits from my loan to pull my family out of poverty," the participants recited in unison. In reply, two women, rising from a bank ledger at the front of the room, pledged to help the poor improve their livelihood and to "accept nothing, not even a glass of water from the members." The language was Ilongo, the village was Bacolod in the Philippine island of Negros, and the gathering a weekly meeting of Project Dungganon, a bank for the poor. The women came to make their weekly loan repayment, to put a peso in their group fund for emergencies, to discuss how to help any member close to default, and to assess loans to new borrowers.

One of those present, Caonisa Esmayan, first came to the bank when her fisherman husband fell sick, making her the family's sole breadwinner. With a $33 loan from Project Dungganon she invested $20 in a pig and the balance in a noodle stall. While the pig was fattening, her noodle stall profits met her weekly debt servicing payments. Four months later, the pig went to market where Caonisa sold it for $40, earning enough profit to add stools and an awning to her stall and a spacious verandah to her dilapidated house. After a year, with the revenues from her noodle stall alone, Caonisa paid off her first loan and set about planning for a second loan. With a 100 per cent repayment record and a growing list of clients across Negros (over 700 women after just one year of operation), Project Dungganon symbolizes a banking revolution sweeping the Third World.

The revolution began in 1976 with Muhammad Yunus, an economics professor at the University of Chittagong in Bangladesh. Unable to convince bankers that the survival skills of the poor made them excellent credit risks, Professor Yunus took out a personal loan and started lending to them himself in an experiment that in 1983 became the Grameen Bank.

Within a decade Grameen became a fully fledged bank, primarily owned by its borrowers, who invested in shares from their accumulated savings. The Grameen Bank today has branches in more than 25 per cent of Bangladesh's 65,000 villages, a staff of 8,000, and 800,000 borrowers whose quarter of a billion dollars in loans have been paid back at a 98 per cent repayment rate. Grameen-type banks have sprung up throughout Asia, Africa, and Latin America, and Dr. Yunus now hosts central bank governors and officials from international aid agencies eager to support similar banking systems.

The Grameen Bank taps peer pressure and peer support to

ensure accountability. Would-be borrowers must form groups of five, of which only two may borrow at a time. These two must repay the loan – average size $60 – in 50 equal weekly install- ments at commercial interest rates. If one member of the group fails to keep up payments, all five are labeled bad risks and cut off from further loans. That way, says Dr. Yunus, the pressure to repay the money comes not only from the bank but also from fellow villagers, who guard against any tendency to invest frivolously, and have an incentive to help a group member in trouble.

Some accuse the Grameen Bank of standing banking prin- ciples on their head: the bank gives loans without collateral, doesn't require guarantors, prefers women clients, lends to illiterates as long as they can sign their name, and forsakes fancy offices for the dusty doorsteps of the village poor. But Dr. Yunus mocks conventional bankers and their blame-the-poor logic that denigrates poor people's skills and reliability as investors:

We are not standing on our head. We are the right way up. It is conventional banking which is upside down.... You will be told with 100 per cent certainty that the poor have to be trained before they can do anything. The poor cannot budget, they cannot save. It is useless to offer anything to poor women, they have no skills. The influence of religion and custom is so strong that they cannot move an inch in any direction.

Quite the contrary, contends Dr. Yunus: "The poor have skills or they wouldn't have been able to survive. All you have to give them is access to capital. Most of them can take it from there."

In a part of the world known for monumental investment disasters, where the international commercial banks are lucky to recover half their loans and state banks require frequent bail- outs, the Grameen's repayment record is exemplary. With its pint-size loans to investments in everything from sewing ma- chines to candy vendor carts, this Third World bank ranks among the most successful in the world. And the successes it finances – the tangible, self-selected investments that the Third

World's poor choose for themselves – have an economic reach and impact unmatched by the billion-dollar megaprojects of the international financiers.

Traditional savings and lending systems have existed in societies everywhere for as long as human beings have made investments. While many have been abusive and unfair, like the notorious money-lending practices that entrap borrowers in a debt-bondage relationship akin to slavery, many systems have been accountable, fair, and successful at bringing savers and investors together to their mutual advantage.

In Africa, such financial institutions – whose activities go unrecorded in the national economic statistics – have thrived out of the limelight of ribbon-cutting ceremonies that glamorize state vanity projects. A system of rotating funds – known as *susu* in Ghana, *sanduk* in the Sudan, and *tontines* in Somalia – generally involves neighbors, fellow workers, or relatives. Nigeria's version, *adichi*, means "system of traditional cooperation among friends" and also "bring, bring."

In *adichi*, each member alternatively acts as a saver and borrower. Salaried workers tend to make monthly deposits, rural workers deposit weekly when they go to market, and city women who work in the markets deposit daily. Members commit to depositing a fixed amount – a salaried worker might decide on 100 nairas a month for 12 months – which, along with everyone else's deposits, is then lent out to borrowers. When the salaried worker needs money, he can receive up to the 1,200 nairas he had committed to depositing.

In most rotating savings associations, members meet regularly to conduct business: to determine the amounts to be contributed by each, to collect the agreed deposits, and sometimes to decide priorities for disbursing loans. The order of rotation might be determined by seniority, election, drawing lots, negotiation, auction, or the urgency of a member's need – but in every case by common consent.

Many associations set aside some savings for a common insurance fund to cover emergencies and social services. Others operate social insurance systems. In Ethiopia's *edirs*, members make periodic contributions that entitle them to benefits in the event of death or sickness, loss of job, or arbitrary imprisonment. Still other associations operate like savings banks, participants entrusting their savings to a treasurer for a fixed period. The funds are then lent, earning interest, to members or non-members for ceremonial expenses, for food and clothing in times of distress, and for consumer durables such as cars and appliances.

Traditional lending practices also finance small businesses needing to invest in income-generating purchases such as trucks or grain-grinding mills, and they facilitate international trade by bringing together foreign exchange earners – exporters or citizens working abroad – with importers who require foreign exchange. In Somalia, much of the import-export business and foreign exchange remittances are channeled through such mechanisms.

These small-scale Third World financial systems are commons, but manageable ones. Because borrowers depend on each other, they ensure a high degree of honesty, vigilance, and caution in individual borrowings and investments. The result is a healthy financial system in which *pacta sunt servanda* – the creed of honoring all contracts so cherished by bankers – reigns. Delinquent though Third World governments may be, their citizens have proved worthy of triple-A credit ratings.

The tragedy of the commons is a tragedy of scale. Commons – in which rights are often informal and self-policed, and where price alone doesn't govern resource use – exist everywhere. Family members manage their own affairs – sharing goods, chores, and incomes – generally without benefit of market incentives, generally with a great deal of security that their interests will be respected. Within many corporations, resources will be shared: people are generally trusted to use the photocopier prudently, and to incur only necessary expenses.

But when the scale enlarges, the system must adapt or become unmanageable: peer pressure and other forms of self-policing no longer ensure accountability. The more distant the relative, the more formal family relations become. Companies

189

become bureaucracies, enforcing discipline through policies, rules, and regulations: photocopies are tracked and billed, operating divisions make their own investment and have their own budgets, and internal markets may be created to control costs.

Enlarge the scale to a national economy – magnify it many million-fold – and the management problems become overwhelming, too overwhelming to handle without decentralized decisionmaking, just laws, and just law-making procedures upholding societally held values. Attempts to manage national economies centrally by directing an ever larger share of investments through ever more regulations from ever larger bureaucracies – as occurred throughout the Third World – culminated in collapse.

Because people everywhere partake in activities large and small, public and private, their communal property and private property must both be protected. Third World entrepreneurs, needing to finance ventures too large for traditional lending associations, and distrusting their countries' unpoliced and politicized financial institutions, took their capital and left, or languished with it, or joined in looting the national commons by using it for bribes. But if assured of the integrity of their financial systems, entrepreneurs would have put their capital to more productive use, generally keeping it in the home market that they knew best. When in need of financing, they would have tapped large-scale capital markets, both at home and abroad.

Nearly a decade after the Mexican debt crisis began in 1982, the country's new-found confidence was performing miracles: Mexican entrepreneurs were bringing back their flight capital from abroad, large-scale privatizations of state-owned enterprises were underway, a North American free-trade agreement was being negotiated, and Mexico's free-wheeling stock market was among the world's strongest performers: the Bolsa index – the Mexican Dow Jones equivalent – was up 250 times over its levels in the early 1980s, and trading became so active that the stock exchange's hours were extended.

The largest stock on the Mexican exchange – the newly

privatized telephone and telecommunications company, Telmex
– was among the star performers, almost doubling in price when
the government decided to give up its majority stake. On the
strength of a business plan promising to increase the number of
telephone lines by 12 per cent over the next four years, ordinary
Mexicans, Telmex employees, and a consortium of Mexican
investors and foreign telephone companies snapped up the new
issue.

Outside the Mexican stock exchange, Telmex in 1991 listed
its shares on the New York Stock Exchange. The issue, oversubscribed by about 50 per cent with over a billion shares sold, was
the largest international equity issue ever made by a Third World
company and, next to a Fiat issue, the largest in the world.
Telmex also arranged Mexico's largest voluntary borrowing in
the international markets since the 1982 debt crisis: $570 million
in credit arranged by Citibank and backed by future receivables
from long-distance calls, not by the national treasury.

Telmex isn't alone among Third World companies to turn to
the private international capital market: companies from the
Philippines and Singapore preceded it, as had Chile's telephone
company, the first Latin American company with a U.S. offering
in 27 years. So high was confidence in Compañía de Teléfonos
de Chile (CTC) – privatized in 1987 – that its share offering,
listed on the New York Stock Exchange, was oversubscribed
fourfold. Having capitalized on foreigners, CTC is now tapping
Chile's own wealthy pension funds, aiming to triple telephone
services by 1996 to 1.6 million lines and more than 2 million
telephones.

Third World enterprises don't need sovereign guarantees to
finance their expansion plans, but they do need sound business
plans that can meet the test of scrutinizing markets: Telmex's
issue was thought to be the most intensively researched market
stock in the world. Reputable investors will flee from any hint
of corruption, but give them a company with transparent operations and a sound balance sheet in a country whose government
provides a regulatory and legal environment in which contractual obligations can be enforced and property rights respected,

and they will invest freely, without coercive government attempts to keep capital at home.

With Mexico's new and empowering economic policies, Mexicans are now investing their savings in their own economy. The country no longer needs to borrow on the foreign market because its needs can be met domestically, as Miguel Mancera Aguayo, the director-general of Mexico's Central Bank was pleased to announce in 1991. The previous year, Mexico had cut its banking debt by $15 billion, or 22 per cent, and the claims on Mexico amounted to $29 billion, about half of the amount owed in 1985.

The financial commons – the free-for-all in which rights were not respected and rules could change arbitrarily and at any time – is ending in Mexico; where it ends, prosperity begins.

THE ENVIRONMENTAL COMMONS will take more time to right itself: damaged ecologies cannot be restored with the same speed as damaged economies. But the same factors empowering people to protect their economies can work to protect their environments too.

Thailand's age-old *muang faai* water management system, beleaguered and almost destroyed by invasions of development experts who came to bring development to the millions living in the country's northern riverine communities, was threatened by more than the new concrete weirs that the Royal Irrigation Department installed. As in Indonesia and other countries, the central government appropriated the forests from the communities that had managed them sustainably, handing them to concessionaires who quickly deforested them.

Branches, logs, and other debris from the logging operations soon clogged the streams, rendering the farmers' traditional irrigation systems useless, leading to crop failure and sometimes to starvation. Deforestation also triggered tragic mudslides that buried villages and farmland under meters of logs, uprooted trees and sand, and killed hundreds.

The worst of the environmental horrors may become a thing of the past. The *muang faai* communities – seeing their neighbors' lands razed and their neighbors impoverished – organized and demanded rights to their land, becoming the vanguard of political change in Thailand. Following two decades of petitions, demonstrations, and legal actions, the central government gave in. In 1989, for the first time, it recognized a local community's right to forests on nationalized land. At the same time, it revoked concessions by banning commercial logging throughout the country. The concessionaires' claim to the commons had ended; control over the environment had come closer to those with an interest in maintaining it.

The commons may reappear in Thailand; its governments have not been stable, nor have they had a long tradition of democracy.

But democracy is on the rise throughout the Third World. Most Latin American juntas have disappeared; the totalitarian regimes in Asia are teetering; even the strong men of Africa are abandoning their one-man dictatorships. Replacing these are newly ascendant democracies, fledgling and struggling, but able to draw from indigenous traditions. Where democracy and accountability are on the rise, so will the unmanageable commons, and all of its consequences, be on the decline.

But democracy, too, can be a commons, and unmanageable if its citizens do not vigilantly protect its very underpinnings: protection for all the rights of all its members, and respect for due process of law.

FORGIVING DEBTS on humanitarian grounds, while compelling because of the plight of the Third World's poor, can only redound to everyone's sorrow. Asking Western taxpayers to relieve both lenders and borrowers – as do all the bailout plans – will only breed cynicism and feed a deadbeat stereotype of the Third World. Third World elites will learn that corruption pays, and devise new means to borrow anew. The banks, receiving bailouts, will learn that they need not act like banks, need not preoccupy themselves with the stability and legitimacy of those to whom they're lending, since taxpayers will backstop them should worst come to worst. First and Third World leaders will

193

continue to sacrifice their taxpayers' pocketbooks and their environments to pet projects or to the exigencies of staying in power.

The Third World should repudiate its debts, not through appeals to charity but by recourse to due process of law. Declaring debts odious will compel the lenders – in order to recover some of the billions they've lost – to seek redress by suing, pursuing and, where possible, seizing the booty of the unrepresentative Third World elites which borrowed so recklessly in the name of their people. In so doing the lenders will be discouraging future elites from similar behavior.

More importantly, declaring debts odious will force lax lenders to be accountable for their mistakes, and ensure that they are never again repeated.

Sources and Further Commentary

Introduction: The Tragedies of the Commons (pages 10-14)

For a wonderful description of the complex functioning of the *muang faai* system see "The *Muang Faai* Irrigation System of Northern Thailand" by Chatchawan Tongdeelert and Larry Lohmann, in *The Ecologist*, vol. 21, no. 2, U.K., March/April, 1991. Also see *Thai Peasant Social Structure* by Jack M. Potter, Berkeley, 1976. For further information on debt bondage see the excellent work of Anti-Slavery International for the Protection of Human Rights, London, a group which traces its origins to William Wilberforce and the movement to abolish slavery in the 1800s. According to the United Nations Supplementary Convention on the abolition of slavery, the slave trade, and institutions and practices similar to slavery (1965), debt bondage is defined thus: "the status or condition arising from a pledge by a debtor of his personal services or of those of a person under his control as security for a debt, if the value of those services as reasonably assessed is not applied towards the liquidation of the debt or the length and nature of those services are not respectively limited and defined."

Chapter 1: The Environmental Legacy of Yesterday's Loans
(pages 16-24)

For the details on the Balbina dam, I am indebted to the prolific and excellent work of Dr. Philip M. Fearnside, a research professor at Brazil's National Institute for Research in the Amazon. See in particular his study *Brazil's Balbina Dam: Environment Versus the Legacy of the Pharaohs in Amazonia*, published by the National Institute for Research in the Amazon (INPA), Manaus, Brazil, 1989. See also, "Amazon rainforest could be wiped out" by Kelly Toughill in *The Toronto Star*, November 5, 1989; "Brazil wants its dams, but at what cost?" by Marlise Simons in *New York Times*, March 12, 1989; articles in *World Rivers Review*, San Francisco, November/December 1987, and July/August 1989; *International Dams Newsletter*, San Francisco, September 1986; "Extracting Power from the Amazon Basin" by John A. Adam in *IEEE Spectrum*, August 1988; *International Water Power & Dam Construction*, U.K., May 1986 and September 1988; Correspondence between the Environmental Defense Fund (Washington) and the World Bank from 1986-1989 as well as EDF Testimony before various congressional committees over the same period.

The World Bank denies that it directly funded the Balbina dam – indeed the bank had earlier rejected a project loan to Balbina on environmental grounds. But the $500 million Power Sector Loan from the World Bank in 1986 – a general loan to be used to help pay for imports for power sector investments – was what the Brazilian government needed to get various stalled dam projects – including Balbina – completed. No sooner had the Power Sector Loan been approved than full-scale work on Balbina was resumed, and just over a year later the dam's floodgates were closed. Furthermore, it is clear from the secret minutes of the Board of Executive Directors meeting, at which the $500 million Power Sector Loan was considered, that the bank knew full well that many controversial projects would be financed with the Power Sector Loan. See "Summary of Discussions at the Meeting of the Executive Directors of the Bank and IDA, and the Board of Directors of IFC, June 19, 1986," from the vice president and secretary of the World Bank to various bank officials including executive directors, the president, vice presidents and department heads.

The Canadian engineering company, Monenco, was involved in the "Design of the 250 MW Balbina, Brazil, hydroelectric project, in consortium with another Brazilian firm." See Monenco *Annual Report* 1977, Montreal, Canada. My requests to Monenco for further information on their involvement in the Balbina dam have not been answered.

For further information on the plight of the 2000 families adversely affected by the toxic-laden waters discharged from the Balbina dam, see the excellent work of the Justice and Peace Office of the Scarboro Foreign Mission Society, Scarborough, Ontario, Canada.

For further details on the Tucurui hydroelectric dam see "The Problems That Plague a Brazilian Dam" by John Barham and Catherine Caufield in *The New Scientist*, London, October 11, 1984; "Hydro dam in Amazon threatens river life" by Augusta Dwyer in *The Globe and Mail*, Toronto, January 3, 1989; various articles in *International Water Power & Dam Construction*, U.K., July 1983, July, September, and November 1984, January 1985, and February 1990 (the last includes a detailed list of the environmental effects of Tucurui). Also see "Brazil's Debt and Deforestation – A Global Warning" by Sandra Steingraber and Judith Hurley, *Food First Action Alert*, Institute for Food and Development Policy, San Francisco, 1990; also see Dr. Philip Fearnside's paper on Balbina mentioned above.

Dr. Fearnside explains how projects like Tucurui operate at the expense of the taxpayer and private electricity ratepayer: "Power tariffs in Brazil are, on average, much lower than the cost of energy production. This discourages energy conservation and provides substantial subsidies to energy-intensive industries such as aluminum smelting. Aluminum production in the Grande Carajás Program area is particularly favored, since Eletronorte has agreed to supply power to the plants at a rate tied to the international price of aluminum, rather than to the cost of producing the energy: for the Alunorte/Albrás plant in Barcarena, Pará (owned by a consortium of 33 Japanese firms together with Brazil's Companhia Vale do Rio Doce), only US 10 mils/kwh is charged, while the power, which is transmitted from Tucurui, is estimated to cost US 60 mils/kwh to generate (Walderlino Teixeira de Carvalho, public statement, 1988). The rate charged the aluminum firms is roughly one-third the rate paid by residential consumers throughout the country, and so is heavily subsidized by the Brazilian populace both through their taxes and their home power bills." From *Brazil's Balbina Dam: Environment Versus the Legacy of the Pharaohs in Amazonia*, page 33.

For information on Singrauli see "Indian Coal Development Creates Hellish Conditions," *Probe Alert* by Probe International, Toronto, May 1990, and the correspondence between the Environmental Defense Fund (Washington D.C.) and the World Bank and EDF's congressional testimony on this subject from 1987 on.

For references on the percentage of debt attributed to energy sector investments see the article by John Adam in *IEEE Spectrum* (as above); *The Foreign Debt and the Energy Sector of Latin America and the Caribbean*, by the Latin American Energy Organization (OLADE), Quito, Ecuador, 1987. Reiner Lock, a legal advisor to the U.S. Federal Energy Regulatory Committee (1985-89), told the U.S. Congressional House Committee on Energy and Commerce in 1989-90 that in most developing countries, "state investments in electric power have contributed to somewhere between 25% and 40% of

their national debt buildups since World War II."
For further details on the Awash River valley development scheme see "Ethiopia: Famine, Food Production, and Changes in the Legal Order" by Peter Koehn, in *African Studies Review*, vol. 22, no. 1, April 1979.

For further reference to Cubatao, Brazil, see "Industrialization of Brazilian village brings jobs at cost of heavy pollution and even death" by Lynda Schuster in *The Wall Street Journal*, April 15, 1985. By 1990, Cubatao, with the help of a half-billion-dollar cleanup, was on the road to recovery. An article in *The Globe and Mail* reported that, according to Sergio Alejandro, regional manager of Cetesb, the Sao Paulo state pollution control agency, "Cubatao is like a sick person who's been moved out of the intensive care unit, but who will have to take certain precautions for the rest of his life." See "Off ecologists' critical list" by Paul Knox in *The Globe and Mail*, Toronto, November 6, 1990. According to the article, of 320 major sources of air, water and soil pollution identified by Cetesb, 286 are now being treated, and the 557 tonnes of dust and noxious gases that used to be released into the air every day, have been cut by 70%. "Clandestine dumps have been found to contain 150,000 tonnes of soil contaminated with organic chlorides, enough to keep the high-temperature incinerator at a Cubatao chemical plant burning almost constantly for the next 10 years," *The Globe and Mail* reported. The worst polluter is a state-owned steel mill.

For details on the environmental consequences of oil development in Mexico, and the report released by the Center for Ecological Development, see "The Cost of Mexico's Filthy Riches" by Mike Rose in *South*, U.K., June 1987. On Mexico City's environmental problems see "Pollution killing thousands in Mexico City" by Linda Hossie, in *The Globe and Mail*, Toronto, November 23, 1988.

Chapter 2: The Environment Strikes Back (pages 25-34)

For details on the various attempts to conquer the Amazon see *The Fate of the Forest: Developers, Destroyers and Defenders of the Amazon* by Susanna Hecht and Alexander Cockburn, Verso, London, 1989 and *Jacques Cousteau's Amazon Journey* by Jacques-Yves Cousteau and Mose Richards, Harry N. Abrahams, Inc. Publishers, New York, 1984. The quotation by the European owners of the Madeira-Mamoré Railway was made by The [British] Public Works Company in 1873, to the British financial assessors, who subsequently issued a harsh post-mortem on the project. More details, including the quotation, can be found in Susanna Hecht and Alexander Cockburn's book, pages 55 and 65.

For details on the Grande Carajás project see Susanna Hecht and Alexander Cockburn (as above); *Bound in Misery and Iron* by Survival International, London 1987; *The Greater Carajás Programme: An Update*, Survival International Information Pack, London, February 1989; "The 'Greening' of the Development Banks: Rhetoric and Reality" by Bruce Rich in *The Ecologist*, vol. 19, no. 2, U.K., 1989; "The Charcoal of Carajás: A Threat to the Forest of Brazil's Eastern Amazon Region" in AMBIO, Sweden, vol. 18, no. 2, 1989; "Grande Carajás, International Financing Agencies, and Biological Diversity in Southeastern Brazilian Amazonia" by David C. Oren, and "Deforestation and International Economic Development Projects in Brazilian Amazonia" by Philip M. Fearnside in *Conservation Biology*, vol. 1, no. 3, October 1987; "The Militarization and Industrialization of Amazonia: the Calha Norte and Grande Carajás Programmes" by David Treece in *The Ecologist*, vol. 19, no. 6, U.K., November/December 1989; "Amazon Rainforest Project Hurtles Towards Disaster" by Catherine Caufield in *The New Scientist*, London, February 26, 1987.

Information on subsidies that have led to rainforest destruction can be found in "A Prescription for Slowing Deforestation in Amazonia" by Philip M. Fearnside in *Environment*, vol. 31, no. 4, U.S., May 1989; "How Brazil Subsidises the Destruction of the Amazon" in *The Economist*, U.K., March 18, 1989; "The Month Amazonia Burns" in *The Economist*, U.K., September 9, 1989; "Plundering the Amazon: Notes on the Greater Carajás Program" by Atila P. Roque in *AMPO Japan-Asia Quarterly Review*, vol. 20, no. 4 and vol. 21, no. 1, 1989; "Time to tackle the threat" by Tom Wicker from *The Globe and Mail*, Toronto, November 29, 1988; *Brazilian Policies That Encourage Deforestation in the Amazon* by Hans P. Binswanger, The World Bank Environment Department Working Paper no. 16, April 1989.

For information on the Polonoroeste Project in Brazil see letters from the Environmental Defense Fund (Washington) and copies of EDF staff lawyers' testimony to the U.S. Congress. Also see the following articles: "Debacle in the Amazon" by Pat Aufderheide and Bruce Rich in *Defenders*, U.S., March-April 1985; "World Bank urged to halt aid to Brazil for Amazon development" by Erik Eckholm, *The New York Times*, October 17, 1984; "Payments stopped on loan to Brazil" by Clyde H. Farnsworth in *The New York Times*, April 9, 1985.

Much has been written about Indonesia's Transmigration Program, especially by Survival International (U.K.), the Environmental Defense Fund (Washington), and *The Ecologist* (U.K.). See in particular, "Transmigration in Irian Jaya: Issues, Targets and Alternative Approaches" by George J. Aditjondro in *Adverse Environmental and Socio-cultural Impacts of World Bank Financed Transmigration Under Replita IV*, April 28-29, 1986; "Indonesia's population relocation: the high costs of failure" by Charles P. Wallace in *Los Angeles Times*, January 6, 1990; *Transmigrasi: Myths and Realities, Indonesian Resettlement Policy, 1965-1985* by Mariël Otten, International Work Group for Indigenous Affairs Document no. 57, Copenhagen, October 1986.

For information on the demise of big dams see the three volumes in *The Social and Environmental Effects of Large Dams* by Edward Goldsmith and Nicholas Hildyard, published by the Wadebridge Ecological Centre, U.K., 1984. The details on hydro dams throughout this book are filed in Probe International's *Hydro File*, a collection of data and articles on approximately

800 hydrodams around the world. For information on the Chixoy project in Guatemala see various issues of *International Water Power and Dam Construction*, U.K., in particular June 1986 and July 1986; *Central American Report* June 3, 1983, January 20, 1984, May 11, 1984, and December 6, 1985. According to the last, after critics publicly charged the National Institute of Electrification with government impropriety and warned that Chixoy's tunnel was doomed to collapse again, General Oscar Sandoval, superintendent of INDE, said that "those who criticize the repairs of Chixoy on the basis of speculation are bad Guatemalans." Also see "Guatemala: A development dream turns into repayment nightmare" by Christopher L. Bryson in *The Christian Science Monitor*, U.S., Friday, May 1, 1987; *Efectos Sobre el Ambiente de Proyectos Financiados Por Bancos Multilaterales de Desarrollo en Guatemala* by Amb. Tulio Monterroso Bonilla and Dr. Oscar R. Murga Solares para Asociacion "Amigos del Bosque," Guatemala, December 1989.

For information on the other dams mentioned see "Prospects for Large and Small Hydro Development in Peru" by P. Wicke in *International Water Power & Dam Construction*, U.K., July 1987; "Debt crisis is inflicting a heavy human toll in Dominican Republic" by Charles F. McCoy in *The Wall Street Journal*, April 20, 1987; "IDB Grants $772,000 for Conservation Study in the Dominican Republic," *Inter-American Development Bank Press Release*, November 15, 1989; "Was Ghana's Akosombo Dam the Best Option?" in *World Water*, U.K., September 1989; "Electricity rationed" in *The Globe and Mail*, Toronto, December 17, 1983. The Balbina dam in Brazil is plagued by more than just an unusually small watershed: according to Philip Fearnside, "Aquatic vegetation, together with the large surface area per volume of water in a shallow reservoir will lead to heavy losses of stored water to evaporation and transpiration." In addition, Dr. Fearnside points out that the residence time of water in Balbina's reservoir will be so long (as long as several years, compared to 1.8 months for Tucurui) that the decomposing vegetation at the bottom of the reservoir will produce acids that will cause corrosion of the turbines. (See *Brazil's Balbina Dam: Environment Versus the Legacy of the Pharaohs in Amazonia*, INPA, Manaus, Brazil, 1989.) For details on India's irrigation record see "The case against big dams" by B.B. Vohra in *Daily Indian Express*, Bombay, March 20, 1989.

For details of the Green Revolution in Asia see "Green Counter-Revolution: Getting Rid of Pesticides" by Ian Steele in *Development Forum*, New York, September-October 1990.

Chapter 3: The Environment Strikes Back: The Economy (Pages 35-40)

For information on the study by the New York Botanical Garden, the Missouri Botanical Garden, and the Yale School of Forestry, see "Valuation of an Amazonian Rainforest" by Charles M. Peters, Alwyn H. Gentry and Robert O. Mendelsohn in *Nature*, vol. 339, June 29, 1989; "Rain forest worth more if uncut, study says" from *The New York Times*, July 4, 1989; "The Real Value of Rainforests," *The TRF Times*, Friends of the Earth, London, U.K. This study counted the value of merchantable fruits and latex, leaving out other "minor" forest products such as oils, fibre, medicinal plants, lianas and small palms because they were too difficult to count. When the value of trees cut for timber on a periodic, selective and sustainable basis – something that is rarely accomplished – was included, the value of the standing rainforest rose to $6,820.

Other studies demonstrate the same economic value from the standing rainforest. The average family on the island of Combu – in a tributary of the Amazon in Brazil's Para state – can earn U.S. $3,300 a month (twice the Brazilian average) by selling rubber, cocoa and acai, the protein-rich fruit of palm trees. And all that in three days or less a week. Research by a University of Pennsylvania biologist found that 6.25 square meters of jungle cleared for cattle grazing will produce a 125 gram hamburger with 0.01% protein. The same area could also support a Brazil nut tree which produces 30 kilos of nuts with 21% protein. For further details see "Amazon Rainforest Riches" in *Environmental Events Record*, vol. 1, no. 9, October 1990.

The theory that any economic activity, no matter how environmentally damaging, adds to national economic wealth was applied by the Exxon oil company. Two years after the company's oil tanker, the *Valdez*, ran aground dumping 11 million gallons of crude oil into Alaska's Prince William Sound – the largest oil spill ever – tarring beaches and killing wildlife, Exxon's director of Alaskan operations declared at a press conference that "The state of Alaska has been impacted but it's all been good." Mr. Otto Harrison, the oil giant's top man in Alaska, was referring to the more than $2 billion that the company spent to hire local families and companies to help clean up the mess. See "Exxon says crude spill windfall for Alaska" by Jerry Dubrowski in *The Globe and Mail*, Toronto, May 9, 1991.

For details on the history of forestry in the Philippines see "Philippine wood industry faces mounting crisis" in *Timber Trades Journal*, (351) no. 5879, U.K., October 7, 1989.

For background on national income accounting and the failure to measure environmental asset degradation see *Wasting Assets: National Resources in the National Income Accounts* by Robert Repetto, William Magrath, Michael Wells, Christine Beer, Fabrizio Rossini, World Resources Institute, Washington, D.C., June 1989; *WRI Publications Brief*, Washington, D.C., June 1989; "Wasting Assets: The Need for National Resource Accounting" in *Technology Review*, U.S., January 1989; "The Economy and the Environment: Revising the National Accounts" in the *IMF Survey*, vol. 19, no. 11, Washigton D.C., June 4, 1990; "Environmental Accounting: Putting a Value on Natural Resources" by John Laird in *Our Planet*, United Nations Environment Programme, vol. 3, no. 1, 1991.

On the basis of its own calculations, the World Resources Institute shows that in most years between 1971 and 1984 resource depletion either exceeded or offset a good part of gross capital formation. With a fuller accounting of natural resource depletion, it says, it might become obvious that in many years depletion exceeded gross investment, and therefore, that "natural resources were being depleted to finance current consumption expenditures." For further background on the treatment of natural resources by various economists, see *The Worldly Philosophers: The Lives, Times and Ideas of the Great Economic Thinkers* by Robert L. Heilbroner, Simon and Schuster, 1972; *Economists And Society: The Development of Economic Thought from Aquinas to Keynes* by Joseph Finkelstein, Alfred L. Thimm, Harper and Row, Publishers, New York, 1973. And for further details on John Maynard Keynes and his role in the design of national income statistics, see *The Life of John Maynard Keynes* by R.F. Harrod, Reprints of Economic Classics, Augustus M. Kelly, New York, 1969; *The Age of Uncertainty: A History of Economic Ideas and Their Consequences* by John Kenneth Galbraith, Houghton Mifflin Company, Boston, 1977.

Chapter 4: The Asset Sale (pages 41-48)

For sources on Mexico's history see *A History of Mexico* by Henry Bamford Parkes, Houghton Mifflin Company, Boston, 1960; *The European Discovery of America: The Southern Voyages 1492-1616* by Samuel Eliot Morison, Oxford University Press, New York, 1974.

For information on Indonesia's rainforests see "Indonesia takes steps to protect rain forests" by Steven Erlanger in *The New York Times*, September 26, 1989; "Indonesia: Suharto's Latest Budget is Bad News for Irian Jaya's Forest" in *World Rainforest Report*, Australia, July 1989; "Too Fast Too Soon" in *Euromoney*, U.K., September 1990.

For information on Cameroon's rainforests see "Cameroon set up for timber sting" by Damien Lewis, in *BBC Wildlife*, March 1990; on Ghana's rainforests see *The Tropical Forestry Action Plan: What Progress?* by Marcus Colchester and Larry Lohmann, The World Rainforest Movement and *The Ecologist*, U.K., 1990; and December 20, 1990 correspondence from CIDA senior vice-president Douglas Lindores in response to an Access to Information request from Probe International. For details on rainforests in general see *Rainforest Action Report* by Friends of the Earth, U.K., Spring 1990.

The details of CIDA's donation of forestry equipment for Ghana's logging operations are contained in CIDA's December 1990 response to Probe International's Access to Information request, including CIDA's "Logical Framework" document.

The U.N. report that encourages Third World nations to boost their commodity exports is called *Africa's Commodity Problems: Towards a Solution*, as reported in "Revitalization of African Commodities" in *Development Forum*, New York, September-October 1990.

For details on Ecuador's shrimp industry see "Shrimps no longer small fry in Ecuador" in *Financial Times*, London, August 18, 1989.

For background on the Philippines see "Marcos's Ghost" by Robin Broad and

John Cavanagh in *The Amicus Journal*, A Publication of the Natural Resources Defense Council, vol. 11, no. 4, New York, Fall 1989; *Fortune*, October 1975.

The brochures handed out by various countries at the annual meetings of the multilateral development banks referred to include: *Venezuela: The Great Turnaround: Rising to New Heights*, A Special Sponsored Report, sponsored by the Oficina Central de Informacion de la Presidencia (OCI), Venezuela, published by International Media Partners, New York, 1990; *Gabon: A Wealth of Resources Fuels New Growth*, A Special Sponsored Report, sponsored by the Finance Ministry of Gabon and published by International Media Partners, New York, 1989.

A good example of sustainable resource extraction is that practiced by the Brazilian *seringueiros*, or rubber tappers and Brazil nut gatherers. Numbering approximately half a million, these forest dwellers depend on the standing rainforest which contains rubber trees and Brazil nut trees that can be continually harvested.

Sources of information on the Mexican *maquiladoras* include "Boom and despair: Mexican border towns are a magnet for foreign factories, workers and abysmal living conditions" by Sonia Nazario in *The Wall Street Journal*, September 22, 1989; "The Maquiladora Boom" in *Mexico Service*, New York, October 3, 1990; "Moving beyond borderline plants" by Madelaine Drohan in *The Globe and Mail*, Toronto, November 22, 1990; "Love Canals in the Making" by Philip Elmer-DeWitt in *Time*, U.S., May 20, 1991.

Chapter 5: The Debt Crisis' Silver Lining (pages 49-58)

Gustavo Esteva has written many books and articles, and has been interviewed extensively by the broadcast media. See in particular "Regenerating People's Space" in *Alternatives*, Special Feature, 1987; "The Informal Economy", transcript of an interview on IDEAS, Canadian Broadcasting Corporation, November 27 and 28, 1990. Esteva offers many examples of environments saved because governments are pauperized. For example, in the late 1980s, Mexico's Rural Development Bank had insufficient funds to force peasants to plant sorghum for animal feed. The result: many communities returned to traditional intercropping of corn and beans, which greatly improved nutritional levels and soil fertility. Similarly hydro dams and pulp mills that would destroy some of Mexico's last remaining natural forests were on hold because of lack of money. Also see my article, "Debt crisis riding to the rescue of Third World environment," in *The Globe and Mail*, Toronto, July 4, 1989.

On Brazil's indebted electric utility system see "Eletrobrás expansion plans hobbled" in *Gazeta Mercantil*, Brazil, December 21, 1987; "Extracting Power From the Amazon Basin" by John A. Adam, in IEEE Spectrum, August 1988; "Financial Problems Delay Brazilian Schemes" in *International Water Power & Dam Construction*, U.K., February 1988; "Eletrobrás:

A Pleasant Shock" in *Gazeta Mercantil,* January 25, 1988; "Tucurui Waters Poisoned" in *International Water Power & Dam Construction,* U.K., July 1984. For details on how Balbina was almost canceled due to austerity measures, see Philip M. Fearnside *Brazil's Balbina Dam: Environment Versus the Legacy of the Pharaohs in Amazonia,* INPA, Manaus, Brazil, 1989; "U.S. Splits With World Bank Over Brazil Hydro Loans" by Glenn Switkes, in *International Dams Newsletter,* vol. 1, no. 5, September 1986.

On Brazil's nuclear power program see "Brazil is well on the way to energy self-sufficiency" by Edwin Taylor, Special Advertising Section in *The Wall Street Journal,* March 21, 1986; *Impacts of Great Energy Projects in Brazil: Comparative Study of Hydroelectric and Nuclear Power* by Luiz Pinguelli Rosa and Otávio Mielnik, published by the International Development Research Centre, Manuscript Report 196e, August 1988; "Bank Officials Check Brazil's Nuclear Ambitions" in *The New Scientist,* February 25, 1989; "West German Investment Outlook" in *Brazil Service,* New York, March 7, 1990; "Datafile: Brazil" in *Nuclear Engineering International,* U.K., April 1990; "Good News for Angra 1 and 2" in *Nuclear Engineering International,* U.K., March 1990:7.

For a description of how the debt crisis slowed Argentina's nuclear power program see "Argentina, short of funds, is likely to halt work on A-plant" by Shirley Christian, *The New York Times,* April 23, 1988.

For an interesting account of megaprojects in the Third World see *Macroproject Development in the Third World: An Analysis of Transnational Partnerships* by Kathleen J. Murphy, Westview Press, Boulder, Colorado, 1983.

For details of the Carhuaquero hydro dam in Peru see "Prospects For Large and Small Hydro Development in Peru" by P. Wicke in *International Water Power & Dam Construction,* U.K., July 1987.

The commotion over the Yacyretá dam was particularly astonishing, especially as President Menem's statement coincided with the IDB loan signing ceremony that took place at the IDB annual meeting in Montreal, 1990. Argentina's Executive Director to the Bank, who had shepherded the loan through to the signing stage, was said to be close to tears upon hearing of his president's condemnation of the dam. See "Billions flow to dam (and billions down drain?)" by Shirley Christian, *The New York Times,* May 4, 1990; "Menem Damns IDB Dam Loan" by Judith Evans in *Annual Meeting News,* vol. 5, no. 4, Montreal, April 4, 1990; "Can Argentina's Third Loan Start Giant Dam Flowing?" in *World Bank Watch,* U.S., May 15, 1989.

Information on the Roseires dam in the Sudan is from "Delay for Sudan's Roseires Scheme" in *International Water Power & Dam Construction,* U.K., November 1986 and from correspondence with Sudanese environmentalists.

For further details on the effect of budget constraints in China see "Energy crisis shuts factories in China" by Julia Leung in *The Wall Street Journal,*

January 6, 1989; "Go-go Chinese regions choking under hard-liners' iron fist" in *The Globe and Mail*, Toronto, March 12, 1990; "China's syndrome: Beijing's economic ills pose a new threat of social upheaval" by Adi Ignatius and Amanda Bennett in *The Wall Street Journal*, August 3, 1989.
Cameroon's forest policy, as recommended by the Tropical Forestry Action Plan, "is essential if the Cameroon is going to be able to meet the demand of the international market." See *The Tropical Forestry Action Plan: What Progress?* by Marcus Colchester and Larry Lohmann, World Rainforest Movement, Friends of the Earth and *The Ecologist*, U.K., 1990.

Details of Nicaragua's ruinous pesticide policy can be found in "Government Pesticide Policy in Nicaragua 1985-1989" by Allan J. Hruska, in *Global Pesticide Monitor*, vol. 1, no. 2, May 1990.

The Brady Plan, launched by U.S. Treasury Secretary Nicholas Brady in March 1989, was designed to use public funds and guarantees to encourage commercial banks to cut their existing Third World debts while continuing lending. It was considered a watershed in the Third World's debt crisis because it marked the first time finance officials from the industrialized countries recognized that some debt forgiveness was required if the Third World was going to get out from under its debt "overhang." Commercial banks were asked to write-down the value of their loans – lower the face value or the interest rates due on their outstanding Third World loans. The role of the public institutions was to collateralize – or guarantee either the principal or the interest – on the balance of the debt.

The Mexico package provides cash flow relief in the form of new money disbursements, a rescheduling of principal obligations, and interest relief resulting from the reduction in contractual interest rates and the elimination of some principal. Specifically, commercial banks holding eligible claims on Mexico were invited to choose from three financing options:
• exchange their existing claims for new 30-year discount bonds worth 65% of the face value of their original loans with full guarantee of principal to be paid back in one installment after 30 years, with 18 months' guarantee on interest;
• convert existing claims to 30-year bonds at par with below-market fixed interest rates and the same guarantee structure as for the discount bonds described above;
• provide net "new money" for 1989-92 amounting to 25 per cent of eligible claims, repayable over 15 years, including 7 years' grace.

The financing package also included options for converting claims into equity in newly privatized enterprises and infrastructural investments. To enhance the debt exchanges Mexico bought U.S. Treasury zero coupon bonds to use as collateral; Mexico also established an interest collateralization account at the Federal Reserve Bank of New York. To pay for these enhancements, Mexico received some $1.7 billion from the IMF, $2 billion from the World Bank, and $2 billion from the Export-Import Bank of Japan.

Part 2: The Queen Comes To Sicartsa (pages 60-64)

I am indebted to the work of Professor Philip A. Wellons from the Harvard Business School on the Sicartsa steel project. Using Sicartsa as a case study, his book, entitled *Passing the Buck: Banks, Governments, and Third World Debt*, from the Harvard Business School Press, Boston, Massachusetts, 1987, shows how special interests (including those of politicians), poor regulation, and a modern-day mercantile system led borrowers and lenders to invest billions in a megaproject that made no economic sense. Professor Wellons describes the relationship between exporters, their bankers, and their governments, the tension between them, and the alliances they form to win massive export credits. The end product, says Professor Wellons, is mercantilism. *Passing the Buck*, which is based on extensive interviews with the various participants in the Sicartsa loans, provides superb detail of the factors and interests that led to the go-ahead for this economic boondoggle.

Other excellent sources of information on Sicartsa include: *Las Truchas: ¿inversión para la desigualdad?* by Ivan Restrepo, Margarita Nolasco, Maria Pilar Garcia, Daniel Hiernaux, Elsa Laurelli, published by Centro de Ecodesarrollo and Ediciones Océano, Mexico City, 1984; "Paths to growth: a steel plant shows how U.S. and Mexico differ on development" by Mary William Walsh in *The Wall Street Journal*, May 2, 1986.

According to reports in *The Financial Times*, U.K., the British government had a lot on the line with Sicartsa: if the deal crashed because of Mexico's financial crisis, "it is the British taxpayer who will suffer, as the government has pledged to compensate in full the leading British company involved, Davy McKee of Sheffield." See "Acapulco welcomes the Queen" and "Dinner awaits Queen in Acapulco fort" in *The Times*, U.K., February 19 and 17, 1983, respectively.

The World Bank made a $70 million loan in 1973 to help finance the first phase of Sicartsa, and $76.3 million in 1984 for improvements in the Lazaro Cardenas Industrial Port. The Inter-American Development Bank lent $54 million in 1973 to finance foreign and Mexican components for the purchase of equipment and for contingencies, price adjustments, interest during construction, inspection and supervision. The IDB subsequently approved a loan in 1976 of $95 million for the second construction stage of Sicartsa but the loan was canceled by Mexico and no disbursements were ever made. See correspondence from Robert Kanchuger, Principal Country Officer, Mexico, World Bank, dated October 12, 1990 to Probe International, and correspondence from William M. McWhinney, Canadian Executive Director, IDB, dated May 17, 1991 to Probe International.

The Overseas Development Administration in London refused to release any information on their involvement in the Sicartsa steel plant "for reasons of client/customer confidentiality." See Unclassified Facsimile from the British High Commission in Ottawa to Probe International dated April 15, 1991.

In early 1991 the Mexican government sought equity participation by Japan's top steelmakers and trading houses in Sicartsa. According to *The Wall Street Journal* the Mexican government is said to have asked the Japanese to buy about $3 billion of its stock, but the reaction was cool. See "Mexico seeks steel backing" in *The Wall Street Journal*, February 27, 1991.

Details on Mexico's nuclear power expansion program and the exporting countries can be found in *The Globe and Mail*, Toronto: "Bidding is keen to supply Mexico's huge nuclear needs," December 14, 1981; "Candu financing plan set for Mexican bid," January 12, 1982; "Candu hopes pinned on Trudeau's journey," January 16, 1982; and "Canada among the battlers for Mexican nuclear plum," January 25, 1982.

Chapter 6: Bankers to the Thirld World (pages 65-74)

Information on the finances of the World Bank come from a variety of sources including: *Moody's Sovereign Credit Report*, New York, 1990, and *Moody's Credit Opinions: Sovereigns Supranationals* August 1989; Standard and Poor's *Supranationals Credit Review*, September 18, 1989; *The World Bank Annual Report* 1989 and 1990; *Information Statement: International Bank for Reconstruction and Development*, September 15, 1989, March 28, 1990 and March 22, 1991.

I use the term "the World Bank" as defined in the bank's 1989 *Annual Report*: "The expression, 'The World Bank' ... means both the International Bank for Reconstruction and Development (IBRD) and its affiliate, the International Development Association (IDA). The IBRD has two affiliates, the International Finance Corporation (IFC) and the Multilateral Investment Guarantee Agency (MIGA). The Bank, the IFC, and MIGA are sometimes referred to as the 'World Bank Group'."

The IBRD was established in 1944, is owned by its 155 member countries, and finances its lending operations primarily from its borrowings in the world capital markets. IBRD loans are made to developing countries with a higher GNP at interest rates just below commercial rates. Each IBRD loan must be made to a government or must be guaranteed by the government concerned, and IBRD loans come with a grace period of five years and are repayable over 15 years or fewer. The International Development Association was established in 1960 to provide assistance for the same purposes as the IBRD, but primarily to the poorer developing countries (those with per capita gross national product of $650 or less). IDA has 138 members, including donors who are in effect lenders, and the borrowing nations. The funds used by IDA, called credits to distinguish them from IBRD loans, come mostly in the form of subscriptions, general replenishments from IDA's more industrialized and developed members, and transfers from the net earnings of the IBRD. IDA credits are made only to governments, carry ten-year grace periods, 40 or 50-year maturities, and no interest. IBRD is thus known as the "hard loan window," IDA as the "soft loan window."

Of the $182 billion owed to the World Bank in 1989, $127.4 billion was owed to IBRD, and $55.5 billion was owed to IDA. Both figures include disbursed and undisbursed loans. Undisbursed loans include those which have been granted to a borrower but have not yet been drawn upon. They are included in the *World Debt Tables 1990-91: External Debt of Developing Countries,* published by the World Bank, as part of the Third World's $1.3 trillion debt. The IBRD's total borrowings from international capital markets equaled $86.5 billion, therefore representing a liability for which IBRD member states are responsible (see Moody's September 1990 *Credit Report*).

Details on the origins of the World Bank and the role that John Maynard Keynes played in setting up the Bretton Woods institutions (including quotations) can be found in the following sources: *The Life of John Maynard Keynes* by R.F. Harrod, Augustus M. Kelly, Publishers, New York, 1969; *The Age of Uncertainty* by John Kenneth Galbraith, Houghton Mifflin Company, Boston, 1977; *The Money Lenders: Bankers In A Dangerous World* by Anthony Sampson, Coronet Books, Hodder and Stoughton, 1981; *The Age of Keynes* by Robert Lekachman, Random House, New York, 1966. While Lord Keynes was preoccupied with the creation of the International Monetary Fund, he threw his full weight behind the World Bank too. In a front-page story in *The New York Times* on July 4, 1944 ("World Bank urged by Keynes as vital") Keynes, chairman of the British delegation to the United Nations Monetary and Financial Conference, was reported to have "urged the delegates and their technical advisers, who had not given as much attention to the bank as to the fund, since they have considered the fund to be the more urgent problem, to speed their consideration of the bank proposals. He asserted that the bank should be ready by the end of the war, so that the liberated countries would know immediately what credit resources they could rely on and thus proceed with their reconstruction programs, get back into production and resume their role in world trade as quickly as possible. Any time lag, he warned, would prevent the establishment of good government and good order and might postpone return of Allied soldiers to their homelands."

Apparently in an attempt to counteract criticism from orthodox American banking circles, which had expressed skepticism of his postwar ideas because of his long-time advocacy of deficit financing, Keynes spoke reassuringly about the soundness of the bank plan. Under the plan, he explained, postwar foreign loans would come mainly from the United States, the world's largest creditor at the time, but the risks for the loans would fall on all the bank's members in proportion to their subscription. The bank, he said, would supervise the spending of borrowed money to ensure that it was used "only for proper purposes and in proper ways," noting that such safeguards against squandering, waste and extravagance were not in place for many of the "ill-fated" loans made after the last war. To counter the fears of those who had declared "both the fund and bank proposals to be of British origin cleverly designed to entrap the United States into playing the 'Santa Claus' role after this war," Keynes said that the plan originated in the United States Treasury.

Although reconstruction would preoccupy the bank in its early years, Keynes explained, it would later shift its duty "to develop the resources and productive capacity of the world, with special attention to the less developed countries, to raise the standard of life and the conditions of labor everywhere, to make the resources of the world more fully available to all mankind and so to order its operations as to promote and maintain equilibrium in international balance of payments of all member countries." The World Bank and the International Monetary Fund, Keynes said, were intended to be permanent institutions.(*The New York Times*, July 4, 1944.) The other influential party to the Bretton Woods Conference consisted of the Americans led by Harry Dexter White working under Secretary of the Treasury Henry Morgenthau.

For elaboration on Keynes's ideas about politics and the management of an economy see R. F. Harrod's biography of Keynes (as above); *Keynes's Vision: A New Political Economy* by Athol Fitzgibbons, Clarendon Press, Oxford, 1988; *The Age of Keynes* by Robert Lekachman, Random House, New York, 1966; *The Keynesian Revolution and Its Critics* by Gordon A. Fletcher, The Macmillan Press, 1987; *Keynes* by D.E. Moggridge, Fontana Books, 1976; *The End of the Keynesian Era* edited by Robert Skidelsky, The Macmillan Press, 1977.

For sources on the structure and facilities of the World Bank, its influence on political institutions in borrowing nations, and why it is unaccountable see: *Articles of Agreement of the International Bank for Reconstruction and Development,* Washington, D.C., (as amended effective February 16, 1989), and *Articles of Agreement of the International Development Association,* Washington, D.C., (effective September 24, 1960); The World Bank *Annual Report 1990,* Washington, D.C.; *Cofinancing,* Office of the Vice President, Cofinancing and Financial Advisory Services, September 1989; *The Impact of International Organizations on Legal and Institutional Change in the Developing Countries,* International Legal Center, New York, 1977, including chapters by Fernando Cepeda Ulloa, John Howard and A.A. Fatouros; "Damming the Third World: Multilateral Development Banks, Environmental Diseconomies and International Reform Pressures on the Lending Process" by Zygmunt J.B. Plater in the *Denver Journal of International Law and Policy,* vol. 17, no. 1, Fall 1988. Also see "Cozy ties: IMF, World Bank aide has dealings hinting at conflict of interest" in *The Wall Street Journal,* December 28, 1990; "Two foes of Mobutu demand inquiry into de Groote's ties to Zaire regime" in *The Wall Street Journal,* December 31, 1990.

Information on the effect of World Bank lending on the electricity systems in Nepal, Colombia, and Panama comes from "Troubled Politics of Himalayan Waters" by Dipak Gyawali in *Himal,* vol. 4, no. 2, Lalitpur, Nepal, May/June 1991; personal correspondence with Dipak Gyawali; "Hydroelectric Power in Colombia" by C.S. Ospina in *International Water Power & Dam Construction,* U.K., July 1987; *Kilowatts and Crisis: Hydroelectric Power and Social Dislocation in Eastern Panama* by Alaka Wali, Westview

Press, Boulder Colorado, 1989.

For details of the megaprojects that the World Bank has supported see *Macroproject Development in the Third World* by Kathleen J. Murphy, Westview Press, Boulder, Colorado, 1983; all World Bank *Annual Reports*.

For details on the World Bank's record of commodity price projections see *The African Debt Crisis* by Trevor W. Parfitt and Stephen P. Riley, Routledge, 1989; "The Berg Report and the Model of Accumulation in Sub-Saharan Africa" in *Review of African Political Economy*, by J. Loxley, 27:8, 1983; "Aid that hurts" by Lawrence Solomon, *The Hamilton Spectator*, July 8, 1985.

Reports on the economic success rate of World Bank projects include *Project Evaluation in Practice: A Statistical Analysis of Rate of Return Divergence of 1,015 World Bank Projects* by Gerhard Pohl and Dubravko Mihaljek, Economic Advisory Staff, the World Bank, December 1989; *The Twelfth Annual Review of Project Performance Results* by the Operations Evaluation Department of the World Bank, 1987; *Between Two Worlds: The World Bank's Next Decade*, edited by Richard Feinberg, Overseas Development Council, Washington, D.C., 1986.

Pablo-Pedro Kuczynski's comment about the Asian Development Bank is from a sponsored supplement prepared especially for the 1987 Asian Development Bank annual meeting in Osaka, Japan, called *The Asian Development Bank* and reprinted from *Institutional Investor*, New York, by the Asian Development Bank.

For details on the World Bank's (and the other development banks') structural adjustment lending and round-trip loans, and the banks' assumption of greater portions of the Third World's debt, see "Escalating the War On Third World Poverty" by Samantha Sparks in *Global Finance*, New York, September 1990; "A Private Quarrel" by Melvyn Westlake in *Euromoney*, U.K., September 1990; "Managing the Debt Crisis in the 1990s" by Stanley Fischer and Ishrat Husain in *Finance and Development*, Washington, D.C., June 1990; "World Bank chief on the hot seat" by Michael Prowse in *The Financial Post*, Toronto, May 3, 1991; "3d-world funds: wrong-way flow" by Paul Lewis, *The New York Times*, February 11, 1988; "Privatize the World Bank" by Melanie Tammen in *The Wall Street Journal*, May 17, 1991; "The World Bank Underwater" by Barry M. Hager in *The International Economy*, September/October 1989; "World Bank: development's foe" by Tom Cox in *The Wall Street Journal*, July 29, 1988; "The World Bank's growing irrelevance" by Roger Altman in *The New York Times*, July 11, 1988; "World Bank confidentially damns itself" by James Bovard in *The Wall Street Journal*, September 23, 1987; "The IMF and World Bank – still needed" by John Gutfreund in *The Wall Street Journal*, September 25, 1990; "The World Bank and IMF are drifting" by Nicholas Eberstadt in *The Christian Science Monitor*, U.S., August 14, 1989; "How creditworthy is the World Bank?" by Nicholas N. Eberstadt in *The New York Times* March 1, 1988; "Will the U.S.

Be Left Holding the Bag On Third World Debt?" by Paul Craig Roberts in *Business Week*, October 16, 1989; "Debt crisis: a familiar fall guy" by Allan H. Meltzer in *The Wall Street Journal*, March 27, 1989.

The IBRD makes about a billion dollars in profits each year: rather than paying a dividend to member countries it puts some of the profits into a $1.5 billion loan loss provision fund against nonperforming loans that now plague the World Bank; it also recycles some to its soft loan window, the International Development Association.

According to the confidential minutes of a World Bank executive directors' meeting on July 9, 1986, an unnamed executive director commented that the proposed $500 million power sector loan under discussion for Brazil "oozed of balance of payments support." See *Summary of Discussions at the Meeting of the Executive Directors of the Bank and IDA, and the Board of Directors of IFC, June 19, 1986* IBRD/IDA/IFC, SD86-35. A follow-up loan in 1988, the second power sector loan, was chided by one bank official as being insufficient to meet Brazil's needs: Brazil's debts had become so serious that "we have to shovel money at them, and million dollar pipelines aren't big enough anymore. We need billion dollar pipelines." See "The World Bank vs The World" by Catherine Caufield in *Joint Annual Meeting News*, Berlin, September 24-25, 1988.

For the quotations from Haitian and Brazilian officials regarding round-tripping of loans see "Haiti retrenches as international aid cut off" by Ellen Hampton in *The Globe and Mail*, Toronto, January 12, 1988; "Nobrega Explains Arrears And Seeks IMF Accord" by Rosemary Werret in *Annual Meeting News*, Washington, D.C., September 25, 1989.

Standard and Poors in their *1989 Credit Review* state: "First, as embodied in the Articles of Agreement of all of the development banks, loans made by these institutions to their borrowing members are not eligible for rescheduling." While it is true that all of the multilateral development banks *have policies against rescheduling their loans* – usually unwritten – it is wrong to say that this principle is embodied in their articles of agreement. In fact, quite the opposite: each of the banks, according to their articles of agreement, are permitted to modify the terms of their loans should borrowers be unable to keep up with their repayments schedules. I confirmed this point in correspondence with each of the banks: based on that correspondence, it appears that only the Asian Development Bank's articles (Article 53) protect it against a moratorium on debt servicing.

The much coveted preferred creditor status of the World Bank also seems to be based on nothing more than an arrangement between borrowers and their rescheduling creditors. According to World Bank Counsel Hugh N. Scott, "The bank's preferred creditor status is reflected in the arrangements between the borrower and its rescheduling creditors. There is no specific commitment to preferred creditor treatment in our Articles of Agreement or loan agreements." From personal correspondence dated June 27, 1991.

For the research on the roadblocks to suing the World Bank I am indebted to Lori Udall from the Environmental Defense Fund in Washington.

For superb detail and analysis of the environmental record of the World Bank see the work of Bruce Rich, senior attorney at the Environmental Defense Fund, Washington, D.C. In particular, see "The Emperor's New Clothes: The World Bank And Environmental Reform" by Bruce Rich in *World Policy Journal*, Spring 1990; "Environmental Reform and the Multilateral Banks" by Pat Aufderheide and Bruce Rich in *World Policy Journal*, Spring 1988; "Conservation Woes at the World Bank" by Bruce Rich in *The Nation*, January 23, 1989.

For excellent examples of the kind of mythology that has become essential to the continuation of the World Bank see the various publications of the Bretton Woods Committee, a bi-partisan group in the U.S. that is organized to build public understanding of the Bretton Woods institutions – the World Bank and the IMF. The committee has more than 400 members throughout the U.S. – including all living past presidents of the U.S. It is a non-profit organization supported by individual and corporate contributions and foundation grants, and actively lobbies for congressional support of the Bretton Woods institutions. Among the many advantages that the World Bank offers the U.S., says the Bretton Woods Committee, one is that "Projects financed by the Bank can be bonanzas for U.S. consulting, manufacturing and engineering firms." See *Banking on Success: The World Bank, the U.S. and the Developing World*, Special Report on the World Bank, Bretton Woods Committee, Washington, D.C., 1988.

Chapter 7: A Credit Union for Countries (pages 75-81)

For basic information on how the IMF operates and its financial history see *1990 International Monetary Fund Annual Report*, Washington, D.C., 1990; *What is the International Monetary Fund?* by David D. Driscoll, IMF, Washington, D.C. (no date); *The IMF and the World Bank, How Do They Differ?* by David D. Driscoll, IMF, Washington, D.C., July 1989; *Ten Common Misconceptions About the IMF*, External Relations Department, IMF, Washington, D.C., 1989; *Helping the Poor, the IMF's New Facilities for Structural Adjustment*, by Joslin Landell-Mills, IMF, Washington, D.C., 1989; *The Alleviation of Poverty Under Structural Adjustment* by Lionel Deméry and Tony Addison, The World Bank, Washington, D.C., 1987. See also "The International Organization of Third World Debt" by Charles Lipson in *International Organization*, vol. 35, Autumn 1981, for a good description of the power the IMF has wielded over the years and why.

Keynes's thoughts turned to setting up an international monetary authority in the early 1940s. In his first draft of an international "Clearing Union" he explained: "We need a central institution, of a purely technical and non-political character, to aid and support other international institutions concerned with the planning and regulation of the world's economic life." After much negotiation with the other advocates of such a system, the Americans, a scheme for the International Monetary Fund emerged. For details of Keynes's early proposal, and the negotiations over the structure of the IMF, see *The Life of John Maynard Keynes* by R. F. Harrod, Augustus M. Kelly, 1969.

For details of the conditions the IMF imposes on borrowers see *Fund Conditionality: Evolution of Principles and Practices* by Manuel Guitián, IMF, Washington, D.C., 1981. See also personal correspondence with Mr. Azizali F. Mohammed, Director of External Relations Department, November 9, 1990, including excerpts from the draft Letters of Intent for Venezuela (March 1989) and Brazil (1990). IMF Managing Director Michel Camdessus's comment about the ability of military expenditures to survive austerity measures was made at a press conference at the annual meeting of the IMF in 1989, Washington, D.C.

Various articles have addressed the issue of the IMF's growing irrelevance, its relaxation of banking standards, and the loss of respect for it in banking circles. They include: "Back It Or Scrap It" from *Euromoney*, U.K., September 1990; "The IMF Dead in the Water?" by Richard E. Feinberg and Catherine Gwin in *The International Economy*, September/October 1989; "Caught in the Muddle," editorial by William A. Orme Jr. in *Latin Finance*, New York, no. 20, September 1990; "Fatter IMF purse won't fatten Third World" by Alan Stoga in *The Wall Street Journal*, June 12, 1990; "Third World interest payments arrears have surged since Bush Plan began" by Peter Truell in *The Wall Street Journal*, October 3, 1990; "Still Exposed After All These Years" by Andrew Froman, in *Latin Finance*, New York, no. 20, September 1990; "Banker's Tapes" in *Annual Meeting News*, Washington, D.C., September, 1990.

For details on the effectiveness of IMF policies, see the following: "IMF is facing the possibility of default on billions of dollars in African loans" by Art Pine in *The Wall Street Journal*, April 10, 1985; "Industrial nations struggle to prevent African defaults on loans from IMF" by Art Pine in *The Wall Street Journal*, July 25, 1985; "IMF's debtors in Third World pay back more" in *The Globe and Mail*, Toronto, February 2, 1988; "Some IMF policies have hurt the poor, report acknowledges" in *The Wall Street Journal*, June 1, 1988; "The Politics of Bread" in A Special Supplement to *Euromoney*, U.K., September 1990; "A Latin American view of the Brady Plan" by Hernando de Soto in *The Wall Street Journal*, May 19, 1989; "Argentina's monetary tango" by Armando P. Ribas in *The Wall Street Journal*, February 16, 1990. Also see *The IMF, the World Bank and the African Debt* vols. 1 and 2, edited by Bade Onimode, Zed Books, London, 1989 for excellent detail on the problems with IMF policies. The IMF's near success at canceling the Balbina dam in the Brazilian Amazon is described in Dr. Philip M. Fearnside's paper, *Brazil's Balbina Dam: Environment Versus the Legacy of the Pharaohs in Amazonia,* INPA, Manaus, Brazil, 1989.

The IMF report which analyzes the effect of IMF programs in seven Third

World countries is called *The Implications of Fund-Supported Adjustment Programs for Poverty: Experiences in Selected Countries* by Peter S. Heller, A. Lans Bovenberg, Thanos Catsambas, Ke-Young Chu, and Parthasarathi Shome, The International Monetary Fund, Washington, D.C., May 1988; also see *Development Issues: Presentations to the 39th Meeting of the Development Committee*, no. 26, Development Committee, Joint Ministerial Committee of the Boards of Governor of the World Bank and the IMF on the Transfer of Real Resources to Developing Countries, Washington, D.C., September 24, 1990.

Chapter 8: The New Mercantilists (pages 82-90)

The contribution of the export credit agencies to the Third World's debt – 15% of the $1.3 trillion – is calculated using figures from the World Bank's Debt and International Finance Division, *The World Debt Tables 1990-91* published by the World Bank; *Financing and External Debt of Developing Countries: 1989 Survey* published by the Organisation for Economic Co-operation and Development, Paris, 1990; *External Debt Statistics: The Debt and Other External Liabilities of Developing, CMEA and Certain Other Countries and Territories* at End-December 1986 and End-December 1987, OECD, Paris, 1988; *Statistics on External Indebtedness: Bank and trade-related non-bank external claims on individual borrowing countries and territories* published by the OECD, Paris and the Bank for International Settlements, Basle, New series, no. 3, July 1989; personal communication with the Institute of International Finance, Washington, D.C. The figure includes amounts owed to the export credit agencies for their various lines of credit, loans, and insurance schemes as well as commercial bank loans guaranteed by the export credit agencies (and which are therefore not included as part of commercial bank exposure).

It is interesting to note that the Canadian Export Development Corporation refused to release any details about the status of its loan to Argentina for the purchase of a CANDU nuclear reactor, even though the president of EDC stated before a parliamentary committee that it was being rescheduled under the Paris Club. Similarly, the British government refused to release details of the financial status of its financing (both through the Overseas Development Administration and the Export Credits Guaranteed Department) for the Sicartsa steel plant. The U.S. Export-Import Bank released detailed financial data on the status of their loan to the Philippine government for the Bataan nuclear reactor. See September 14, 1990 letter from EDC to Probe International; April 15, 1991 facsimile from the British High Commission in Ottawa to Probe International and July 5, 1991 letter from ECGD to Probe International; August 10, 1990 letter from the Export-Import Bank of the United States to Probe International.

Margaret Thatcher's quotation can be found in the Hansard for the British House of Commons, October 26, 1981, page 562, or in *Passing the Buck: Banks, Governments, and Third World Debt* by Philip A. Wellons, Harvard Business School Press, 1987, which offers superb analysis of the role of the export credit agencies in international trade wars in general, and of Britain's Export Credits Guarantee Department in Sicartsa in particular.

The official title for the Pearson Commission report is *Partners in Development: Report of the Commission on International Development*, Lester B. Pearson, Chairman, Praeger Publishers, New York, 1969.

For details of the role that export credit agencies played in promoting exports throughout the 1970s and 1980s see "Recent International Borrowing by Developing Countries" in *Finance & Development*, Washington, D.C., March 1987; "Export Credits and the Debt Crisis" by Miranda Xafa in *Finance & Development*, Washington, D.C., March 1987. The quote comparing trade to modern warfare is from "For No One's Benefit: Canada's Use of Foreign Aid to Subsidize Exports" by Richard C. Owens, in *University of Toronto Faculty of Law Review*, vol. 46, no. 1, Winter 1988. This article also quotes the author of the French report which condemns export credits: P. Messerlin, "Export-Credit Mercantilism à la Française" (1986) 9 *The World Economy*. The estimate of the importance to export credit in the 1990s is from "U.S. hits at rivals in tying aid to exports" in *The Globe and Mail*, Toronto, May 17, 1990.

For details of the importance of export credit to Boeing's foreign business see *Debt Trap: Rethinking the Logic of Development* by Richard W. Lombardi, Praeger, New York, 1985.

The environmental problems caused by the Sicartsa steel complex can be found in *Las Truchas: ¿inversión para la desigualdad?* by Ivan Restrepo, Margarita Nolasco, Maria Pilar Garcia, Daniel Hiernaux, Elsa Laurelli, published by Centro de Ecodesarrollo and Ediciones Océano, Mexico City, 1984. For details on the environmental review procedures (or lack of them) of the export credit agencies see correspondence from the Canadian Minister for International Trade, August 9, 1990 to The Honourable Charles Caccia, Member of Parliament, Canada. For the U.S. Export-Import Bank see May 17, 1990 letter from John W. Wisniewski to Probe International and *Federal Register* vol. 44, no. 170/ Thursday, August 30, 1979/ Rules and Regulations, Export-Import Bank of the United States 12 CFR, Part 408, National Environmental Policy Act Procedures; *Federal Register* Part III, Department of State, Unified procedures Applicable to Major Federal Actions Relating to Nuclear Activities Subject to Executive Order 12114, November 13, 1979.

For further information on Canada's Export Development Corporation and the Canada Account see the corporation's *1990 Annual Report*, and prospectuses issued regularly; "Controversy comes with demands of job as top man at EDC" by Andrew Cohen in *The Financial Post*, Toronto, February 20, 1990; "EDC helps Canadian suppliers, consultants stake export claim" by Kara Kuryllowicz in *Pulp and Paper Journal*, February 1990. In both his 1989 and 1990 reports to the Canadian House of Commons, the Auditor General criticized the Export Development Corporation for inadequately recognizing their sovereign risk. By late 1990, the Canadian government had added some $8.4 billion to the national debt, thereby acknowledging that many of the EDC's loans were unlikely to be repaid. No sooner had the government done this than the value of claims paid out by EDC to exporters for losses from buyers who couldn't pay jumped. See "Exporters left holding the bag" by Peter Morton in *The Financial Post*, Toronto, April 20, 1991. For details of how adding to EDC's provisions against loan losses increased the national debt see "Ottawa's debt rises $8B at stroke of pen" in *The Financial Post*, Toronto, October 30, 1990, as well as EDC's *1990 Annual Report*.

Further information on the U.S. Ex-Im Bank's financial woes can be found in "Loan-loss reserve at Export-Import Bank established" by Eduardo Lachica in *The Wall Street Journal*, January 5, 1990; "Bank loss reserve" in *The Globe and Mail*, Toronto, January 5, 1990; "Look Whose Turn It Is To Bite The Bullet" by Lenny Glynn in *Global Finance*, New York, March 1990. The aggressive bid to promote U.S. exports is described in "U.S. hits at rivals in tying aid to exports" in *The Globe and Mail*, Toronto, May 17, 1990.

The near demise of Britain's Export Credits Guarantee Department is described in the following articles: "Call for break-up of ECGD" in *The Times*, U.K., June 6, 1989; "ECGD sale may raise £100m" by Colin Narbrough in *The Times*, U.K., November 9, 1989; "Report opposes ECGD sale" by Colin Narbrough, in *The Times*, U.K., December 19, 1989; "British export credit agency spared axe" by Paul Melly in *The Globe and Mail*, Toronto, January 3, 1990.

For a terrific explanation of rescheduling, the role of the Paris Club, the contribution of public bodies to the Third World's debt crisis, and Eugene Rotberg's quotation, see "Look Whose Turn It Is To Bite The Bullet" by Lenny Glynn in *Global Finance*, New York, March 1990.

Chapter 9: Givers and Takers (pages 91-94)

Once again, the report of the Pearson Commission provides extremely valuable insight into the role of foreign aid in the Third World's debt crisis. See *Partners in Development: Report of the Commission on International Development*, Lester B. Pearson, Chairman, Praeger Publishers, New York, 1969.

The various figures for the sums owed to bilateral aid agencies and how much they have forgiven can be found in *The World Debt Tables 1990-91* published by the World Bank, and in *Development Co-operation: Efforts and Policies of the Members of the Development Assistance Committee* of the OECD, Paris 1990. The total owed to national aid agencies were also compiled with the help of data provided by the World Bank's Debt and International Finance Division.

The Treasury Board report that estimated tied aid prices were inflated is called *The Economic Effects of an Untying of Canadian Bilateral Aid* by the Effectiveness Evaluation Division, Planning Branch, Treasury Board Secretariat, Canadian Government, July 1976.

A copy of Mr. Haines's comments can be found in *Annual Consultations* of the Canadian Export Association and the Canadian International Development Agency, June 10-11, 1986.

For more detail on the Paris Club see *The Paris Club: An Inside View* by David Sevigny, published by The North-South Institute, 1990; Jeffrey Sachs's comment can be found in "Look Whose Turn It Is To Bite The Bullet" by Lenny Glynn in *Global Finance*, New York, March 1990. President Bongo's regrets were quoted in "Ottawa pledges $17 million more to French Africa" by Graham Fraser in *The Globe and Mail*, Toronto, September 4, 1987.

Chapter 10: The Petrodollar Recyclers (pages 95-102)

Statistics on bank earnings from Third World loans come from *The Debt Trap: Rethinking the Logic of Development* by Richard W. Lombardi, Praeger, New York, 1985, as does the reference to the Salomon Brothers report, which is called *U.S. Multinational Banking: Current and Perspective Strategies*, New York, 1976.

Mexico's Minister of Finance was quoted in a Canadian parliamentary report entitled *Canada, the International Financial Institutions and the Debt Problem of Developing Countries*, Report of The Standing Senate Committee on Foreign Affairs, April 1987.

For general background on the role of the commercial banks in the Third World's debt crisis I used several publications in particular, including: Richard Lombardi's book (as above); *The Money Lenders* by Anthony Sampson, Coronet Books, Hodder and Stoughton, 1982; *Latin American Debt* by Pedro-Pablo Kuczynski, The Johns Hopkins University Press, Baltimore and London, 1988; *Passing the Buck: Banks, Governments and Third World Debt* by Philip A. Wellons, Harvard Business School Press, 1987; *The Debt Threat: The Dangers of High Real Interest Rates for the World Economy* by Tim Congdon, Basil Blackwell, 1988; *The Debt Squads: The U.S., the Banks and Latin America* by Sue Branford and Bernardo Kucinski, Zed Books, London and New Jersey, 1988; *Disaster Myopia In International Banking* by Jack M. Guttentag and Richard J. Herring, Essays in International Finance, no. 164, International Finance section, Department of Economics, Princeton University, New Jersey, September 1986.

The figures on Citibank's losses on foreign loans come from Guttentag and Herring.

One of the most interesting displays of the banks' confidence that the public sector would bail them out if things went wrong appeared in a December 1975 *Euromoney* article by David I. Levine (executive director of Chase Manhattan) entitled "Developing countries and the $150 billion Euromarket financing problem" in which he said: "On the one hand, a purely technical analysis of the [non-oil developing countries'] current financial position would suggest that defaults are inevitable: yet on the other hand, many experts feel this is not likely to happen. The World Bank, IMF and the governments of major industrialized nations, they argue, would step in rather than watch any default seriously disrupt the entire Euromarkets apparatus with possible secondary damage to their own domestic banking systems, which in many cases are already straining under their own credit problems."

Walter Wriston's now legendary quotation appeared in an article he authored in *The New York Times*, called "Banking against disaster," September 14, 1982.

Information on country risk analysis comes from Pedro-Pablo Kuczynski's book, while details on syndicated loans and the banks' dependence on a handful of high-risk countries come from Philip Wellons' book in particular. Also see "Banks showing more caution regarding Third World loans" by John Kohut in *The Globe and Mail*, Toronto, August 7, 1987. One particularly good review of what went wrong was written by Donald Fullerton, CEO of the Canadian Imperial Bank of Commerce in "Banks have lessons to learn from debtor nations in financial crisis" in *The Globe and Mail*, Toronto, November 25, 1989. For good descriptions of the build-up to the Mexican debt crisis, the measures banks took to protect themselves, and the IMF plan, see Pedro-Pablo Kuczynski's book, *Latin American Debt*; Philip Wellons' book; *A Fate Worse Than Debt* by Susan George, Penguin Books, 1988; and *The Economic Effects of an Untying of Canadian Bilateral Aid*, Effectiveness Evaluation Division, Planning Branch, Treasury Board Secretariat, Canadian Government, July 1976.

For the early history and prices of various Third World country loans on the secondary market see Pedro-Pablo Kuczynski's book: also see "Return of the Living Debt" by Lee C. Buchheit in *International Financial Law Review*, May 1990. Much has been written on the loan-loss provisions that commercial banks have been setting aside, and the sales of Third World loans on the secondary market. Just a few of the many good articles include: in Canada, "Top six Canadian banks plan to double reserves against Third World debt" by Gord McIntosh in *The Globe and Mail*, Toronto, July 7, 1987; "Bank chairmen tackling issue of global debt" by Virginia Galt in *The Globe and Mail*, Toronto, January 23, 1988; "Third World loans still haunt banks" by Sonita Horvitch in *The Financial Post*, Toronto, January 19, 1990; "Banks' loan-loss woes coming to an end" by Jacquie McNish in *The Globe and Mail*, Toronto, December 8, 1989; "Canadian banks reducing exposure to Third World" by Satinder Bindra in *The Globe and Mail*, Toronto, October 30, 1990. For European and Japanese banks see "The Debt Squad Pays the Price" in *South*, U.K., April 1990; "Third World debt woes likely to lead to weak '89 results for big U.K. banks" by Craig Forman, in *The Wall Street Journal*, February 12, 1990; "British banks move on debt by Third World" by Craig Forman in *The Wall Street Journal*, November 10, 1989; "Third World debt starts to hurt Japan's banks" by Marcus W. Brauchli in *The Wall Street*

Journal, February 7, 1990. For the U.S. banks see "Banks' reserve action may make debt crisis even more vexatious" by Peter Truell in *The Wall Street Journal*, July 2, 1987; "Corporate profits fell 18% in third quarter, for first drop since '87" by Lindley H. Clark Jr. in *The Wall Street Journal*, November 6, 1989; "Morgan adds $2 billion to reserve for loans to developing nations" by Robert Guenther in *The Wall Street Journal*, September 9, 1989.

Just a sample of the bankers' anger over the Brady Plan can be found in the following: "Debt condition of developing nations seems to further unravel, Moody's says" by Peter Truell in *The Wall Street Journal*, August 31, 1989; "Banking On A Better Future" in *Euromoney*, U.K., September 1989; "Brady plan ill-conceived, banker says" by Paul Melly in *The Globe and Mail*, Toronto, August 4, 1989; "Whose Pound Of Flesh?" by David Shirreff, in *Annual Meeting News*, Washington, D.C., September 25, 1989; "Carrot and Stick" by David Shirreff in *Risk*, vol. 2, no. 8, London, September 1989; "Brady strategy: rest in peace" in *The Wall Street Journal*, January 22, 1990, "Bankers' barbs at Brady" by Hobart Rowen in *The Washington Post*, February 8, 1990; "Third World interest payments arrears have surged since Bush Plan began" by Peter Truell in *The Wall Street Journal*, October 3, 1990; "The Background to Brady's Initiative" by Lee C. Buchheit in *International Financial Law Review*, April 1990.

Bank of Nova Scotia President Cedric Ritchie's comments about the banks' role in lending to risky sovereign borrowers are from his address to the 158th Annual General Meeting of Shareholders of the Bank, January 16, 1990, Halifax, Nova Scotia.

Part 3: Ponzi Writ Large (pages 104-109)

Information about Charles Ponzi came from "Ponzi Dies In Brazil" in *Life Magazine*, January 31, 1949, and from "Tax Implications of Fraudulent Income Earning Schemes: Ponzi and Others" by Robert Grafton and Clyde Posey in *American Business Law Journal*, vol. 27, no. 4, Winter 1990.

The First National City Bank senior vice-president quoted is G. A. Costanzo from his article, "Latin America – Myths and Realities" in *Barron's*, New York, May 31, 1965.

For interesting insights from a commercial banker see *Loans in the Brazilian Environment* by Andrew Satterthwaite, Maureen James and Ian Leung, in their thesis for Innis College, University of Toronto, 1988.

See *Limits to Growth: A Report For The Club of Rome's Project on The Predicament of Mankind* by Donella H. Meadows, Dennis L. Meadows, Jorgen Randers, William W. Behrens III, Universe Books, New York, 1972 for predictions of resource shortages.

For details of the role that the public sector paid in the debt build-up see *Latin*

American Debt by Pedro-Pablo Kuczynski, The Johns Hopkins University Press, Baltimore, 1988, and the *World Debt Tables 1990-91* published by the World Bank. Also see Kuczynski's book for details of how interest rates and inflation rates made massive borrowing irresistible.

For details of the industrial expansion program in Brazil see *The Debt Squads: The U.S., the Banks, and Latin America* by Sue Branford and Bernardo Kucinski, Zed Books, London, 1988.

I am indebted to the excellent work of Nick Eberstadt on uneconomic and unsustainable investments in the Third World. His work is published in many places, but the sources I most used were "Investment Without Growth, Industrialization Without Prosperity" in *Journal of Economic Growth*, vol. 3, no. 4, Washington, D.C., Summer 1989, and "Foreign aid's industrialized poverty" in *The Wall Street Journal*, November 8, 1989.

Information about the accounting practices of Latin American state enterprises comes from *Latin American Debt* by Kuczynski. For details on the Brazilian Congress's mandate to investigate the whereabouts of the billions borrowed, see Article 26 in the new Brazilian Constitution, promulgated in October 1988. Clause 2 of Article 26 says that after an investigation, if an irregularity is proved, the Congress shall propose to the Executive that a declaration of nullity be made, and shall proceed to file a competent law suit with the Attorney General. In the end, the congressional committee struck to carry out this task could not get the loan contracts necessary to investigate the nature of and signatories to the loans. For popular Brazilian reaction to the debt see *Report of the Brazilian National Conference on the Foreign Debt* Final Statement, Brasília, D.F. Brazil, September 13-15, 1989.

For a few details on Swiss moves to reveal and release illicit money deposited by the Marcos family in Swiss bank accounts see "Marcos money" in *The Wall Street Journal*, December 22, 1989; "$1.3-billion frozen" in *The Globe and Mail*, Toronto, May 31, 1991.

Chapter 11: The Business of the State (Pages 110-118)

For an excellent review of the costs of the Colombian electricity sector, for the quotation opening the chapter, and for specific information on the Guavio dam, see "El agujero negro" and "Un elefante llamado Guavio", both in *Semana*, Colombia, April 4, 1989. Also see *International Water Power & Dam Construction*, U.K., July 1987, February 1988, and May 1990 for further information on the Guavio dam. In addition to funding from the Inter-American Development Bank, Guavio was also funded by the Canadian International Development Agency and the Canadian Export Development Corporation.

Sources for the estimates of how much of the Third World's debt was accounted for by electric utilities and state energy companies include *Economic and Social Progress in Latin America, 1989 Report* published by the Inter-American Development Bank, 1989; *Latin American Debt* by Pedro-Pablo Kuczynski, The Johns Hopkins University Press, Baltimore, 1988.

For Brazil, in particular, data on the debt accumulated by Brazilian state enterprises comes from "Extracting Power From The Amazon Basin" by John A. Adam, *IEEE Spectrum*, August 1988; "Too Big, Too Bad" in *The Economist*, U.K., March 12, 1983; "Losses Grow As Payrolls Blossom" in A Supplement to *Euromoney*, U.K., September, 1989. For details on Itaipu's borrowings see "Hydro project is to receive $103 million" in *The Globe and Mail*, Toronto, June 1, 1984; "Itaipu celebrates completion amidst financial crisis" in *The Financial Times*, U.K., May 7, 1991; "Brazil: Itaipu dam has 'critical problem,' says official" in *Gazeta Mercantil*; *Swaps: The Newsletter of New Financial Instruments*, vol. 3, no. 8, Washington, D.C., August 1989.

For more information on Zaire's Inga-Shaba hydroelectric project, see *Debt Trap* by Richard Lombardi, Praeger, New York, 1985; *A Fate Worse Than Debt* by Susan George, Penguin Books, London, 1988.

Details on Brazil's nuclear power program can be found in "Datafile: Brazil" in *Nuclear Engineering International*, U.K., April 1990, and *Impacts of Great Energy Projects in Brazil* by Luiz Pinguelli Rosa and Otávio Mielnik, International Development Research Centre, Ottawa, August 1988. On Mexico's nuclear power program see "Mexico's Nuclear Paradox" by Michael Redclift in *Energy Policy*, February 1989; "Mexico: Nuclear Debaters Fired" in *IFDA dossier 74*, Switzerland, November/December 1989; "Storm gathers over Mexico A-plant" in *The New York Times*, May 2, 1987.

For details on Pemex see *Latin American Debt* by Kuczynski; "Well of nationalism: oil's role in Mexico raises tricky issues for a free-trade pact" by Matt Moffet in *The New York Times*, November 26, 1990. For information on Petrobrás see "Latin paradox: lofty crude-oil prices drive Brazil's producer deeper into the hole" by Thomas Kamm in *The Wall Street Journal*, October 25, 1990. In a special advertising supplement in *The Wall Street Journal* entitled "Petrobrás: a catalyst for Brazil's development," March 21, 1986, Helio Beltrao, president of Petrobrás, said: "Brazil's debt problem doesn't affect Petrobrás credit and operations. All the important banks extend credit to us. As a matter of fact, we can't use all the credit we are offered."

The detail on Mexico's Sicartsa steel plant comes from "Paths to growth: a steel plant shows how U.S. and Mexico differ on development" by Mary Williams Walsh in *The Wall Street Journal*, May 2, 1986 especially. A description of the reach of the public sector into Mexico's economy, primarily as a result of the bank nationalization in September 1982, appears in "Disposing of banks' holdings a problem for Mexico" in *The Globe and Mail*, Toronto, September 17, 1982.

On the steel industry see "Losses Grow As Payrolls Blossom" in A Supplement to *Euromoney*, U.K., September, 1989; *Latin American Debt* by Kuczynski; "What Brazil's new president will face" in *The Globe and Mail*, Toronto, November 15, 1989; "Brazil to sell state-owned CSN once it's pulled out of the red" by James Brooke in *The Globe and Mail*, Toronto, June 4, 1990; "Debt-burdened Venezuela set to sell off investment offspring" by Simon Fisher in *The Globe and Mail*, Toronto, December 26, 1989. Details of Togo and Nigeria's steel saga are from *Debt Trap* by Richard Lombardi (as above). About Zaire's Maluku steel facility see *A Fate Worse Than Debt* by Susan George (as above).

Sources on the dismal record of state vanity projects include *The Debt Threat* by Tim Congdon, Basil Blackwell, London, 1988. See also *Oil Windfalls: Blessing or Curse?* by Alan Gelb and associates, published for the World Bank by Oxford University Press, 1988.

Information on the expense of Argentina's state enterprises comes from "Argentina trains, economy spin wheels" by Roger Cohen in *The Wall Street Journal*, March 2, 1989; "Will reality force the hand of Argentina's Peronists?" by Manuel Tanoira in *The Wall Street Journal*, June 9, 1989; "Privatization campaign in Argentina bogs down" by Thomas Kamm in *The Wall Street Journal*, October 25, 1990; "Argentina: Menem Ditches the Dogma" in A Supplement to *Euromoney*, September 1990.

For the total economic costs of state enterprises in Latin American economies see *Latin American Debt* by Kuczynski; "Brazil may lay off 400,000 to curb government costs" in *The Globe and Mail*, Toronto, May 10, 1990; "Billions come and go" in *The Globe and Mail*, Toronto, October 6, 1986.

Information on the Ivory Coast's sugar complex comes from *Debt Trap* by Lombardi. Details on Ghana's, Egypt's, and Malawi's state enterprises come from "African Privatization: How's It Going?" by Colleen Lowe Morna in *Development Forum*, vol. 18, no. 6, New York, November-December 1990; A Special Supplement to *Euromoney*, U.K., September 1990. See also "Blame Africa's own leaders for 'black elephant' aid" by George B.N. Ayittey in *The Globe and Mail*, Toronto, August 4, 1988; "African leaders put power first says Conable" by Peter Riddell in *The Financial Times*, U.K., April 26, 1990; *Industrialization in Sub-Saharan Africa: Strategies and Performance* by William F. Steel and Jonathan W. Evans, World Bank Technical Paper no. 25, The World Bank, 1984.

One of the main reasons for privatizing state enterprises is to reduce the state deficits. For further information see "Privatization Fever Hits Latin America" by Lenny Glynn, in *Global Finance*, New York, March 1990; "Privatization, Venezuelan style" by Carlos Ball, in *The Wall Street Journal*, June 1, 1990; "The Future Looks Brighter" in *The IDB*, Inter-American Development Bank, November 1990; *Privatization and Public Enterprises*, by Richard Hemming and Ali M. Mansoor, IMF, January 1988; "Privatisation Can Be A Complicated Process" in *Euromoney*, U.K., September 1990; *Privatization:*

An Overview of Worldwide Experience With Implications For The Electric Utility Industry In The United States, by Russell L. Klepper, for the Power Supply Policy Group, Edison Electric Institute, Washington, D.C., 1989; "Privatization in Honduras Called Lesson for Latins" in *World Bank Watch*, U.S., February 26, 1990; address by Miss Zélia Cardoso de Mello, Minister of the Economy, Finance and Planning, Brazilian governor to the Inter-American Development Bank Annual Meeting, Montreal, April 2, 1990; *Privatizing the World: A Study of International Privatisation in Theory and Practice* by Oliver Letwin, Cassell, London, 1988; "Caribbean & Central America Give Privatization Bandwagon a Push" by Richard C. Schroeder, in *Annual Meeting News*, Washington, D.C., September 25, 1989.

Chapter 12: Money for the Military (pages 119-123)

For statistics on the portion of the Third World's debt that can be attributed to military expenditure see: "Arms and the Third World" in *The Globe and Mail*, Toronto, June 26, 1990; "Our Alms For The Poor Fall Into The Wrong Pockets" by John Gellner in *Executive Magazine*, Canada, May 1984; "Research Communication: The Military Related External Debt of Third World Countries" by Michael Brzoska, in *Journal of Peace Research*, vol. 20, no. 3, 1983; "Military-Related Debt In Non-Oil Developing Countries, 1972-82" by Rita Tullberg in *World Armaments and Disarmament, Stockholm International Peace Research Institute Yearbook 1985*, Taylor & Francis, London and Philadelphia, 1985; "Debt, Financial Flows and International Security" by Somnath Sen in *SIPRI Yearbook 1990: World Armaments and Disarmament; Address by Barber Conable to the Board of Governors of the World Bank Group*, Washington, D.C. September 26, 1989.

Another excellent source of information on military expenditures is *World Military and Social Expenditures* by Ruth Leger Sivard, published by World Priorities, Washington, D.C. I have relied on Sivard's annual reports starting in the late 1970s for virtually all of my statistics. See the latest, the 14th edition, issued in 1991 for current data, and the 1989 report for the quotation about domestic use of military might.

For information on Argentina's military expenditures see "Argentine debt: a case study" by Edward Schumacher in *The New York Times*, May 12, 1984; "Argentina sends more weapons to Central America" by Jackson Diehl in *The Washington Post*, June 10, 1984; "Plans to boost arms exports" in *Latin America Weekly Report*, WR-84-26, July 6, 1984; "Argentina selling defence industries" by Paul Knox in *The Globe and Mail*, Toronto, September 17, 1990.

Africa spends more on its military as a percentage of GNP than do other regions of the Third World, with the exception of the middle east. See Sivard, 1991. Also see "Aid Donors to Africa: Fewer Guns, More Security" by Samantha Sparks in *Development Forum*, New York, September-October 1990.

For rates of growth in military expenditures see Tullberg (as above) from *SIPRI Yearbook 1985*.

For statistics on the combined expense of the military and debt servicing, and the decline in military expenditures in the 1980s, see Somnath Sen in *SIPRI Yearbook 1990* (as above). Also see "Tightening the Belt" by Husain Haqqani in *The Far Eastern Economic Review*, July 14, 1988 for details on Pakistan's military and debt servicing expenses. Also see "The Trade In Major Conventional Weapons" by Thomas Ohlson and Elisabeth Sköns from *SIPRI Yearbook 1987: World Armaments and Disarmament*, 1987.

Regarding the World Bank and the IMF's position on military expenditures in Peru see "Peru tightens belt to reduce debt" by William Chislett in *The Globe and Mail*, Toronto, January 16, 1984; for other countries, see "IMF urging cuts in military spending," *The Globe and Mail*, Toronto, May 4, 1991; Barber Conable's September 26, 1989 speech (as above). For the World Bank quotation criticizing Third World military expenditures see "The world's poorest get poorer" in *The Toronto Star*, September 17, 990.

Statistics on arms exports from industrialized countries come from Sivard, 1991.

For further details on pressure being applied by Western donors on Zaire's government see "Redistributing the Blame in Africa" by Stephanie Cooke in *Institutional Investor*, New York, September 1990.

For SIPRI's expression of hope that financial constraints would finally reduce Third World military expenditures, see Somnath Sen in *SIPRI Yearbook 1990* (as above). Despite promises to adopt arms control measures, the U.S. administration announced soon after the end of the 1991 Gulf War that it was going to ask Congress to authorize the Export-Import Bank to underwrite sales of military goods for the first time since the 1970s. According to "White House sides with arms industry" in *The Globe and Mail*, Toronto, March 19, 1991, "A Pentagon-administered military credit guarantee program was suspended in the late 1970s after too many customers went into arrears, with their loans either forgiven or rescheduled."

Chapter 13: Despots on the Dole (pages 124-131)

Each year *Forbes* and *Fortune* magazines conduct surveys of the richest people in the world: *Forbes* examines only those in the private sector, while *Fortune* documents the wealth of both the private sector and royalty. I have relied on "The World's Billionaires," *Forbes*, U.S., July 23, 1990 for my data on the former, and "Shrewd Managers of Regal Riches" in *Fortune*, U.S., October 12, 1987, for information on the latter. See also "The World's Billionaires" in *Forbes*, July 25, 1988; "The Enigma Behind the Saudi Billions" in *Euromoney*, U.K., September 1990.

For details of the wealth accumulated by the Marcos family see "Marcoses want property back" in *The Globe and Mail*, Toronto, March 12, 1991. This article describes how Imelda Marcos and her children demanded that her family's property seized by President Corazon Aquino's government be returned. In a petition filed by their lawyers with the Supreme Court, the Marcos family contended that the property should be returned to them "in the same manner that the heirs of the known gangsters in the United States, Al Capone, Dillinger ... inherited their fortunes" without losing a dollar of the assets to the U.S. government. In another article in *The Wall Street Journal* on March 12, 1991 about the same application to the Supreme Court, the family of the late President Ferdinand Marcos was reported to have estimated their family's wealth to be worth $75 billion. See also "Marcos money" in *The Wall Street Journal*, December 22, 1989. Another excellent survey of how much money the Marcos family stole from the Philippine people, and how, is *The Revolving Door? External Debt and Capital Flight: A Philippine Case Study*, by James K. Boyce, Department of Economics, University of Massachusetts, June 1990.

For details on the Bataan nuclear reactor and President Marcos's $80 million fee see the excellent investigative work of Fox Butterfield in "Filipinos say Marcos was given millions for '76 nuclear contract" in *The New York Times*, March 7, 1986. For even more detail on this case see *The Bataan Nuclear Power Plant*, by Consortium Research on Fraudulent Loans, Mae Buenaventura, Ed Santoalla, and Roberto Verzola, (draft), June 15, 1990.

As a result of this corruption the Aquino government filed a formal complaint on December 1, 1988, for money damages and equitable relief and demand for jury trial against Westinghouse before the U.S. federal court of New Jersey. Specifically the Aquino government demanded that respondents Westinghouse Electric, WIPCO and Burns and Roe Enterprises be tried for: obtaining their respective contracts with the NPC through rough bribery and other fraudulent, illegal and improper conduct; wrongful interference with the fiduciary duty owed by Marcos to the Filipino people by paying bribes to the former president to obtain their contracts; "unconscionable commercial practices, fraud, deceptions, misrepresentations, concealment or suppression of material facts" in violation of the New Jersey Consumer Fraud Act; breaches of contract for failure to supply the goods and services necessary for a "complete, safe, licensable, and operable nuclear power plant," improper charge for services, and failure to complete the plant by the warranted completion date of January 25, 1985; negligence for failure to fulfill their promises to function as "highly experienced and skilled in design, procurement, manufacture, installation, quality assurance, start-up and testing, and overall management of nuclear power plant projects"; and civil conspiracy among themselves and with Marcos, Disini, and some 20 Filipinos and Philippine companies.

For details on how Marcos and his cronies siphoned money from the state oil company see "Marcos crony returning despite fraud evidence" by Fox Butterfield in *The New York Times*, March 24, 1986.

For details of Mrs. Marcos's reputation see "How Hot Money Has Beggared The Third World" by Lenny Glynn in *Report on Business Magazine* from *The Globe and Mail*, Toronto, September 1985. The Filipino businesswoman quoted is Aurora Pijuan-Manotoc, and the quotation is from her article "Invest in the Filipino people, not their government" in *The Wall Street Journal*, January 28, 1985.

For sources on the extent of the corruption of Zaire's President Mobutu, including his run-in with the IMF, see *The African Debt Crisis* by Trevor W. Parfitt and Stephen P. Riley, Routledge, London, 1989; *Hot Money and the Politics of Debt* by R.T. Naylor, McClelland and Stewart, 1987; "Congo drums" in *The Wall Street Journal*, March 7, 1990; *A Fate Worse Than Debt* by Susan George, Penguin Books, 1988. Mobutu's complaint about being overlooked as the seventh-richest man was described in "Redistributing the blame in Africa" by Stephanie Cooke in *Institutional Investor*, New York, September 1990; *World Bank Watch*, U.S., July 3, 1989.

Chapter 14: Corruption in High and Not-so-High Places (pages 132-143)

The Public Broadcasting System ran their program "In Search of the Marcos Millions" on *Frontline* in 1987. See transcript no. 511 from the Public Broadcasting System/WGBH-Boston. This interview, plus various details about the workings of behest loans, are contained in *The Revolving Door? External Debt and Capital Flight: A Philippine Case Study* by James Boyce, Department of Economics, University of Massachusetts, June 1990.

For details of how money went astray through state finance development banks in Bangladesh, see "Bad loans cast cloud over Bangladesh" by John Elliot in *The Globe and Mail*, Toronto, February 13, 1984. And in Latin America, see "A Case Against Coddled Credit" in *The IDB*, the Inter-American Development Bank, January-February 1990. Also see "A Private Quarrel" in *Euromoney*, U.K., September 1990; "Escalating the War on Third World Poverty" by Samantha Sparks, in *Global Finance*, New York, September 1990; "Lending institutions stall Latin American progress," by Manuel F. Ayau, in *The Wall Street Journal*, November 18, 1983; "Report cites high level of insolvencies in financial area in developing nations" by Peter Truell, in *The Wall Street Journal*, July 5, 1989; "Lenders Repent at Leisure" in *South*, London, September 1989.

Details on corruption in Argentina come from "Argentine bankers in £78m scandal" by Eduardo Cué in *The Times*, U.K., September 30, 1986; *Hot Money* by R.T. Naylor, McClelland and Stewart, 1987; *The Debt Threat* by Tim Congdon, Basil Blackwell, 1988. The "lost" Argentinean debt is described in *Hot Money*, and also in "Argentina: Menem Ditches The Dogma" in A Supplement to *Euromoney*, U.K., September 1990.

On Nigeria's corruption, material comes from *The African Debt Crisis* by Trevor W. Parfitt and Stephen P. Riley. Also see *Hot Money* by R.T. Naylor and "The real foreign debt problem" by George B.N. Ayittey in *The Wall*

Street Journal, April 8, 1986. Details on Malaysia's use of over-invoicing can be found in *World Financial Markets*, Morgan Guaranty Trust Company, March 1986.

Details on corruption in Venezuela came from several sources: "Venezuelan aluminum project wrapped in profligacy" by Tyler Bridges in *The Wall Street Journal*, November 11, 1988; "Venezuela's cleanup" editorial in *The Globe and Mail*, Toronto, August 26, 1989; "Calm After The Storm?" in *Euromoney*, U.K., September 1989; "Venezuelan scandal may involve billions of dollars" by Simon Fisher in *The Globe and Mail*, Toronto, May 1, 1989; "Many executives flee Venezuela in scandal of foreign exchange" by Jose de Cordoba, in *The Wall Street Journal*, August 24, 1989.

The importance to corruption of state vanity projects, especially those financed with foreign funds, is described in "World debt woes spring from lack of democracy" by Arvind K. Jain in *The Globe and Mail*, Toronto, April 4, 1988.

An excellent source of information on capital flight is "Where The Money Went: Third World Debt Hoax" by James Henry in *The New Republic*, April 14, 1986. See this article also for details of how many U.S. dollars Venezuelans reported carrying on entering the U.S.

The apt description of swapping pesos for foreign currencies as "the bicycle" comes from *The Debt Squads: The U.S., the Banks and Latin America* by Sue Branford and Bernardo Kucinski, Zed Books Ltd., London, 1988.

The story about the frozen duck stuffed with cash is from "How Hot Money Has Beggared The Third World" by Lenny Glynn in *Report on Business Magazine* from *The Globe and Mail*, Toronto, September 1985.

Details of diamond smuggling come from "The real foreign debt problem" by George B.N. Ayittey in *The Wall Street Journal*, April 8, 1986.

The story of La Quina in Mexico comes from "Modernization at Gunpoint" by David Gardner in *Latin Finance*, U.K., February, 1989.

The extraordinary tale of Canadian bribes in connection with the sale of a Candu nuclear reactor to Argentina comes from the following sources: "The Big Payoffs: Good Business? Or Bad?" in *Maclean's*, Toronto, December 13, 1976; *Vote and Proceedings*, Third Session, 30th Parliament, No. 69, House of Commons, Canada, Monday, February 27, 1978; "$4 million bribe given on Candu Argentina says" in *The Toronto Star*, June 14, 1985; "AECL's Argentina deal over nuclear reactors netted minister millions" by Ross Howard in *The Globe and Mail*, Toronto, June 14, 1985.

Information on the Yacyretá dam in Argentina comes especially from "Billions flow to dam (and billions down drain?)" by Shirley Christian in *The New York Times*, May 4, 1990.

227

For details of France's enterprising first family see "Besides the presidency, Giscard d'Estaings holds other key posts, companies run by relatives of the French president play big role in Africa" by Jonathan Kwinty in *The Wall Street Journal*, April 23, 1981.

Stephen Lewis's quotation is from "Redistributing the Blame in Africa" by Stephanie Cooke, in *Institutional Investor*, New York, September 1990.

Octavio Paz's quotation is from *The Debt Threat* by Tim Congdon, Basil Blackwell, 1988 but originally from "After the Cultural Delirium" in *Encounter*, July/August, 1986.

Chapter 15: The Nether Borrowers (pages 144-150)

Details of the Perón's flight capital come from "Will we see a cartel of Third World debtor countries?" by Gwynne Dyer, in *The Toronto Star*, July 30, 1984, and *Eva Perón, The Myths of a Woman* by Julie M. Taylor, Basil Blackwell, Oxford, 1979. The extent of flight capital from Argentina comes from "How to Resolve Latin America's Debt Crisis" by David Felix, in *Challenge*, November-December 1985.

For Morgan Guaranty Trust Company's analysis see "LDC Capital Flight" in *World Financial Markets*, Morgan Guaranty Trust Company, March 1986.

For other good descriptions of the extent of capital flight, and the forces that created it, see "Has Capital Flight Made the U.S. a Debtor of Latin America?" in *Business Week*, U.S., April 21, 1986; "How Hot Money Has Beggared The Third World" by Lenny Glynn, in *Report on Business Magazine*, from *The Globe and Mail*, Toronto, September 1985; "Capital Flight from Developing Countries" by Mohsin S. Khan and Nadeem Ul Haque, in *Finance & Development*, Washington, D.C., March 1987; *Hot Money and the Politics of Debt* by R.T. Naylor, McClelland and Stewart, 1987

One of best sources of information on capital flight is "Where The Money Went" by James S. Henry, in *The New Republic*, April 14, 1986. See Henry for details of Mexico's capital flight. Also see *A Fate Worse Than Debt* by Susan George, Penguin Books, 1988, especially for details on Mexico's capital flight. According to George, Antonio Ortiz Mena, a Mexican and past president of the Inter-American Development Bank, estimated that Mexicans had sent roughly $90 billion abroad during President Portillo's administration – more than the $85 billion debt at the time.

Officials from the World Bank and the IMF concur with Henry's assessment of the coincidence between foreign loans and capital flight: "The ease with which residents engage in capital flight is obviously directly related to the availability of foreign exchange, which in itself is a function of foreign borrowing. Exchange controls may increase the implicit costs of moving funds abroad, but experience shows that such controls can be circumvented.

Common ways of doing this are underinvoicing of exports, overinvoicing of imports, and even outright smuggling of currencies or foreign exchange-earning commodities." See "Capital Flight from Developing Countries" (as above).

See *Debt Trap* by Richard W. Lombardi, Praeger, New York, 1985 for details of Nigeria's missing $1 billion.

For descriptions of how economic mismanagement fuelled capital flight see *Debt Trap* by Lombardi (as above); *The Debt Threat* by Tim Congdon, Basil Blackwell, 1988; "Capital Flight from Developing Countries" (as above); "When inflation rate is 116,000 per cent, prices change by the hour," by R. Nazario in *The Wall Street Journal*, European Edition, February 8, 1985; "How to Resolve Latin America's Debt Crisis" by David Felix, in *Challenge*, November-December 1985.

For details of how President Marcos of the Philippines frightened capital away from the country he governed see *The Revolving Door? External Debt and Capital Flight: A Philippine Case Study*, by James K. Boyce, Department of Economics, University of Massachusetts, June 1990.

See "Where the Money Went" by Henry (as above) for a description of the extent to which non-Americans hold "Yanqui" dollars.

For details on Brazil's capital flight see "Inflation Reaches the Boiling Point in Brazil" in *Swaps, The Newsletter of New Financial Instruments*, Washington, D.C., vol. 3, no. 8, August 1989.

The details of Mexican capital flight came from "Mexico's capital flight still wracks economy, despite the Brady Plan" by Matt Moffett, from *The Wall Street Journal*, September 25, 1989; "Mexicans fall into step on bank moves" by Matt Moffett, in *The Wall Street Journal*, May 25, 1990; and from Henry's article in *The New Republic*, as above.

For George Ayittey's and Walter Wriston's quotations see "The real foreign debt problem" by George B.N. Ayittey, in *The Wall Street Journal*, April 8, 1986.

Chapter 16: Unchecked Governments (pages 151-156)

For an analysis of the contribution of the oil crisis to the Third World's debt, see *International Debt: Systemic Risk and Policy Response* by William R. Cline, Institute for International Economics, Washington, D.C., 1984; *The Debt Squads: The U.S., the Banks and Latin America* by Sue Branford and Bernardo Kucinski, Zed Books, London, 1988.

For an excellent description of how increasing interest rates and declining commodity prices squeezed Third World countries see *Latin American Debt* by Pedro-Pablo Kuczynski, The Johns Hopkins University Press, Baltimore,

1988. See Kuczynski also for the contribution of state subsidies to government deficits.

On the subject of state subsidies to agriculture see *Mexico Service*, A Publication of International Reports, vol. 10, no. 9, New York, April 25, 1990; "Government role in farming is big issue in Salvador, too" by Virginia Prewett, in *The Wall Street Journal*, March 8, 1985; "Survey: The Third World" in *The Economist*, U.K., September 23, 1989; "World Bank sows bad advice in Africa" by Melanie S. Tammen, in *The Wall Street Journal*, April 13, 1988; "Tanzania: Again Squandering Foreign Aid" by Melanie Tammen, *Backgrounder*, The Heritage Foundation, Washington, D.C, no. 62, 1/7/88; "Grain Marketing Policies and Institutions in Africa" by Peter Hopcraft, in *Finance & Development*, Washington, D.C., March 1987.

For the details on the diversion of agricultural credit to other investments in Brazil see especially "National Business, Debt-Led Growth and Political Transition in Latin America" by Sylvia Maxfield, in *Debt and Democracy in Latin America*, edited by Barbara Stallings and Robert Kaufman, Westview Press, Boulder, 1989; "Too Big, Too Bad" in *The Economist*, U.K., March 12, 1983.

Regarding state payrolls in Brazil, see "Losses Grow As Payrolls Blossom" from A Supplement to *Euromoney*, U.K., September 1989; "Deficit-cutting wage curb blocked by Brazil's army" in *The Globe and Mail*, Toronto, March 7, 1988; "Brazil may lay off 400,000 to curb government costs" in *The Globe and Mail*, Toronto, May 10, 1990. For public sector layoffs in Zaire, see *The African Debt Crisis*, by Trevor W. Parfitt and Stephen P. Riley, Routledge, London, 1989.

Sources describing the growth in budget deficits and the increasing difficulty of maintaining them come from "Last days of an African survivor?" by Hugh McCullum, in *The Globe and Mail*, Toronto, July 26, 1990. See *Latin American Debt* by Kuczynski for an excellent description of the commercial banks' retreat to short-term loans.

The crushing cost of servicing the debt is described ably in the publications and communiques of the Swiss Aid Agencies Coalition, including the various publications of its coordinator Richard Gertser; "Debt Crisis – Where Now?" by Sue Branford in *Friends of the Earth – Tropical Rainforest Times*, Spring, 1989; "World Bank looking for more belt-tightening" by James Rusk, in *The Globe and Mail*, Toronto, September 1, 1989; *Philippine Debt To Foreign Banks* by John E. Lind, Northern California Interfaith Committee on Corporate Responsibility, November 1984; the regular publications of *PAID! People Against Immoral Debt*, Official Newsletter of the Freedom From Debt Coalition, Philippines.

Much has been written about the contribution of government budget deficits to the Third World's debt crisis. Here is a sample of the sources I have used: "China's budget deficit yawns wider," from *The Globe and Mail*, Toronto,

August 21, 1990; "A no-growth future for Zimbabwe" by Dan Griswold, in *The Wall Street Journal*, September 26, 1985; *Nigeria and the IMF*, by T.A. Oyejide, A. Soyode, M.O. Kayode, Heinemann Educational Books (Nigeria), 1985; "Angola, an economic ostrich" by Julian Ozanne, *The Financial Post*, Toronto, May 10, 1991; "The Federal Deficit" in *Brazil Service*, A Publication of International Reports, vol. 10, no. 9, New York, May 2, 1990; "Can Salinas Avoid Mistakes of the Past?" in *Mexico Service*, A Publication of International Reports, New York, October 3, 1990; "Aid, the Public Sector and the Market in Less Developed Countries" by Paul Mosley, John Hudson and Sara Horrell, in *The Economic Journal*, 97, September, 1987; "Reviving Growth in Latin America" by S. Shahid Husain, in *Finance & Development*, Washington, D.C., June 1989; "Why Asia boomed and Africa busted," by Keith Marsden, in *The Wall Street Journal*. An article about Bolivia's attempts to curtail its budget deficit explained the difficulty for leaders: "The danger is that the government may end up shying away from unpopular measures. Fernando Illanas de Rivas, former minister of hydrocarbons and ambassador to the U.S. who was responsible for implementing the buy-back of the Bolivian debt, asserts: 'The budget was a typical example. The President said we must make the government more efficient and shrink its spending, but then a budget was produced increasing spending by 50 per cent, in the search for popularity. The President also feels the need to be loved.'" See "Bolivia: Holding Steady But Growth Proves Elusive" by Kevin Rafferty, in *Annual Meeting News*, IDB Annual Meeting, Montreal, April 3, 1990.

The effect of Mexican budget deficits is described in "Mexican crisis shocks financial community" by Alan Freidman, in *The Globe and Mail*, Toronto, August 24, 1982; "Mexico's president breaks the banking taboo" by Sergio Sarmiento, in *The Wall Street Journal*, May 4, 1990.

Sources of analysis and data on the extent and effect of inflation in the Third World are from *The Debt Threat* by Tim Congdon, Basil Blackwell, London, 1988; "Daily inflation struggle obsesses Brazil" by Thomas Kamm, in *The Wall Street Journal*, January 29, 1990; "Brazil's moves to curb its inflation also curb U.S. concerns' profits" by Robert L. Rose in *The Wall Street Journal*, July 25, 1990; "Bolivia's inflation triumph holds perils" by Jonathan Kandell, in *The Wall Street Journal*, September 11, 1989.

Part 4: Illegitimate Debts (pages 158-161)

The story from the "Information Newsletter" of the Brazilian Evangelical Lutheran Church has been cited in many places, including Susan George's book, *A Fate Worse Than Debt*, Penguin Books, 1988. The information about the study on nutrition levels in north-eastern Brazil also came from *A Fate Worse Than Debt*.

For UNICEF's position, see *The State of the World's Children 1989*, United Nations Children's Fund, Oxford University Press, 1989. UNICEF's figures of social spending are per capita, unlike the figures in Chapter 12 on the military, which are as a percentage of GNP.

Information on Canada's debt came from numerous newspaper articles and from "Foreign Investment in the Canadian Bond Market, 1978 to 1990" by Lucie Laliberté, in *Canadian Economic Observer*, Canada, June 1991, which states that Canada's net liability to non-residents is $259 billion, representing 38 per cent of gross domestic product. Brazil's total external debt of $111 billion is 24 per cent of gross national product.

Word of the Japanese offer to assume Brazil's debt in return for mineral rights to gold in the Amazon shocked everyone: it came at a time when concern for protecting the Amazon from damaging activities like gold mining was at its height; most were surprised that the debt could be retired so easily; the offer seemed unconscionable. For further information see "Japanese offer to buy Brazil's debt" in *The Globe and Mail*, Toronto, February 5, 1990.

Chapter 17: The Doctrine of Odious Debts (pages 162-170)

For an interesting description of the lead-up to the American-Spanish War, see *Civilization in the Western World: 1815 to the Present* by J. Russell Major, J.P. Lippincott Company, Philadelphia and New York, 1966.

The peace negotiations at Paris that followed the end of the Spanish-American war are described in a number of places, including: *Public Debts and State Succession* by Ernst H. Feilchenfeld, J.U.D. (Berlin), The Macmillan Company, New York, 1931; *Les Effets des Transformations des États sur leurs Dettes Publiques et Autres Obligations Financières* by A.N. Sack, Recueil Sirey, Paris, 1927; "Effects of State and Government Succession on Commercial Bank Loans to Foreign Sovereign Borrowers" by James L. Foorman and Michael E. Jehle, in *University of Illinois Law Review*, vol. 1982, no. 1; *The Law of State Succession*, by D.P. O'Connell, Cambridge At The University Press, 1965; *State Succession In Municipal Law and International Law*, vol. 1, Internal Relations, by D.P. O'Connell, Cambridge At The University Press, 1967; "Legal Problems of the Overindebtedness of Developing Countries: The Current Relevance of the Doctrine of Odious Debts" by Günter Frankenberg and Rolf Knieper, in *International Journal of the Sociology of Law*, 1984, 12; and "Through a Glass Darkly: Reflections Upon The History of the International Law of Public Debt In Connection With State Succession" by M.H. Hoeflich, in *University of Illinois Law Review*, vol. 1982, no. 1. The quotation from the Spanish negotiators is from the last citation.

The debts in question consisted of bonds which had been sold on the international market and held by the nations of a number of major powers, including France and Belgium.

The precedents cited by the Spanish commissioners included the payment by Spain's former colonies in Central and South America of that part of Spain's public debt properly attributed to the colonies when they achieved independence. They also noted that after the American Revolution the thirteen original colonies paid over £15,000,000 to Great Britain in discharge of the colonies' debts. The American Commissioners vigorously refuted the Spanish Commissioners' position, saying: "The American commissioners are not acquainted with the works of the publicists who maintain that the thirteen original United States paid to Great Britain 15,000,000 pounds sterling, presumably for the extinguishment of colonial debts. The American Commissioners, however, feel no interest in the matter, since the statement is entirely erroneous." From Hoeflich, as above.

The American arguments are cited in *Les Effets des Transformations des États sur leurs Dettes Publiques et Autres Obligations Financières* by A.N. Sack (as above), p. 159 and in *Public Debts and State Succession* by Ernst H. Feilchenfeld (as above), p. 340. They can also be found in J.B. Moore, *Digest International Arbitrations*, vol. 1, pp. 358-359, as cited in Sack, p. 159.

For the quotation regarding the risk that the creditors must have known they were taking, see "Through a Glass Darkly" by M.H. Hoeflich (as above).
For the conclusion to the Paris peace negotiations see *Treaty of Peace between Spain and the United States, signed at Paris*, concluded at Paris December 10, 1898. Also see Ernst H. Feilchenfeld (as above), p. 340. It can also be found in J.B. Moore, *Digest International Arbitrations*, vol. 1, p. 343. Feilchenfeld says "The Spanish proposals were not, therefore, adopted in the final treaty, nor were any Spanish debts assumed by Cuba or by the United States after the Treaty of Paris went into effect."

A.N. Sack's contribution to the subject of public debts and state succession is, according to Feilchenfeld, "perhaps the most profound treatise ever written on the subject and is unrivaled in its careful analysis of the details of the problem." Also see *La Succession Aux Dettes Publiques D'Etat* by A.N. Sack, 70, 1929; "Diplomatic Claims Against the Soviets" by Alexander N. Sack, New York University School of Law, Contemporary Law Pamphlets, Series 1, Number 7, *New York University Law Quarterly Review*, New York, New York, 1938. The portion of Sack's definition of odious debts that I have quoted in English appeared originally in French, pp. 157-8 (1927):

I. – DETTES ODIEUSES POUR LA POPULATION DE L'ÉTAT ENTIER

Si un pouvoir despotique contracte une dette non pas pur les besoins et dans les intérêts de l'État, mais pour fortifier son régime despotique, pour réprimer la population qui le combat, etc., cette dette est odieuse pour la population de l'État entier.

Cette dette n'est pas obligatoire pour la nation; c'est une dette de régime, dette personnelle du pouvoir qui l'a contractée, par conséquent elle tombe avec la chute de ce pouvoir.

La raison pour laquelle ces dettes "odieuses" ne peuvent être considérées comme grevant le territoire de l'État, est que ces dettes ne répondent pas à l'une des conditions qui déterminent la régularité des dettes d'État, à savoir celle-ci : les dettes d'État doivent être contractées et les fonds qui en proviennent utilisés pour les besoins et dans les intérêts de l'État.

Les dettes "odieuses", contractées et utilisées à des fins lesquelles, au su des créanciers, sont contraires aux intérêts de la nation, n'engagent pas cette dernière – au cas où elle arrive à se débarrasser du gouvernement qui les avait contractées – sauf dans la limite des avantages réels qu'elle a pu obtenir de ces dettes. Les créanciers ont commis un acte hostile à l'égard du peuple; ils ne peuvent donc pas compter que la nation affranchie d'un pouvoir despotique assume les dettes "odieuses," qui sont des dettes personnelles de ce pouvoir.

Quand même un pouvoir despotique serait renversé par un autre, non moins despotique et ne répondant pas davantage à la volonté du peuple, les dettes "odieuses" du pouvoir déchu n'en demeurent pas moins ses dettes personnelles et ne sont pas obligatoires pour le nouveau pouvoir....

On pourrait également ranger dans cette catégorie de dettes les emprunts contractés dans des vues manifestement intéressées et personnelles des membres du gouvernement ou des personnes et groupements liés au gouvernement – des vues qui n'ont aucun rapport aux intérêts de l'État.

Further details of the Russian debt repudiation can be found in James L. Foorman and Michael E. Jehle, 1982 (as above); "Through a Glass Darkly" by M.H. Hoeflich (as above); A.N. Sack, 1927 and 1938 (as above).

The meaning of the Soviets' repudiation of the tsarist debts is by no means clear, and much disagreement about the principle on which they based their arguments persists to this day. Indeed, Sack (1938) says international law was violated by some of the Soviet decrees. Interestingly, it appears that in a bid for international recognition, the White Russian provisional government, in 1921, announced its intention to honor tsarist debts. It lost its bid to govern, as did Russia's creditors to their claims, until 1987 when the new government in the Soviet Union decided to honor the old bonds. According to "Russian bond holders face payments puzzle" in The Times, U.K., October 30, 1987, a thriving market for Russian bonds as collectors' items was forcing holders to choose between collecting on their ancient debts or hanging on to their certificates for their novelty value. But the Russian repudiation of debts greatly influenced Sack to write his monumental treatise (1938), which he opens by saying: "The study of the Russian revolution of March 1917 has brought me to examine the effects of a political transformation of the State on its public debt."

References to ultra vires contracts and their effect on the enforceability of state debts can be found in Sack's book (1927), pp. 24-25, where he says that debts of the state must be incurred by appropriate governmental services, conforming to legal procedures. See also "Legal Problems of the Overindebtedness of Developing Countries" by Frankenberg and Knieper (as above). For details of the Venezuelan contracts that were declared ultra vires, see "Repudiation of Ultra Vires State Contracts and the International Responsibility of States" by Theodor Meron, in International and Comparative Law Quarterly, vol. 6, April 1957.

For details of the failure of oil concessions and loans in which Costa Rican President Frederico Tinoco engaged, see Meron (as above); also see Foorman and Jehle (as above). For the final decision of Chief Justice Taft, see *Annual Digest of Public International Law Cases*, Years 1923 to 1924, edited by Sir John Fischer Williams and H. Lauterpacht, Longmans, Green and Co., London, 1933.

For further details on the tendency to hold successor states and governments responsible for old debts incurred even by agents with apparent authority, see Meron (as above).
The lawyers at The First National Bank of Chicago, James L. Foorman and Michael E. Jehle, are quoted from their 1982 article (as above).

Sack's original statement on the use of borrowed money to subjugate or colonize a population appeared thus:

Lorsque le gouvernement contracte des dettes afin d'asservir la population d'une partie de son territoire ou de coloniser celle-ci par des ressortissants de la nationalité dominante, etc., ces dettes sont odieuses pour la population indigène de cette partie du territoire de l'État débiteur.
See Sack, 1927 (as above), p. 158.

Chapter 18: Mercantile Law Versus The People (171-178)

For insight into Indonesian policies that affect traditional property rights and the environment see *Environesia*, the newsletter of Friends of the Earth Indonesia. In particular, see "Consolidation of Power in the Forestry Industry" in vol. 4, no. 2, April/August 1990, for the quotations cited. Also see "Who Is Violating Whose Law?" in the same issue, which further explains the subjugation of *adat* law by the national law.

Hernando de Soto's remarkable book is called *The Other Path: The Invisible Revolution in the Third World*, Harper & Row, New York, 1989. Also see "Informals key to Third World growth" by Hernando de Soto, in *The Toronto Star*, June 30, 1990; "A Latin American view of the Brady Plan" by Hernando de Soto, in *The Wall Street Journal*, May 19, 1989; "Peru's Informal Sector" in *Swaps: The Newsletter of New Financial Instruments*, Washington, D.C., vol. 3, no. 11, November 1989. See the transcript of an interview with Hernando de Soto and Gustavo Esteva, "The Informal Economy," on IDEAS, Canadian Broadcasting Corporation, November 27 and 28, 1990.

The United Nations Report referred to is *Human Development Report 1991*, published for the United Nations Development Programme, Oxford University Press, New York and Oxford, 1991.

On the need for better laws and better government also see the recent statements of Pope John Paul II: "Profitability over people decried in encyclical" by Jack Kapica, in *The Globe and Mail*, Toronto, May 2, 1991; "Guatemalans chastised for making up their own minds" by Mart Altolaguirre, in *The Wall Street Journal*, August 10, 1990; "Central America moves toward capitalism" by David Asman, in *The Wall Street Journal*, March 25, 1991; *Economic Reform and Democracy in Latin America and the Caribbean*, Proceedings of The North-South Institute Seminar held in collaboration with the Inter-American Development Bank, March 31, 1990, Montreal, Quebec, 1990; *Land and People*, a newsletter of the Society for Participatory Research in Asia, New Delhi, India. The lead story of the no. 6, July-September 1989 issue, "The Right To Know," is about the need for access to information legislation in India.

The Charter on Environmental Rights and Obligations of Individuals, Groups and Organisations, drafted by 300 citizens groups in Asia, is contained in *An Agenda for Common Future*, and published in *Pakenviron*, Special Issue, Environmental Management Society, Friends of the Earth – Pakistan, 1990. It lays out the incentive structures and mechanisms for bringing about developments such as sustainable energy use, industrial activity, and natural resources management. It also examines the economics of sustainability, and recommends reforms to guarantee access to information, legal protection and compensation for environmental damages, and public participation in government policies and projects.

Chapter 19: The Virtues of Taxation (pages 179-184)

For Chinese dissident Fang Lizhi's views on foreign financing, see "Chinese dissident advocates divestment" by Joe Cuomo, in *The Wall Street Journal*, April 26, 1989. Mr. Fang made one exception to his appeal for foreign divestment from China: he thought World Bank and other loans should continue for education projects. Also see "Free to Speak" in *The Far Eastern Economic Review*, August 2, 1990. Guyana's former prime minister, Cheddi Jagan, described his view of foreign financing in a letter to the editor of *The Toronto Star*, "Guyana founders under IMF austerity plan," April 29, 1989. In "Guyana austerity plan will provoke turmoil opposition head says," in *The Globe and Mail*, Toronto, October 4, 1989, Jagan, referring to an economic austerity program in his country, said that the country would be willing to face sacrifices if there were fair elections to produce a government with broad support. Electoral reform, he said, was an important demand of a coalition of five political parties in Guyana.

For the Guatemalans' quotations see "Foreign aid inhibits market ideas in Guatemala" by Fernando Monterroso in *The Wall Street Journal*, November 3, 1989.

For further details on the Ptolemic tax burden see *The Lessons of History* by Will and Ariel Durant, Simon and Schuster, 1968, New York. Sir William Petty's description of public reaction to taxes is from *The Basic Teachings of the Great Economists* by John W. McConnell, The New Home Library, New York, 1943. Adam Smith talked extensively about taxes in the second volume of his 1776 treatise *The Wealth of Nations*, published by J.M. Dent and Sons, London, 1910.

For a very interesting discussion of the political effects of deficit financing see several chapters in *The End of the Keynesian Era*, edited by Robert Skidelsky, The Macmillan Press, London, 1977. See in particular "The Political Meaning of the Keynesian Revolution" by Robert Skidelsky; "Can Democracy Manage an Economy?" by Samuel Brittan; "Keynes and the Developing World" by Harry G. Johnson; "Keynes and the Pax Americana" by David P. Calleo.

For the economic impacts of persistent deficit financing in the Third World, see "Why Asia boomed and Africa busted" by Keith Marsden, in *The Wall Street Journal*, June 3, 1985.

For the statistics on Africa see *Sub-Saharan Africa: From Crisis to Sustainable Growth*, A Long-Term Perspective Study, by The World Bank, Washington, D.C., 1989; also see "Africa, The Long Good-bye" by David Ewing Duncan, in *The Atlantic*, U.S., July 1990.

Claude Ake's quotations are cited in "Redistributing the Blame in Africa" by Stephanie Cooke, in *Institutional Investor*, New York, September 1990.

Information about the state of foreign aid in Nepal comes from "Nepal faces economic 'shambles' of poverty and addiction to aid" by Sanjoy Hazarika, in *The Globe and Mail*, Toronto, May 15, 1990; "A White Lie" by P.C. Joshi and Ramesh Manandhar, in *Impact*, Philippines, May 1990; and from personal correspondence with Dipak Gyawali.

The Manila Declaration on People's Participation and Sustainable Development was drafted in June 1989, and published in IFDA Dossier 75-76, (International Foundation for Development Alternatives), Switzerland, January/April 1990.

Conclusion: Commons No More (pages 185-194)

The story of the Project Dungganon, and of Caonisa Esmayan, comes from "Reproducing Success – Grameen Travels Abroad" by Helen Todd, *Third World Network Features*, 700/90, based in Malaysia. This news syndication service is provided by the Third World Network, a grouping of organizations and individuals working on Third World and development issues.

Dr. Yunus, founder of the Grameen Bank, has become a legend in his own time. For sources of quotations, and for further information on the Grameen bank revolution see the following: "Novel bank serves poor of Bangladesh" by Susan Delacourt, in *The Globe and Mail*, Toronto, October 15, 1986; "Bank lending to Bangladesh poor a trail-blazer" by David Stewart-Patterson, in *The Globe and Mail*, Toronto, July 9, 1987; "Your bank just roared past in a cloud of dust" by Kristin Helmore, in *The Christian Science Monitor*, U.S., January 25-31, 1988; "The Grameen Bank," transcript of an interview with Dr. Yunus, on IDEAS, Canadian Broadcasting Corporation, March 5, 1991; "Micro-loans to the world's poorest" by Clyde H. Farnsworth, in *The*

New York Times, February 21, 1988; "Loans help tiny Third World businesses thrive" by Robert Brehl, in *Toronto Star*, March 31, 1991; "For Bangladeshi Banker, Credit is a Basic Human Right" by Halinah Todd, in *Development Forum*, New York, November-December 1989.

The Grameen Bank has many publications as well, including: *Grameen Dialogue*, a newsletter published by the Grameen Trust, Bangladesh; *Participation As Process* by Andreas Fuglesang and Dale Chandler, Grameen Bank, 1988; and The Grameen Bank's *Annual Report*, which lists loans for everything from blacksmithing, cart repairing, maddy latrine construction, well digging and rubber stamp making to napkin weaving.

Grameen Bank equivalents are springing up all over the Third World. See "Third World debt that is almost always is (sic) paid in full" by Brent Bowers, in *The Wall Street Journal*, June 9, 1991.

Details on traditional African lending systems come from *Sub-Saharan Africa: From Crisis to Sustainable Growth*, The World Bank, Washington, D.C. 1989. The system described in Nigeria comes from personal communication with Kole Shettima, a political science graduate student in Toronto.

For details of Mexico's booming economy see the following articles by Matt Moffett in *The Wall Street Journal* : "Long-sickly Mexico has investment boom as trade hopes grow," May 24, 1991; "Mexican conglomerate cuts costs and learns there's life after debt," July, 26, 1991; "Mexico boosts role of private investment," July 12, 1990; also see "Finance Minister of the Year" in *Euromoney*, U.K., September, 1990.

For more information on the Mexican stock market see *Mexico Service, A Publication of International Reports*, vol. 11, no. 8, New York, April 10, 1991 and vol. 11, no. 2, January 16, 1991. For considerable detail on the privatization of Telmex (and other privatizations) see *Mexico Service*, going back to December 14, 1989. For further information on Telmex's credit arrangement with Citibank see *Mexico Service*, vol. 11, no. 4, February 13, 1991; "Carnival Time Again For Latin Borrowers" in *Euromoney*, U.K., September 1990.

For details of how privatizations of state enterprises are lowering budget deficits, see *Mexico Service*, vol. 10, no. 24, November 28, 1990 and vol. 11, no. 5, February 27, 1991; "Mexico's Telmex rings up a first" by Linda Sandler, in *The Globe and Mail*, Toronto, June 10, 1991.

For an indication of the investment optimism in other Third World countries, including Chile, see "Looking for a Bigger Market" by E. Guthrie McTigue, in *Global Finance*, New York, September 1990; "Smart Money Goes South," by Melvyn Westlake, in *Risk*, vol. 4, no. 1, London, December 1990-January 1991.

For Mexico's Central Bank Executive Director's quotation see "Mexico's borrowing position" in *The Globe and Mail*, Toronto, June 11, 1991.

An excellent source that describes the grassroots movement to reclaim community forests and lands in Thailand is "National Assessment Study on Environment in Thailand" by W. Permpongsacharoen, Project for Ecological Recovery and A. Usher, *The Nation*, Bangkok.

Index

245